THE THINGS SHE CARRIED

THE THINGS SHE CARRIED

A CULTURAL HISTORY OF THE PURSE IN AMERICA

KATHLEEN B. CASEY

OXFORD
UNIVERSITY PRESS

Oxford University Press is a department of the University of Oxford.
It furthers the University's objective of excellence in research, scholarship,
and education by publishing worldwide. Oxford is a registered trade mark of
Oxford University Press in the UK and in certain other countries.

Published in the United States of America by Oxford University Press
198 Madison Avenue, New York, NY 10016, United States of America.

© Oxford University Press 2025

All rights reserved. No part of this publication may be reproduced, stored in a retrieval system, transmitted, used for text and data mining, or used for training artificial intelligence, in any form or by any means, without the prior permission in writing of Oxford University Press, or as expressly permitted by law, by license or under terms agreed with the appropriate reprographics rights organization. Inquiries concerning reproduction outside the scope of the above should be sent to the Rights Department, Oxford University Press, at the address above.

You must not circulate this work in any other form
and you must impose this same condition on any acquirer.

Library of Congress Cataloging-in-Publication Data
Names: Casey, Kathleen B., author.
Title: The things she carried : a cultural history of the purse in America / Kathleen B. Casey.
Other titles: Cultural history of the purse in America
Description: New York : Oxford University Press, 2025. | Includes bibliographical references and index.
Identifiers: LCCN 2025015761 (print) | LCCN 2025015762 (ebook) | ISBN 9780197587829 (hardback) | ISBN 9780197587843 (epub)
Subjects: LCSH: Handbags—United States—History. | Handbags—Social aspects.
Classification: LCC GT2180 .C37 2025 (print) | LCC GT2180 (ebook) | DDC 391.4/4—dc23/eng/20250417
LC record available at https://lccn.loc.gov/2025015761
LC ebook record available at https://lccn.loc.gov/2025015762

DOI: 10.1093/oso/9780197587829.001.0001

Printed by Sheridan Books, Inc., United States of America

The manufacturer's authorized representative in the EU for product safety is
Oxford University Press España S.A., Parque Empresarial San Fernando de Henares,
Avenida de Castilla, 2 – 28830 Madrid (www.oup.es/en).

Portions of Chapter 1 were originally published in *The Cultural Construction of Hidden Spaces: Essays on Pockets, Pouches and Secret Drawers*, edited by James Brown, Anna Jamieson, Naomi Segal (Leiden: Brill, 2024), 37–51.

Portions of Chapter 5 were originally published in "Pickets, Protests, and Purses in the American Civil Rights Movement," *Gender and History* 35, no. 3 (October 2023): 1070–1088.

*To my mother and father,
Ann and Dennis*

Contents

Acknowledgments	ix
Introduction: The Possibilities of Purses	1
1. "This Sack So Full": Enslaved Women's Use of Bags in Antebellum America	15
2. Purses and Pathbreaking Women at the Turn of the Century	36
3. Space, Privacy, and the Pocketbooks of Working Women	61
4. The Bag and the Body: Purses and Personal Hygiene, 1920s–1940s	81
5. Pickets, Protests, and Purses in the Civil Rights Movement	108
6. "Keith Carried a Clutch": Queer Communities and Purses in the Late Twentieth Century	132
Epilogue	155
Notes	161
Bibliography	201
Index	215

Acknowledgments

This effort was supported by so many people that I'm bound to forget someone, but let me start with librarians, archivists, and curators. Research is not possible without the help of these amazing professionals, who silently sustain the work of so many researchers, writers, and students all over the world. I am no exception. Your work is so important, and so many of you helped me gain access to the primary sources that are the backbone of this book. More specifically, I want to thank Stephen Leist, head librarian at Virginia Wesleyan University, who always found a way to get me whatever strange sources I requested in the middle of the night. When I began working at Furman University in the summer of 2023, Mary Fairbairn also helped me gain access to the last batch of sources I needed to finish this book.

Connie Frisbee Houde, of the textiles and clothing department, and Jennifer Lemak, Chief Curator of History, both helped me the first time I started working with purses by giving me access to the purses and bags housed at the New York State Museum in Albany, New York. Lucia Floriana Savi, the curator of the "Bags: Inside Out" exhibit at the Victoria and Albert Museum, made time to let me pick her brain over Zoom when I had to cancel my trip to the museum because of the global pandemic. I also want to thank Catherine G. Buckland and Lotte Schwillens of the (now closed) Tassen Museum in the Netherlands for their extensive knowledge of pockets and purses and their excellent company. Tomeka Myers helped me access key photographs through the Library of Congress. I want to thank Lisa Marine and Fred and Phyllis Blackwell for helping me publish Fred's famous photograph of the Woolworth's protest from Jackson, Mississippi, in 1963. I'm also grateful to Doug Remley, Carrie, and other staff members at the National Museum of African American History and Culture, as well as the staff at the New York Public Library. Thank you to Jon Crispin for granting permission to use three of his magnificent photographs of the patient suitcases and bags that remained in storage at Willard State Hospital long after the institution had closed its doors.

I've always found research to be fun, but the writing has always been the hardest part for me (have you ever written 300 words, then deleted 600?). The chapters that constitute this book have benefited from the careful review of many readers who thus created a web of support for this project. My dear friend Aviva Dove-Viebahn read the Introduction and Chapter 6 and, more importantly, believes in me. Dan Howland, my close friend and confidante, reads anything I ask him to and helped me talk through the ideas expressed here before I wrote a word; he also looked at several sections of this book over many years. Two anonymous peer reviewers gave me detailed, constructive feedback on the manuscript for an article that later formed the basis of Chapter 5. Victoria Wolcott, who taught me as an undergraduate and graduate student and continues to inspire me, also read and helped me to improve Chapter 5. Alison K. Lange provided feedback on a very early version of Chapter 2, and Laura Prieto of Simmons College gave me valuable comments at the Berkshires Conference in Boston in June 2017. My neighbor Kim Lewandowski read several sections of this book and kept reminding me that she couldn't wait to read it. She passed away in 2024, and I'm sorry that she never got the chance. My parents read much of this manuscript and gave me gentle advice as I plodded along, even as they complained about the cost of ink from printing so many pages of drafts. My remarkable dog Betsy kept me company during all the years I spent researching, writing, and revising this work.

This kind of research also requires a lot of time and money, and this work would not have been possible without support from several resources. In 2015, I was fortunate to participate in a National Endowment for the Humanities summer institute on nineteenth-century American material culture in New York City. At the Bard Graduate Center, I met and was inspired by others studying material culture, including Katherine Fama and the late David Jaffee.

In 2016, I received the Mednick Memorial Fellowship, awarded annually to one professor at each of the independent colleges of Virginia. I was also awarded a summer faculty development grant by colleagues at Virginia Wesleyan University in 2022. This funding paid for a research trip to San Francisco, where I met Bruce Colton and Alfredo Esponda, the best Airbnb hosts a person could ask for (when the airline lost my luggage, Bruce and Alfredo gave me their own clothing, which I then wore to the archives!). At the GLBT Historical Society in San Francisco, I was helped by the amazing author and archivist Isaac Fellman, who introduced me to Victoria Schneider's story and helped me gain access to two images from Chapter 6.

Jeremy Cass at Furman University allowed me time to finish this book as I began an exciting new job as the Director of the Women's, Gender, and Sexuality Studies Program at Furman University. The Furman Humanities Center awarded me a book development grant in September 2024, which helped defray the cost of acquiring the images that are so key to this book. I am thankful for all my new colleagues at Furman University, but especially Lane Harris and all my colleagues in the History Department and the Women's, Gender, and Sexuality Studies Program, including Kylie Fisher, Scott Henderson, Nick Radel, and many others. Sarah Cochran's indomitable spirit, energy, technical savvy, and photography helped me get this book across the finish line.

I also want to thank those who listened to various iterations of this research at multiple conferences, including the American Studies Association, the American Historical Association, the National Women's Studies Association, the Berkshires Conference of Women's Historians, and several universities where I gave talks over the last several years. At each venue, a copanelist, chair, or audience member pointed me in deserving directions.

Danielle Stern regularly lifted my spirits, and shared laughter and tears with me over the last several years. Emily Taylor is generous and puffs me up. Savita Nair, who passed away in November 2024, provided a model of warmth and kindness at Furman and still does. Lynn Gordon, who passed away in 2012, still peers over my shoulder, reminding me to write what women before me could not. Though I now live in South Carolina, I am also thankful to the feminist community that coheres around Eleanor's Norfolk in Norfolk, Virginia, and am especially grateful to its intrepid owner, Erin Dougherty. Golan Moskowitz, organizer of Tulane's Working Group on Jewish Gender Performance and Drag, gave me a new intellectual home for a year and helped expose me to new texts and thinkers.

My colleagues and co-conspirators at Virginia Wesleyan University buoyed my spirits and made me feel as if I was part of a team. Richard Bond commented on an early version of Chapter 1 and wrote me a letter of recommendation for the National Endowment for the Humanities summer institute that helped get this project off the ground. Sara Sewell, my comrade and supporter, urged me to persist after I presented this research at the Berkshires Conference of Women's Historians and sustained me with encouragement and slices of delicious cake. I also thank Taryn Myers, Jen Slivka, Leslie Caughell, Kellie Holzer of the Gender, Women's, and Sexuality Studies Program at Virginia Wesleyan University. I am additionally thankful to Kathy Merlock Jackson, Joe Jackson, Jeff Toussaint, Annette Clayton, Gabi Martorell, Kathy Stolley, and too many others to name. Keep on getting in good trouble.

I am especially indebted to those who agreed to sit down and share their lives with a stranger in an oral history interview. I wish to thank Roberta ("Bobbi")

Yancy who generously gave me hours of her time. Joan Trumpauer Mulholland made an indelible mark when she invited me into her home and gave me access to her personal archives just before the pandemic began.

I want to thank all of my students. You remind me that what I'm doing is worthwhile and help me balance the many directions in which my brain moves. Callum Foley and Riley Conrad stand out. Former students Melissa Fisher, Karlee Fretz, and Abigail Peterson all helped me collect valuable primary sources for this project.

I wish to thank the following editors: Cheryl Warsh, James Brown, Naomi Segal, Anna Jamieson, Nancy Toff, Susan Ferber, Chelsea Hogue, and everyone at Oxford University Press.

Finally, I thank you, reader, for your care and curiosity.

Introduction
The Possibilities of Purses

A purse has always felt like a burdensome and overdetermined object to me, a sort of red flag of femininity. Despite my aversion to purses, I have long needed a container larger than the paltry pockets that irregularly come built into women's clothing. While still in graduate school in the early 2000s, I began carrying around my identification, overdrawn debit card, keys, lip balm, and a bottle of water in an army-green burlap shoulder bag that might more aptly be described as a "sack." Somehow this sack felt like a good compromise between a proper purse and a practical container I needed for the devices and detritus of my life.

Figures I.1A and I.1B. This army green burlap sack kept the author company most days from 2005 until approximately 2017. It has torn and ripped in many places and has taken on the shape of a book. (Photographs by Sarah Cochran, August 2024.)

Unlike most commercially produced purses made over the last century, my burlap sack was not made of anything durable like leather or plastic, and it lacked any secure closing mechanism, like an outer zipper or button to snap shut. Thus, it never made a reassuring "click," "zip," or "snap" sound that told me my belongings were safely secured inside. As a result, the contents of my sack occasionally and embarrassingly spilled out before uninvited audiences.

As I navigated private and public spaces with my sack for more than a dozen years, I noticed the strong reactions it elicited from those around me. One of my three sisters told me that it was so odious that it needed to be destroyed. On at least one occasion, she threatened to stick it in the garbage disposal; on another, she offered to do me the favor of setting it on fire. Over the course of this bag's lifetime, I set it down on dirty floors, precariously balanced it on toilet paper dispensers in public restrooms, and took it across state lines and national borders where it functioned as a miniature, mobile version of my home. Even though it offered limited material security, it provided me with a sense of sameness in unfamiliar places. As it became increasingly ragged, though, it became the butt of jokes among my friends. Once I was at a restaurant in Berlin and, as I left my seat, I asked a friend to "watch my purse" while I went to the restroom. With a knowing smile, she said, "Don't worry. No one will ever steal that."

Every time I wore the sack, I slung it over my left shoulder, letting it cleave my chest in two, which I imagined would make it harder for a purse snatcher to abscond with than if I wore it hanging haphazardly from one shoulder. It generally rested on my right hip and rhythmically bopped at my side as I walked. I continued to carry my sack even after it got caught on doorknobs and displays at the ends of grocery store aisles, unexpectedly lurching me back in space each time. As it acquired stains and developed large yawning holes, revealing its thin black lining, it transmitted material evidence of my clumsiness, failure to securely seal a bottle of water, and apparent refusal to put a cap back on a pen. My daily habit of carrying a book with me eventually began to change the shape of the bag, pulling at its corners. On a few occasions, things got dire, and I found some thick blue thread and hastily performed a series of small surgeries on my sack to keep it in one piece. The older my bag got, the more women I had never met came up to me, telling me that my bag was "boho-chic" and had a desirable lived-in aesthetic, like the well-worn "distressed" denim for which some shoppers pay a premium. In fact, the more holes the sack accumulated, the more other women seemed to want to know where I had purchased it.

I began to realize that purses, bags, pocketbooks, and sacks mattered. Whether American women love or hate their bags (and there is ample evidence of both sentiments and everything in between), they are not simply inert receptacles. Instead, they are items of apparel—adaptable toolkits—that lead multidimensional lives of their own. Sometimes they pass through the hands and closets of multiple owners. Sometimes they are invaded by the fingers of foreign sets of hands, as my mother's purse had been in the mid-1960s when a man snuck up behind her and grabbed it. In a moment of defiance that surprised even her, she white-knuckled the straps of her purse until her assailant finally let go and ran off. As it had for my mother and my mother's mother, my sack helped shape how my body moved, what parts of it were visible to others, how I navigated space, and how I conceptualized danger, dignity, and my own safety.

I now carry a black book bag, preferring to have my laptop and at least a couple books with me at all times. I retired my green burlap sack years ago when it ceased to serve as a reliable vessel. But even from the back of my closet, it is still silently making statements (judgments?) about me. I cannot imagine throwing it out, as it continues to signal my feelings about gender expression, my age, my socioeconomic status, my feelings about fast fashion and wastefulness, the number of items I feel like I "need" to have with me, and how secure I need them to be (apparently, not very). This sack carries vivid memories of my days as a broke graduate student and a woman who was beginning to abandon gendered scripts, which I had been alternately following and fighting my whole life. It is also a tangible representation of my intellectual investment in the study of gender and culture, and it is the inspiration for this book.

* * * * *

Purses and bags have always been much more than a fashion accessory. For millennia, they have enabled humans to morph into marsupials. And for just as long, these items have been telling stories about their owners. Perhaps because these seemingly mundane objects appear everywhere, they have not yet become entirely visible as objects of particular value. Nonetheless, as corsets, detachable collars, and bloomers have come and gone, the purse has remained a critical and highly adaptable object that Americans have used to achieve a host of social, cultural, and political objectives over the last two centuries.

Because purses are so adaptable, there is no single way in which carriers used and conceptualized these objects over time and no specific, stable set of items that purse-owners placed inside them. However, purses have long provided far more than carrying capacity; perhaps more than any other accessory, they have been uncommonly useful in helping their carriers create privacy in public. In nuanced ways, purses have served ornamental, utilitarian, psychological, linguistic, aesthetic, symbolic, and economic functions in American culture. "Purses," "pocketbooks," and "handbags" (terms that vary by style, size, region, and generation) have functioned not simply as accessories but as objects with agency. Women (and some men) have used these objects to construct their identities and execute their own agendas. As toolkits, purses have helped disparate carriers improve their lives and, in some cases, even emancipate themselves from marginal positions.

Although humans have used external containers to carry goods throughout human history, the origin of the purse is tied to the history of pockets. In the seventeenth century, women wore pockets like modern underwear, that is, underneath their clothing and next to the skin. For women of average means, pockets were often made of cotton or linen and were typically bell- or pear-shaped, worn in pairs, and contained an open vertical slit in the middle. This shape and the fact that some women wore their pockets in front of their pelvis or even between their thighs brought forth associations with women's bodies (specifically their genitalia) and sexuality more generally.[1] Incrementally, purses also would adopt such associations. Because pockets were rarely integrated into women's clothing, however, many women relied on a pair of sizable tie-on pockets that wrapped around the waist and could be taken on and off. These pockets varied in size and style, though larger tie-on pockets were often worn by working women, who needed access to tools to ply their trades and manage their homes. Most pockets, however, were hidden, accessible only through slits in women's skirts under folds of fabric. In fits and starts, however, the slim fit of neoclassical dresses eventually made interior pockets aesthetically undesirable.[2] Although some women began to wear integrated pockets in the 1850s and 1860s when silhouettes once again expanded, this trend did not last. According to design historian Hannah Carlson, dressmakers began tucking pockets in the backs of bustles, which were virtually unreachable.[3] By the end of the nineteenth century, tie-on pockets had mostly become obsolete.[4]

Although some women had carried items like sweet bags since the sixteenth century, in the early 1800s, elite women carried small, often flat, miniature purses, then called "reticules," outside the body.[5] Reticules caused quite a stir since they were associated with undergarments.[6] According to one historian, "[T]he idea of a woman parading her personal belongings in a visible pocket was an act akin to lifting up her skirts and publicly revealing her underwear."[7] Indeed, men mocked reticules, calling them "ridicules." Unlike tie-on pockets, these objects were far smaller than the average mid- to late-twentieth-century leather purses or pocketbooks. Largely ornamental, they were often constructed of delicate embroidered fabrics and typically held only small, lightweight items like calling cards and fans.

In the mid-nineteenth century, several other kinds of bags became popular and, though some women adopted them, many were originally designed for men. "Miser's bags," also known as "gentleman's purses" or "long purses," were popular in the seventeenth century and reemerged in the mid-nineteenth century. They contained two compartments for storing different kinds of coins. These sections were separated by one or two rings that closed a small slit. Accessing one's money through a miser's purse was quite inconvenient, hence the name. Most popular in the 1850s and 1860s, these knitted purses were still carried by some individuals in the early 1910s.[8] "Carpetbags" were also originally designed for men, becoming popular during and after the Civil War. In the 1870s, as American railroads and travel expanded dramatically, carpetbags, known for their durability and lightness, spared railroad travelers from lugging heavy trunks across the country.[9] Many will remember how Julie Andrews carried a magic carpetbag that contained endless wonders in turn-of-the-century London in the iconic Disney film *Mary Poppins*.[10]

In the early 1900s, some women keenly felt that it was unfair that men had multiple integrated pockets. A few women's rights activists even published critiques highlighting this inequity.[11] Feminist writer and suffragist Charlotte Perkins Gilman noted the "supremacy" of men's pockets, which leave them far more ready to navigate daily life.[12] Others associated with the suffrage movement believed that the lack of integrated pockets left them at a distinct disadvantage. In 1887, a writer for *The Boston Daily Globe* complained that women "are deprived."[13] For the most part, ready-made women's clothing would not begin to contain integrated pockets until the 1940s, when functionality took precedence over fashion during World War II. But even these integrated pockets were never as consistent or as large as men's pockets. Thus, purses remained necessary. Instead of disappearing, purses expanded in size and durability.

Reticules, miser's bags, carpetbags, sacks, pocketbooks, handbags, and purses name different objects, though each of these terms refers to a human-made personal container designed for the daily purpose of carrying items outside the home. The language Americans have used to describe the containers they carry has been constantly evolving, and each term has its own history. According to the *Oxford English Dictionary*, the term "purse," which comes from the Latin word "bursa," is older than handbag or pocketbook, having been in use as early as the fourth century.[14] However, others trace its first use to the American colonies in 1700.[15]

The term "pocketbook," on the other hand, has been used to describe different objects depending on when the term was used. The word originally referred to a small book that could fit inside a pocket. By the early 1800s, the meaning of this term expanded, and it was used to describe a book-sized leather case with multiple storage compartments for small objects, bills, and papers.[16] Both men and women carried these objects, but when pocketbooks more fully absorbed associations with women's bodies in the 1920s and 1930s, American men largely abandoned them.

Of course, this connection between bags and women was not entirely new; several ancient cultures associated pouches and purses with the womb.[17] But these associations became more specifically gendered over time. In the United States, the term "bag" was associated with promiscuous women at least as early as the 1920s.[18] Of course, the term "baggage" also has negative connotations of emotional excess. Aging women, in particular, have been derogated as "old bags" since at least the 1940s.[19] It is not a coincidence, then, that the word "pocketbook" was also used in the 1940s as a euphemism for a woman's vagina.[20]

Historically, the term "handbag" is newer than both pocketbook and purse. It was often used to describe small baggage carried by hand and first came into its present-day use in the middle of the nineteenth century.[21] Linguists found that "pocketbook" was more commonly used in the east, while "purse" was commonly used in the west, and "handbag" was most commonly used by Americans over the age of 60.[22] The terms pocketbook, purse, and handbag all refer to a relatively lightweight movable, personal container carried primarily in women's hands from the late nineteenth century through the present day. However, the women who carried these bags might have chosen one term over the other to indicate a difference in style, construction, or size. As a reflection of Americans' wide-ranging use of this diverse terminology, I use the terms most often used by my subjects in each historical period.

Despite several recent studies on the history of clothing and textiles, a social, cultural, and material history of the purse in America is long overdue.[23] This work has benefited from multiple books written by curators and collectors that feature glossy pictures of Hermès, Chanel, Birkin, Judith Leiber, and Louis Vuitton bags, but these studies primarily examine purses as icons of high fashion and often do so from a European perspective.[24] When such books do focus on women, they almost exclusively examine white women. Other books entertainingly explore the aesthetic qualities of purses but leave out much of their history.²⁵ By contrast, this book primarily examines commercially manufactured purses and studies how women (and some men) used them both in the everyday world and as the materials of their activism. It is not a comprehensive survey of all bags, materials, and brands, and there are many intriguing kinds of bags—including parfleche, beaded bags, mesh bags, and chatelaines—that this book leaves out.²⁶ This book does not examine the production processes of these bags either. Instead, *The Things She Carried* uses an intersectional lens to examine how a variety of bags and purses became meaningful for Americans often ignored in studies of fashion, whose possessions are largely left out of museum artifact collections. As a cultural biography of a particularly potent object, it focuses on distinct episodes in the cultural history of bags and purses, illuminating the many ways that both ordinary and extraordinary Americans used their purses to disrupt existing social, cultural, economic, and political structures.

* * * * *

A 1976 issue of *Vogue* suggested that "the only thing more revealing" than the inside of a woman's purse is a medicine cabinet, but for millions of Americans, the purse reveals much more than that. Americans have long used items of apparel such as hats and shoes to express aspirations, amplify differences, and alleviate anxieties, but only the purse—with its cavernous, pocketed interior—has also provided women with much-needed space and privacy. Unlike items of apparel placed directly on the body, purses provide an extension of the body, allowing women to carry a miniature version of the home that they could fill with tools to cope with the challenges of a shifting landscape. In fact, the purse has simultaneously functioned as a medicine cabinet, a mobile home, safe, church, bank, armory, office, powder room, companion, and confidante. Perhaps most of all, the purse is a symbolic and material representation of the female body.²⁷

When I began this research, I learned that bags have been telling compelling stories about their owners for millennia, if only we would pause and pay attention. For example, when in 1940 two archeologists discovered the corpse of a man in his forties in a Nevada cave, they also discovered three closely woven, diamond-plated, almost entirely intact bags next to him that were made of leather, juniper, sage, and bird feathers. Radiocarbon tests revealed that this man, dubbed the "Spirit Cave Man," had died 9,400 years earlier. His bags proved that humans in post–Ice Age North America had developed advanced weaving technologies much earlier than scholars previously supposed.²⁸ The Spirit Cave Man's bags make clear that handheld personal containers were not always considered feminine.²⁹

Historians and other scholars of material culture often begin with the archive. Unfortunately, what gets saved is too often the product of accident or the elitist thinking of previous generations. Ordinary women's items, especially the seemingly mundane objects used and worn by those most disenfranchised, have been among the least likely to be saved. In fact, until the 1960s (and often longer), the items used and worn by enslaved, immigrant, undocumented, lesbian, and working-class women have largely been considered historically insignificant. Such people's lives too often remain "archivally unknown."[30]

In my efforts to study bags, sacks, and purses that shed new light on individuals and communities otherwise overlooked in history, I most often traveled to smaller museums and libraries to find purses carried by working- and middle-class women. My trip to examine the sprawling collections of the now-closed Tassen Museum of Bags in Amsterdam, which held one of Margaret Thatcher's iconic bags among many other treasures, is a notable exception. But for the most part, I focused on smaller, almost incidental collections of purses. Rather than whole archives, many libraries and museums have a handful of bags in a collection associated with an individual or group. Early on in my visits to archives, I stopped at the Schlesinger Library at Harvard University. Once there, I found myself handling two cream-colored canvas bags that suffragists slung over their shoulders and necks. I noted the suffragist colors as I placed one over my own neck in an attempt to determine how the bags would have moved with their bodies. The larger of the two bags was likely used to hold and distribute suffragist newspapers.

One of my earliest stops at an archive was in 2015 at the New York State Museum in Albany, where I was introduced to a collection affiliated with the Willard Asylum for the Insane in Willard, New York. This stately Victorian hospital began accepting patients in 1869 and did not close its doors until 1995, when it was abandoned.[31] Along with the gurneys left in hallways, empty chairs perched in the beauty salon, and operating tables still standing in the morgue, the belongings of former patients had been stored in suitcases, bags, and purses in the attic of the hospital's workshop where they remained entombed for years. When the building was set to be demolished, two hospital workers guided a curator to the attic in a scramble to save historically significant objects. They discovered a trove of men's suitcases on the left and women's on the right, each side labeled and alphabetized by the owner's last name.[32] The hospital's patients were largely poor men and women, many of whom were immigrants who died at the asylum and whose personal effects were never retrieved by family or friends. Fortunately, the hospital's staff had been reticent to dispose of their belongings and the curator managed to save 427 of the bags.[33]

Figure I.2. This archival box held at Harvard contains two canvas suffragist bags, the smaller of which features a green and purple stripe and measures 9 inches wide by 6 inches tall. Its strap is only 15 inches long, similar to the length of a necklace. It features no interior pockets and no closing mechanism. The larger bag contains three small interior pockets and is 17 inches wide and 14.3 inches high. The much wider shoulder strap is 1.5 inches wide and 38 inches long. Circa 1913–1920. (Author's photograph, August 2016, Schlesinger Library on American Women, Harvard University.)

After their discovery, photographer Jon Crispin spent 6 years visually documenting the suitcases and their contents.[34] Some were empty, but others contained shoes, hats, gloves, postcards, shoe polish, watches, buttons, and items as intimate and ephemeral as Band-Aids. Some suitcases, like Anna B. H.'s, also contained several purses.[35] In addition to a beaded coat outfitted with a fur collar, her brown suitcase contained multiple small purses, including a white bag embellished with brown and blue beads and a small, black snap purse with a purple, pocketed interior and a corroded gold-colored frame.[36] At some point, Anna B. H. found herself at Willard. She may have been brought there against her will. Thus, the objects she left behind must speak for her.

When I arrived at the New York State Museum, one of the curators kindly laid out some of the purses found inside the suitcases on a white table. I began by attempting to put aside my assumptions about these objects, instead asking questions about each object's sensory and physical properties, orientation, and potential interactions with the body. What would patients have packed inside these receptacles on their way to the asylum, if they even knew where they were

Figure I.3. This brown suitcase with heavily worn corners belonged to Anna B. H., a resident of the Willard Insane Asylum whose full name has been obscured. This suitcase contained at least two smaller purses seen in the next two photos. (Jon Crispin, 2012, "Willard Suitcases/Anna B.H.")

Figure I.4. This second purse was found inside the brown suitcase with a velvet black exterior and lined purple interior. It contains an internal pocket and the handwritten inscription, "A.B. H--- 24." (Jon Crispin, 2012, "Willard Suitcases/Anna B.H.")

Figure I.5. An interior view of a much smaller purse containing hairpins found inside Anna B. H.'s brown suitcase. The attached label marked this item as hers. (Jon Crispin, 2012, "Willard Suitcases/Anna B.H.")

headed? Some certainly had no idea they were about to be admitted to an institution with little or no hope of release. I put on my white gloves and closed and opened each flap, listening for snaps and zips, checking to see how secure each object would have been inside its private container. I felt each object for softness and stiffness, pliability and texture. In one, I found a loose key, with no clue as to what it unlocked. These queries gave me hints as to the life of the object, how often it was used and worn down by contact with the oils from human hands. Finally, I measured each bag and took photographs so that I could later return to these images and compile a comparative record of the appearance and dimensions of the objects.

I hoped to catch what was distinctive about each item and its owner. I considered each bag's potential social, economic, spatial, spiritual, ideological, gendered, and racialized value among a constellation of other objects, always keeping in mind that these objects were meant to be mobile despite their long respite in the hospital's attic. I was also keenly aware of the invasive nature of my activity and wondered, if they could bear witness, what the owners of these objects would make of my excavations of their belongings.

These purses, bags, and suitcases remind me that, when our bodies fail and get buried in the ground, what remains are our objects. Perhaps others will uncover those objects and consider what they reveal about our lives; if we are lucky, perhaps a stranger will document, preserve, or give new life to them. While they are not the subject of this book, the owners of the suitcases and purses in Willard have been tucked away and forgotten by polite society. Yet, their bags refuse to let us forget about their owners, even though we are often unable to identify their graves. Most importantly, they generate questions we may never have bothered to ask.

This book includes some purse-centered stories about famous women like Nellie Bly and Susan B. Anthony (whose purses have been preserved) and Rosa Parks (whose purses have not). However, it centers how ordinary women and some men used purses in the pursuit of space, privacy, and power. Ordinary people used purses to transgress boundaries across gender, class, race, and sexuality. For this reason, the purse carriers in this book are just as important as the things they carried.[37] When I could access purses, I borrowed from the methods used by scholars of material culture. Yet, this is primarily a work of cultural history that synthesizes images and texts to fill in archival gaps. As dress historian Lou Taylor has explained, the process of "twinning text" with material culture allows us to probe, hear, see, and feel stories that we might otherwise miss.[38] Pairing sacks, bags, and purses with photographs, advertisements, illustrations, newspaper stories, trial transcripts, trade journals, and oral histories (and relying on the latter when the artifacts are inaccessible) creates a vivid picture of the cultural lives of purses, uncovering new narratives about the persistence and resilience of marginalized people.

* * * * *

This book is organized both chronologically and topically, beginning in the mid-nineteenth century and ending with an epilogue that ventures into the twenty-first century, when women and other gender and sexual minorities have arguably experienced some of the most profound changes in American history. Geographically, it focuses on the United States and moves primarily between the South, Midwest, Northeast, and West Coast. It highlights urban settings because these are the crowded contexts in which purses provided working- and middle-class women with critical space and much-needed privacy. In fact, purses provided privacy for those most subjugated by their class, race, citizenship, and sexuality. This book finds purses at fraught moments, uncovering untold narratives while revealing new angles on familiar stories. Ultimately, it charts how women and some men effectively deployed purses in their efforts to move from the margins of society to the middle.

In the mid-nineteenth century, privacy was deeply circumscribed by racial, economic, and gender privilege. In this context, enslaved Black women were the least likely group to enjoy privacy and the most likely to have their bodies violated in myriad ways. While curators most often showcase how upper-class white women wore decorative reticules in the antebellum period, Chapter 1 decenters that narrative by analyzing how enslaved women used sacks to manufacture their own concealed spaces, creating small but critical measures of power and privacy in an environment designed for their brutal exposure and vulnerability. Enslaved women used sacks in a variety of ways, but often repurposed them to create private toolkits that aided their survival and liberation. Analyzing the role these sacks played allows us to see not only how structures of power operated in antebellum America but also how enslaved women used textiles to fashion secret containers and proto-purses that disrupted those structures. In doing so, they were able to negotiate some of the most oppressive conditions of their lives.

Purses played an important role in shaping the modern identities of their holders in visual culture. Photographs, illustrations, and films featuring women holding purses serve as visual autobiographies. At the same time that purses helped women construct an idealized sense of self through imagery in the late nineteenth century, scores of newspaper articles highlighted growing anxiety over the phenomenon of "purse-snatching." To keep unchaperoned women safe, inventors even patented "burglary-proof" purses and purse-sized vanity cases shaped like guns, while others used their purses to steal from department stores. Chapter 2 situates purses as a central site of both identity construction and criminal activity in a highly visible world.

When critical masses of American women took on new roles as waged workers in the early twentieth century, no other single item symbolized women's newfound independence and autonomy more than the purse. As working women spent more time outside the home, purses grew in size and were increasingly made out of leather, making them more durable and useful for women who were expected to perform many different roles in multiple places. Purses offered expanding numbers of waged women an increasingly gendered, intimate space that they strategically used to navigate a masculine, public world. Chapter 3 illustrates how pocketbooks aided immigrant working women who were employed at New York City's Triangle Shirtwaist Factory as they moved between the private and public sphere. Oral histories and trial transcripts demonstrate that, when this space was invaded by male bosses, women felt physically and psychologically violated. And yet they still viewed their purses as critical to their own well-being.

In the 1920s and 1930s, purses became the sole property of women in America, with sales increasing dramatically starting in 1921. More women bought and carried pocketbooks in the 1920s, while seemingly discouraging men from doing so. Chapter 4 explores how purses offered women the opportunity to take a personal hygiene kit and veritable medicine cabinet everywhere they went. As purse-sized personal products began to saturate the consumer market, women could freshen their makeup, reapply perfume, swallow Midol, smoke a cigarette on their commute to work, carry cash, and stay away from home for longer periods of time. Women began relying on their purses to manage both their bodies and rising hygienic expectations. Most importantly, new menstruation technologies played an important role in this process. In the same year that sales of purses in America began to skyrocket, Kotex began selling disposable sanitary napkins. As new products like sanitary napkins and (later) tampons became available to women who could afford them, these items formed a seemingly organic partnership with purses. In these decades, the purse became fully feminized and served as a proxy for women's bodies.

Civil rights activists—both the legendary and lesser known—used purses to appear to play the part of well-dressed, respectable ladies while attending sit-ins and marches. Yet, many women in the 1950s and 1960s simultaneously used their purses to hide items they needed to protect themselves as they voted, sat-in, and integrated schools. Women activists deployed their purses in highly fraught environments and within particular groups such as the Student Nonviolent Coordinating Committee (SNCC), the Montgomery Bus Boycott Movement, and the National Association for the Advancement of Colored People (NAACP). By examining activists' purses, Chapter 5 reveals that Black women's participation in the armed self-defense movement was far more significant than we have appreciated. Purses were critical to ensuring the safety of white and Black female activists, though white women were often more able to maintain control over their purses.

Purses held potential as both defensive and offensive weapons for the LGBTQ+ community as well. The final chapter of this book notes that, in the early gay rights movement, many gay men felt pressure to act and dress "straight." However, by the late 1960s, small but highly visible numbers of gay men increasingly used the purse to announce their subversive sexuality, while trans women and sex workers hid bricks and bottles in their handbags to protect themselves from would-be harassers and assaulters. Contrarily, most butch lesbians were emphatically averse to purses, believing that they were incompatible with "the butch ensemble."[39] However, in a pinch, butch lesbians could grab a more feminine friend's purse to avoid getting arrested for "cross-dressing," a crime many American cities outlawed in the late nineteenth and early twentieth centuries.[40]

Purses continue to offer their carriers intimate, cavernous, critical spaces, even if they sometimes feel burdensome in the twenty-first century. The recent origins of the "murse" (man-purse) in America and items like Fisher-Price's My Pretty Learning Purse (marketed to baby girls) are indications that purses remain as pervasive and gendered as ever. Despite the warnings of critics who predicted that COVID-19 would be the death knell of purses as fewer people left their homes, purses persist, remaining a complex but vital object in American culture.

I

"This Sack So Full"

Enslaved Women's Use of Bags in Antebellum America

On January 18, 1937, a woman living 100 miles east of Atlanta, Georgia, answered her door and welcomed a strange man into her home. Her visitor, John Booth, was an employee of the Federal Writers' Project (FWP) and he had come on behalf of the U.S. government to collect stories about enslavement. Though the woman he wanted to speak with, Charlotte Raines, had passed away, Booth conversed with a woman who was probably her niece. One part of the discussion focused on how Aunt Charlotte, who had been enslaved by a man named Swepson H. Cox, surreptitiously used flour sacks during enslavement.[1]

The woman painted Booth a vivid picture: "My mother and my grandmother both say that they have seen her pull up her skirts and drop things into a flour sack which she always wore tied round her waist just for this purpose." Indeed, the sack Raines carried under her skirts was large and often full of food. The woman noted, "I myself have seen this sack so full that it would bump against her knee." Yet she added that her aunt used homemade pockets to steal more than food: "She would also take personal belongings. Another servant in the household once found one of Aunt Charlotte's granddaughters using a compact that she had stolen from her young mistress." Soon after, the compact was quietly returned to its owner but "nothing was ever said to Aunt Charlotte although everyone knew she had stolen it." Though the woman viewed her aunt's actions as evidence of her incorrigibility, Raines did not keep these illicit items for herself. In fact, enslaved women like Raines used homemade pockets they fashioned from cotton, flour, or tobacco sacks and other materials to redistribute resources otherwise denied to their families. Indeed, these sacks helped enslaved women supplement the meager diets of their family and offer objects that represented moments of freedom, privacy, and pleasure.

During the Great Depression, FWP employees like John Booth conducted oral history interviews with formerly enslaved people and their descendants throughout the South.[2] In fact, between 1936 and 1938, FWP workers interviewed over 2,000 formerly enslaved people in their seventies, eighties, and nineties, and their recollections offer much of the most direct testimony about American enslavement available. Those who were too young to have experienced or remembered slavery directly also shared family stories that provide additional critical insight. FWP interviewers were given approximately twenty questions to use as guidelines, though only one of these questions specifically asked about clothing.[3] Yet, interviewees often volunteered additional information about textiles while responding to other questions about food, shelter, medicine, and more.

Transcripts of these interviews only rarely include the words "purse" or "pocketbook," terms that were infrequently used in the United States before the Civil War, especially by enslaved people. Indeed, purses and pocketbooks became more pervasive in American life after the Civil War, when detachable pockets were increasingly externalized into small bags. In a few oral history interviews, formerly enslaved people used the terms purses and pocketbooks but in ways that suggested these items were primarily the province of white people.[4] Nonetheless, many of the oral history interviews conducted by the FWP in the 1930s prove enslaved people regularly used whatever textiles they could find to construct private, movable containers and they used these items for a variety of purposes.[5]

In nineteenth-century America, privacy was deeply determined by race, class, and gender. Most enslaved women did not have reticules, which were tiny, ornamented bags that hung from the wrist and served a decorative purpose. Like all women, their clothing also lacked integrated pockets. In this context, enslaved women who manufactured their own concealed spaces under their skirts created small but critical measures of power and privacy in a world designed for brutal exposure and vulnerability. They used these spaces as vehicles for pursuing small and large rebellions and escaping the oppressive eyes of masters who sought to limit their movements and freedoms. In the antebellum period, enslaved women used sacks to enhance their lives and attempt self-liberation.[6]

Most enslaved people had limited access to clothing, which was closely monitored by enslavers. Indeed, enslavers sought to control every aspect of the lives of those they enslaved while expanding profit margins wherever possible. As early as the 1730s, in states such as South Carolina and Louisiana, legislators even sought to eliminate the potential for individual expression while reinforcing white supremacy by instituting dress codes that outlined what materials enslaved people could and could not wear.[7] These sumptuary codes sought to ensure that all enslaved people would appear in homogenous, loose-fitting, drab-colored clothing that obscured their individuality and visually marked them as unfree.

Historians typically date the ready-made clothing revolution to the nineteenth century, though it came decades earlier for men than for women.[8] However, clothing for enslaved people was arguably the first mass-produced ready-made clothing. This apparel was typically constructed of scratchy "Negro cloth," which was generally imported in order to clothe enslaved people as cheaply as possible. Most enslaved people wore cloth imported from Europe around the revolution, though this practice may have stopped during the homespun movement.[9]

After the revolution, much of the clothing that enslaved people on large plantations wore was produced on-site by enslaved women who spun, wove, and sewed the material themselves. Though this loose, untailored clothing was a sign of enslaved peoples' servitude, ironically, it also helped women like Charlotte Raines hide large sacks through which they ferried food, textiles, talismans, medicine, and other materials to their families. In some cases, enslaved people were able to save money and buy Sunday clothes after selling the products of small home gardens or being hired out. Nonetheless, the majority of enslaved people's clothing was produced at home.[10]

Enslaved people who were highly visible were often given special, higher-quality clothing and a few even wore custom-made livery.[11] Elite men like Thomas Jefferson assigned a special person—in Jefferson's case, Mrs. Randolph—to order the clothing for enslaved house servants like Sally Hemings, with whom he fathered six children. Meanwhile, other enslaved people who worked outside wore "colored plains" ordered by Mr. Higginbotham. George Washington ordered cloth from Great Britain for the people he enslaved, and he expressed frustration when he had to resort to buying them locally after a shipment was delayed. He also complained that his enslaved seamstresses worked too slowly, and he suspected them of theft, an accusation women who worked with textiles would face for many decades to come.[12]

Washington may have had good reason to worry about theft. Enslaved women who knew how to make clothing could and did sneak away extra fabric and use it to enhance their family's clothing, especially their undergarments, which were less likely to be seen by overseers. Those who knew how could use dye to create clothing in new colors. In fact, they could create an entirely new costume in different colors to wear or bring with them when they ran away.[13] Those who worked in the house could also use hand-me-downs their mistresses thought no longer fit to wear.

Although enslaved people who were forced to work inside white homes were typically given better-quality clothing than those who labored in fields, interviews confirm that most enslaved people were given only one to two changes of clothing per year.[14] Critically, these clothes were sometimes made directly out of sacks. Adeline Marshall, who was born enslaved in Texas, recalled being given "a plain cotton slip with a string 'round de neck, de stuff dey makes pickin' sacks of. Summer or winter, dat all we gits to wear."[15] Likewise, Albert Todd, who had been enslaved as a child in Kentucky, recalled wearing "a long shirt, made out of a meal sack. That's all I wore them days."[16] Other enslaved people who were given more formal clothing wore sacks when they washed their clothes on Sundays. Jenny Proctor, who was born in Alabama in 1850, recalled wearing "gunny sacks wid holes cut for our head and arms" while other clothes were washed.[17]

Beyond prescribing what enslaved people could wear, legislators in the state of South Carolina so rigidly circumscribed enslaved people's mobility and privacy that they made it illegal for them to leave plantations without documented permission provided by a visible badge or written letter from their enslaver.[18] Isaiah Butler, who was enslaved in South Carolina and was 9 or 10 years old when Union soldiers arrived during the Civil War, recalled, "You couldn't travel unless de boss give you a pass. De Ku Klan had 'patrol' all about in de bushes by de side of de road at night. And when dey caught you dey'd whip you almost to death!"[19] Such rules applied to both men and women. Enslaved people occasionally found ways to get around these rules by bribing white children to write letters granting permission for them to leave.[20]

Some enslavers even used devices to audibly monitor the movements of enslaved people. In Alabama, one enslaver forced those who had been caught running away to wear a large iron rod with a collar around their neck and belt around their waist to prevent them from moving without emitting sound. Other enslavers used iron collars that fit around an enslaved person's neck and were outfitted with two bells, one extending over each shoulder. Both devices were designed to prevent enslaved people from making any unauthorized movements.[21]

Although enslaved women did not have access to pocketbooks and purses as twenty-first-century Americans conceive of them, oral history interviews prove that, in addition to using sacks as clothing, they regularly used tow, crocus, and burlap sacks constructed of natural fibers to create private, movable containers. These containers functioned as disruptive spaces—pockets and proto-purses—that could be strategically used for a variety of purposes. Unlike purses, though, these objects had the advantage of being both silent and hidden.

Enslaved women accessed sacks in a few different ways. Sacks were distributed to enslaved women for picking crops like cotton, but enslavers also used them as containers to distribute food rations. Enslaved people repurposed sacks originally created to carry heavy amounts of flour, seed, salt, sugar, and other staples. On larger plantations, some enslaved women were assigned to construct these sacks, as well as to create the clothing to be worn by their enslaved peers. After the invention of the sewing machine in the 1840s, products made with sewing machines used a double-locking chain stitch that would not tear apart even under the weight of heavy materials.[22] This made them quite useful as a kind of makeshift luggage.

However they acquired them, women repurposed these sacks, fashioning them into private pockets, additional layers of clothing, and emergency bags to be packed in preparation for running away. Just as their daughters and granddaughters would use pocketbooks in the late nineteenth and twentieth centuries, enslaved women used these sacks in versatile and inconspicuous ways. In fact, sacks allowed enslaved women to carve out multiple spaces for themselves at a time and place in which the law did not recognize their humanity, ownership of their own bodies, or guardianship of their children. Indeed, in the hands of enslaved women, these seemingly mundane sacks functioned as both symbols and sites of resistance.[23]

In addition to providing resources for their resistance, the sacks that enslaved people used to collect crops were emblems of their oppression. Sacks used for picking cotton symbolized the enormous physical labor people in bondage were regularly coerced into performing. On cotton plantations, they functioned as material representations of the brutalities that enslavers would visit upon the bodies of enslaved people if they failed to sufficiently fill their sacks.

Narratives written by those who experienced and escaped enslavement, including Harriet Jacobs, Frederick Douglass, and Solomon Northup, provide invaluable insight into the lives of enslaved people. However, they typically only represent the experiences of people who successfully escaped slavery and were literate or had literate friends. Thus, they are not necessarily representative of the millions of people who endured enslavement in the United States. In addition, very few of these narratives were written by women, so they often provide a male-centered view of slavery. Nonetheless, passages in these narratives bear witness to women's actions and provide valuable insight into the daily lives of enslaved people. One such narrative includes Solomon Northup's *Twelve Years a Slave*, published in 1853.[24] Northup's story is particularly exceptional because he was a free man who worked as a professional violinist before he was kidnapped and sold into slavery in 1841. His narrative provides rich descriptions of what it felt like to carry these sacks full of cotton while laboring "as soon as it is light in the morning . . . until it is too dark to see."[25] He notes that some enslaved people were allotted only ten to fifteen minutes to stop to eat lunch with no break for dinner. In such a context, storing food inside homemade pockets would have helped save scarce time.[26]

Northup also recalled that some enslaved people carried these sacks over their shoulders, while others hung them from their necks. He described the sacks he used to collect cotton in detail. Northup recalled that every August each enslaved person was given a sack: "A strap is fastened to it, which goes over the neck, holding the mouth of the sack breast high, while the bottom reaches nearly to the ground."[27] Once assigned a sack, Northup soon found himself attempting to negotiate a "long, cumbersome sack swinging from side to side in a manner not allowable in the cotton field."[28] Working his way through the narrow rows of crops, Northup consistently struggled to fill the sack to the minimum weight, a staggering 200 pounds for both men and women. When each sack was full, each picker was ordered to transfer the contents of their sack into a basket and start the process all over again. Those who failed to meet the daily weight by the end of the day were routinely whipped. In his narrative, Northup marveled at how an enslaved woman named Patsey managed to use the aforementioned strap to hang her sack from her neck so she could utilize both her right and left hands to pick very quickly. Northup was able to collect only 95 pounds on his first day, but he noted that "five hundred pounds a day was not unusual" for Patsey.[29]

Northup's recollections coincide with those of other formerly enslaved people who marveled at how much enslaved women picked and hauled. At the time of his FWP interview, Richard Orford, who had been enslaved in Georgia, claimed that "women in dem days could pick five-hundred pounds of cotton a day wid a child in a sack on dere backs."[30] Sarah Ashley, who was born in Mississippi, sold on an auction block in New Orleans, and was 19 when the "burst of freedom come," proudly remembered the amount of cotton she picked, as well as how far she managed to carry the heavy sacks full of cotton: "I used to have to pick cotton and sometime I pick 300 pound and tote it a mile

Figure 1.1. Formerly enslaved woman Sarah Ashley sits outside for a photograph in Texas on May 28, 1937. (Portraits of African American ex-slaves from the U.S. Works Progress Administration, Federal Writers' Project slave narratives collections. Library of Congress Prints and Photographs Division, LC-USZ62-125165.)

to de cotton house. Some pick 300 to 800 pound cotton and have to tote de bag de whole mile to da gin." Ashley proudly noted, "I never git whip, 'causa I allus git my 300 pound."[31] Irella Battle Walker faced a similarly daunting task from a young age. Walker told her FWP interviewer that, at the age of 12, she was already picking and carrying approximately 150 pounds of cotton a day.[32]

Multiple sources note that women regularly picked substantially more cotton than men. It is possible that women became accustomed to picking and carrying heavier loads of cotton while doing so through pregnancy and while carrying babies and small children on their backs. White enslavers certainly perpetuated the idea that, unlike delicate white women, Black women were preternaturally strong. White observers in Africa marveled at how easily they believed childbirth was for African women, remarking that they could both give birth and return to work in the field on the same day.[33] In the American colonies and after the American Revolution, white enslavers' self-serving belief that Black women did not feel pain and were able to engage in back-breaking labor was critical to racist logic.[34] Black women's ability to pick as much or more than their male peers was a core part of this racist ideology but also a point of pride for some enslaved Black women.

Though enslaved women like Patsey, Sarah Ashley, and Irella Walker were forced to carry hundreds of pounds of cotton on a daily basis, one enslaved young boy deployed his sack in another memorable way. Joe Clinton, who would have been approximately 8 to 11 years old and enslaved in Mississippi when the Civil War started, told an interviewer about an enslaved boy named Henry who boldly burned the sack he had been ordered to fill with cotton. Clinton described how, on a Friday, enslaver Harvey Brown decided that Henry had not picked enough cotton and, as punishment, gave "Henry er lashin' out in de field." Later that evening, Henry burned his sack and ran away, taking refuge along the bayou. Not to be deterred, Brown sent two overseers who succeeded in finding Henry. When he reluctantly returned, Brown asked, "Henry, where your sack?" Offering no apology for his actions, "Henry say he done burnt he sack up."[35]

In taking this action, Henry demonstrated a willingness to destroy his enslaver's property, a refusal to pick cotton again, and perhaps the feeling that this sack was not a critical item to be repurposed. Rather than claim to have lost or ripped the sack as a safer form of sabotage, Henry forthrightly stated that he burned it, altogether erasing one of the most important material signifiers of his enslaved status on a cotton plantation. Brown found this act intolerable and proceeded to "lit into him like a bear, lashin him right and left." As Henry attempted to run, Brown then grabbed a piece of wood and nearly beat him to death.[36] For "days en days," Henry languished in the sick house, while another slave tended to him, picking maggots out of his sores. While several women used sacks to carry babies and adapted them into detachable pockets because their loose-fitting skirts could hide sacks full of food and other materials, Henry demolished his sack, eliminating evidence of its very existence.

Sacks continued to hold symbolic value as emblems of unfreedom for both men and women even as the Civil War was ending. Rube Witt was 87 and living in Marshall, Texas, at the time of his FWP interview. On September 7, 1937, he stood squinting into the sun on the uneven floorboards of his porch in what appeared to be a ready-made light blazer, a white button-down shirt, rolled-up dark pants, and shoes. Witt told interviewers how clothing made out of sacks represented bondage.[37] He vividly remembered enslaved people in Texas gleefully removing their clothing as soon as they learned of their newfound freedom: "Master [Jess Witt] calls up all the slaves and says we was free, but if we stayed and worked for him we'd have plenty to eat and wear, and if we left, it'd be root, hawg or die." While Witt stayed for one year, most others left, rejecting Witt's offer of food and clothing. "You'd ought to seed 'em pullin' off them croaker-sack clothes when master says we's free."[38] Clothing constructed from sacks was not only uncomfortable, but a material manifestation of the bondage that enslaved women and men were eager to cast off in their first moments of freedom.

Unlike enslaved men, by the nineteenth century, most free men enjoyed access to pants with private pockets. In fact, according to one historian, men had access to integrated pockets for more than 400 years, transitioning from carrying pouches to wearing pants with integrated pockets around the sixteenth century.[39] There are multiple theories about why such a large discrepancy existed between men's and women's access to pockets. But perhaps there is no simpler explanation than the fact that women have nearly always been given less space than men, even among the most privileged classes.

Free Black men who had access to secondhand clothing made strategic use of private pockets. The incredible story of a free Black man named David Walker demonstrates the power of pockets most vividly. Though Walker is believed to have been born free in North Carolina, he witnessed the brutal slayings of enslaved people who were discovered planning a slave rebellion. After living in Charleston sometime between 1822 and 1829, Walker moved to Boston, where slavery had already been banned.[40] There, he opened up a secondhand clothing store, where he sold clothing to free men, including sailors. In September 1829, he published a fiery manifesto that called white enslavers hypocrites and directly encouraged Black people to engage in violent revolution. Boldly, he signed his real name and printed thousands of copies of his pamphlet.[41]

David Walker's "Appeal" managed to find its way into the hands of Black people in South Carolina, Georgia, and Louisiana. How did it get there? Walker had been stuffing copies of his pamphlet into the pockets of pants he sold to sailors in his store.[42] Such men may not have realized what they had in their pockets when they embarked on their ships and sailed south. Unsurprisingly, Southerners began to call for Walker's arrest and rumors began circulating that a bounty of 3,000 dollars had been placed on his head. Within one year, Walker was found dead in the doorway of his store, possibly the victim of a poisoning.[43] Just as Black women would use purses to ferry guns throughout the South during the Civil Rights Movement and trans women and gay men used pocketbooks to carry bricks to protect their bodies in the second half of the twentieth century, Walker used pockets to distribute a revolutionary message.

Enslaved Black men and women created their own pockets using repurposed sacks, but they also used sacks at points of departure. Whether burning a sack before running away or using one to store provisions in preparation for an escape, sacks often signified a prelude to a goodbye. To be sure, dropping a sack for the last time would have provided an immediate sense of physical and mental relief for enslaved people and free whites recognized this too. In 1853, when a lawyer first arrived at the Louisiana plantation on which Solomon Northup had been enslaved, it is particularly poignant that, upon first sight, Northup remembered the lawyer commanded him to "throw down that sack."[44] The act of dropping a heavy sack was a potent gesture that signified the loosening of enslaved bodies from their enslavers' immediate grasp.

For many, the material trappings of slavery were not easily left behind. After the Civil War, most newly freed people were given no new clothes and had nothing to wear but the clothes on their backs. In her memoir *First Days Amongst the Contrabands,* Elizabeth Botume, a white woman who published her recollections of teaching newly freed people in South Carolina, vividly described how her students were dressed: "The refugees . . . had literally nothing to wear." The women, she noted, "came to me with only a skirt on made of coarse bagging, or 'crocus' tied together with twine and a nondescript item over the shoulders, something between a shawl and a sack made of old bits of carpeting."[45] In addition, many enslaved women were issued clothing so infrequently that they learned to save, mend, and reuse such materials until they degraded beyond repair. For these reasons, surviving examples of pockets, sacks, and clothing worn by enslaved people are comparatively rare in museum collections.

Before slavery was abolished, enslaved mothers also used sacks to prepare to say goodbye to family members. When enslavers died, their property was often divvied up among surviving family members or sold off to pay outstanding debts. From the perspective of an enslaved person, then, an enslaver's death was a particularly frightening event because it most often precipitated the forced separation of family members. Such goodbyes might be temporary, or perhaps last forever, but sacks often played a part in the process.

In *All That She Carried*, historian Tiya Miles examines the remarkable journey of a sack beginning in the hands of an enslaved Black mother named Rose who was living in Charleston, South Carolina. When Rose learned in 1852 that her 9-year-old daughter Ashley would be sold away, she grabbed a sack made out of cotton and filled it with "a tattered dress, three handfuls of pecans, and a braid of her own hair" to give to her daughter.[46] Functioning like luggage, the sack was nearly 3 feet long and 16 inches wide, making it far larger than most nineteenth-century detachable pockets and several times larger than the integrated pockets found in most women's clothing today.[47] Of course, this sack was also much larger than the reticules that free white women carried in the nineteenth century.

After giving her the sack, Rose never saw Ashley again, yet the sack would provide a pivotal link between four generations of Black women. In 1921, Rose's great-granddaughter Ruth Middleton embroidered the story of the sack's origins onto the sack itself. The history of the sack is remarkable; its intact survival, embroidery, disappearance, and its 2007 rediscovery at a flea market in Tennessee are even more so.[48] However, in revealing the multifaceted significance of a sack for one family, Miles also hints at a larger story borne out by a close examination of sacks in other primary sources. Slave narratives and oral history interviews prove that at least some enslaved people, and women in particular, strategically and effectively deployed sacks in their pursuit of agency and autonomy not just in South Carolina, but in Arkansas, Georgia, Mississippi, Missouri, Oklahoma, Texas, and Virginia.

After or before a sale, enslaved people like Ashley were sometimes forcibly walked in coffles, chained to each other as they marched deeper into the bowels of the South. Illustrations of these coffles show enslaved people shouldering "tow sacks," which were similar to burlap bags.[49] These sacks provided their only opportunity to bring the most meaningful material possessions of their previous lives to their uncertain new ones. In fact, one formerly enslaved Virginian recalled witnessing "droves of Negroes brought in here on foot going South to be sold. Each one of them had an old tow sack on his back with everything he's got in it."[50]

Enslaved women were practiced in the art of creating something out of nothing, and they found ingenious ways of making use of scrap materials.[51] Starting in the nineteenth century, Black women used scraps from sacks and other items to create quilts to keep warm, but these quilts also featured abstract designs with vivid colors. In the segregated farming area of Gees Bend, Alabama, generations of rural Black women had made quilts when, in 1966, approximately 85 Black women formed the Freedom Quilting Bee, a sewing cooperative to support their families during the struggles of the Civil Rights Movement.[52] Beginning in the 1970s, these quilts have been widely recognized as a distinctive and exceptional African American art form.[53]

In the nineteenth century, enslaved women also used sacks to fashion additional clothing, bedding, and extra layers of clothing that could help them stay warm in the winter months. Fannie Tatum, who was born enslaved in the middle of the Civil War along the Ouachita River in Arkansas, often turned to sacks intended for flour and tobacco, sometimes referred to as "backy sacks." Tatum recalled creating stockings by "wrapping sacks and rags around her legs" to keep them warm in the winter.[54] Tatum also described making a bed out of sacks: "I slept by the jamb of the fireplace on a sack of straw and covered with saddle blankets."[55] Decades later, Fannie Wheeler was in the process of making a bedspread out of "backy sacks" when a writer working for the Works Progress Administration (WPA) knocked on the door of her Arkansas home in the 1930s.[56]

Rosa Simmons, who was 15 years old when the Civil War began, attested to how sacks could be used to simulate some semblance of private domestic space where none existed, even functioning as doors or walls. The cabin in which Simmons was forced to lived had no door, so "just had a balin' sack hangin' in the door." One night she woke up, startled to find a bear beside her; the bear had wandered through the sack "door."[57] Obviously a sack provided a poor alternative to a door, but at least a sack could prevent prying eyes from seeing inside the home.

Some of the strategies enslaved women used to appropriate sacks for purposes beyond their most obvious uses as containers for crops and rations survived long after the institution of slavery officially ended. For example, in the midst of the Great Depression, one interviewer described Laura Bell, who was 73 years old and living in a two-room house in Raleigh, North Carolina at the time of her interview, as "a tall Negro woman clad in burlap bags."⁵⁸

As enslaved people and their descendants attest, the practice of wrapping sacks around one's legs created warmth in cold winters when clothing was often scarce. However, this practice may also have served a second purpose for women. Indeed, enslaved women may have adopted this practice to achieve a greater sense of bodily privacy and security, hoping to prevent white enslavers from visually consuming their bodies as they worked and moved about plantations. In an environment in which enslaved women were regularly sexually assaulted, clothing was often minimal, and enslaved children were left only partially clothed or altogether nude, providing an extra layer of cover could be critical. In this context, one can imagine that wearing a sack underneath a loose and transparent shirt or dress could help conceal one's legs. Given that enslaved people endured being oiled, propped upon auction blocks, stripped, and probed at slave markets, having this extra barrier between their skin and enslaver may have provided a symbolic and material layer of protection.⁵⁹

In addition to providing extra clothing and privacy, sacks permitted enslaved women to supplement food supplies. In particular, enslaved women who worked inside white homes used sacks to acquire food reserved only for white people. For example, Tom Hawkins recalled that on Johnny Poore's plantation in South Carolina, enslaved women who served as cooks "tied sacks 'roun deir waisties under deir skirts, and all thoo' de day dey would drap a little of dis, and some of dat, in de sacks. When dey poured it out at night, dere was plenty of good somepin t'eat."⁶⁰ While enslaved in Oklahoma, Ida Henry, who was born in 1854, similarly recalled how she "would put biscuits and pieces of chicken in a sack under me dress dat hung from me waist, as I waited de table for me Mistress." She added that later she "would slip off and eat it as dey never gave de slaves none of dis sort of food."⁶¹

White enslavers seemed to both know and fear that enslaved women were using hidden sacks to appropriate goods. They wanted to make sure enslaved women were never encouraged, even indirectly, to do so. Waters McIntosh, who had been born during the Civil War in South Carolina, told an FWP interviewer that when an itinerant white preacher was given permission to preach to a group of enslaved people, he urged them to "[B]e honest: When you go to the mill, don't carry along an extra sack and put some of the meal or the flour in for yourself." Yet, the preacher singled out women in particular, advising that "when you women are cooking in the big house, don't make a big pocket under your dress and put a sack of coffee and a sack of sugar and other things you want in it."[62] Apparently angered that the preacher had seemingly given the enslaved women suggestions for stealing (suggestions of which they were almost certainly already aware), McIntosh revealed that white enslavers then took the preacher and "hanged him for corrupting the morals of the slaves."[63] It is possible that the enslaved people who heard the preacher's sermon were only told that the preacher had been hanged to instill fear in them, or that the story had been embellished over the decades. Nonetheless, the story clearly conveyed the message that using sacks for illicit purposes could result in severe punishment or even death.

In the 1930s, one formerly enslaved woman bemoaned the loss of large detachable pockets made out of sacks. During an interview at her home in Athens, Georgia, 90-year-old Lina Hunter stood up to display the opening of a pocket on the front left side of her dress: "See here, Chile," she said to the FWP interviewer, "here's a sho 'nough pocket. Jus' let me turn it wrong-side-out to show you how big it is. Why, I used a whole twenty-five-pound flour sack to make it."[64] Six decades later, Hunter was using the same methods enslaved people had used to create commodious private spaces. Hunter found these pockets to be far superior to the small ready-made inset pockets that only occasionally appeared in women's clothing by the 1930s. "I don't lak none if dese newfangled little pockets," she insisted. "Dis pocket hangs down inside and nobody don't see it."[65] Unlike a front pocket on an apron or visible pocketbook that was carried outside the body, Hunter's pocket afforded more storage space while remaining hidden.

In addition to using sacks to create pockets, enslaved people also made use of sacks while planning their escapes to freedom, carefully considering what to take with them and what to leave behind. In advertisements for runaway slaves, the newspapers often circulated images of runaway slaves absconding with a sack full of materials. In fact, advertisements for runaway slaves often featured thumbnail-sized images of an enslaved person carrying a sack while on the run. These images were known as "stereotypes." Many antebellum printers relied on a variety of these stock images when attempting to depict runaways.[66] Though some newspapers used one stock image of a nondescript silhouette carrying a shouldered stick with a bag tied to it to depict all runaways, many used separate images for women and men. For men, newspapers often used an image of a man running—midstride—at a nearly a 45-degree angle with a walking stick. By contrast, women were often portrayed carrying a bag as they pursued their own liberation.[67] Runaway advertisements offered detailed descriptions of the clothing runaways were wearing and took with them.[68] Far fewer enslaved women ran away than enslaved men; many believe that women were unwilling to leave their enslaved children behind and unable to successfully escape with them. Nonetheless, these images suggest at least the perception that enslaved women did not leave their possessions behind when they ran away.

Images paired with advertisements for enslaved women often feature a woman wearing a headwrap, dress, and walking with a bag. Like a chatelaine, the bag was sometimes tied to her waist, rather than carried in her hand. She was often depicted as moving at a slower pace than the man, perhaps slowed down by her baggage. Just as a modern-day shoulder bag frees the arms of its carriers, an enslaved woman who tied a bag around her waist could keep her hands free, making it easier for her to move through woods, wade through rivers, scale or climb uphill terrain, or fend off attackers. Images of an enslaved woman with a bag also emphasized the enslaved woman's mobility as well as the ability to take goods with her. This was a point of frustration for enslavers who wished to keep enslaved women locked down and within sight. Yet, a bag filled with unknown contents also pointed to the small measure of privacy enslaved women carved out for themselves as they slowly planned to self-liberate.

The texts of these advertisements repeatedly emphasized the significance of women who were suspected of absconding with a bag full of clothing, as this made them much more difficult to identify. In June 1836, Simon Abbott purchased an advertisement searching for "Sarah," a 23-year-old woman whose "dress is not known, as she carried off several suits with her."[69] Baggage allowed her to disguise herself differently at various points of her journey. At least two enslaved women famously escaped by disguising themselves as men, a feat that could not be pulled off without access to men's clothes. These escapes often took years of planning and months to execute. In 1848, Ellen and William Craft, an enslaved couple, fled their plantations in Macon, Georgia. Ellen, who was lighter-skinned than William, disguised herself as a white man named William Johnson, who was traveling with his servant/slave (William). In one iteration of the story, Ellen planned to cut off her hair and wear men's clothes as they rode a train for four days to freedom.[70] Anna Maria Weems also successfully escaped slavery in 1855 by disguising herself as a male carriage driver; her access to a driver's uniform, bow tie, and hat was critical to her ability to do this.[71]

In September 1845, the *Milledgeville Federal Union* published an advertisement that featured an image of a woman with poor posture walking; her head

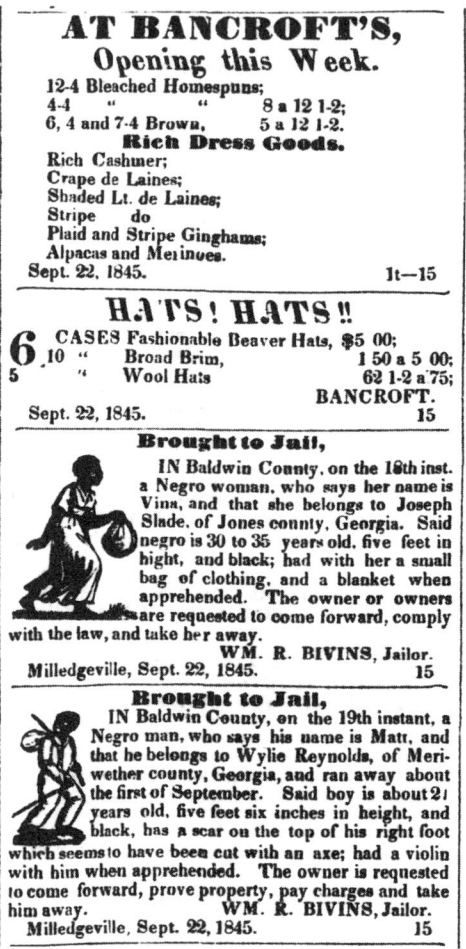

Figure 1.2. In September 1845, a Georgia newspaper featured separate advertisements for an enslaved woman and man who were presumed to be runaways. The top illustration depicts a Black woman with short hair or perhaps a head scarf in a dress with a bag in her hand. She has poor posture and is pictured moving at a slow pace from left to right. An advertisement for an enslaved man found with a violin appears below her, though he is represented by a figure with a walking cane and a knapsack suspended from his shoulder. The juxtaposition of ads for bulk fabric and "Hats! Hats!!" alongside human beings suggests that advertisers saw these categories of goods similarly. (*Milledgeville Federal Union*, September 23, 1845, 3, Georgia Historic Newspapers.)

is bare, and she is carrying a sack in her left hand. The advertisement described the discovery and arrest of a "negro woman" who, when captured, had with her a "small bag of clothing."[72] Among other newspapers, *The Charleston Mercury*, the *Charleston Courier*, the *Raleigh Register*, and *The Daily Picayune* used similar images for their runaway advertisements.

In 1847, T. J. Pretlow of Southhampton County, Virginia, took out at least five advertisements in two different newspapers in pursuit of an enslaved woman he valued at the price of 50 and later, 100 dollars. He described her as highly skilled, literate, and a "first-rate sempstress" [*sic*] who took with her a "Portmanteau or Travelling Bag." Though she had previously called herself Martha Payn, Pretlow noted her real name was Elizabeth Scott and stated that "some of her clothes are probably marked with E. S."[73] A change of clothes could have been critical to her successful escape, enabling her to trade spare clothing for food and shelter. Though having her clothes marked with her initials could have given her away, it also signaled that the clothes were *hers*.

Though enslaved people did not legally own their bodies or their labor, in some cases, legal practices tied ownership of clothing to the person wearing it, even when that person was enslaved. This was true in the case of accessories as well. In fact, clothes and other textiles were perhaps the most important property that a runaway slave could carry with them. If caught, however, an enslaved person could be charged with two crimes: running away and theft. But enslaved people sometimes fought those charges, insisting that they owned their clothing. In 1805, an enslaved woman named Caty ran away and took clothing with her. When she was caught and brought to court, she acknowledged running away but insisted the clothing she took was her own.[74]

Other runaway slaves prioritized money over a change of clothing. Much like Rose gave her daughter Ashley a sack just before she was to be sold away, Harriet Jacobs described the importance of a small bag she carried on her long journey to freedom in her narrative, *Incidents in the Life of a Slave Girl* (1861). She recounted an incident when her grandmother entered the room after Jacobs announced her plan to run away, saying "she came in with a small bag of money, which she wanted me to take. I begged her to keep a part of it... but she insisted, while her tears were falling fast, that I should take the whole." In yet another example of a Black maternal figure using a sack to care for her progeny, Jacobs's grandmother argued, "'You may be sick among strangers,' she said, 'and they would send you to the poorhouse to die.'" Reflecting back, Jacobs noted, "Ah, that good grandmother!"[75]

Perhaps no figure embodies the journey of self-liberation for enslaved Black women better than Harriet Tubman. Multiple sources suggest that, after liberating herself from enslavement in Maryland in 1849, Tubman carried a reticule while traveling. Reticules were most often used by upper-class white women in the late eighteenth and early nineteenth century. These bags were very small in size and largely ornamental in purpose. Reticules typically closed with a drawstring and were often embroidered and constructed of satin or netting. They frequently contained a fan and calling cards, or *cartes de visite*, and sometimes included a small vial of perfume or aromatic oils and cosmetics.[76] Unlike handbags in the twentieth century, they were rarely used to carry money. Until the Regency era ushered in slim, clinging profiles and empire waists, white women had carried detachable pockets worn under their clothing, much like the ones enslaved women fashioned from sacks. While men ridiculed women and their need to carry supposedly trivial items, women like Harriet Tubman subversively used reticules as both a marker of freedom and a toolkit for survival.

One of the first physical descriptions ever published of Harriet Tubman appeared in William Wells Brown's book *Rising Son* in 1859. Brown described Tubman as "a black woman of medium size . . . attired in coarse but neat apparel, with an old fashioned reticule or bag by her side."[77] Tubman was seen with a small reticule dangling from her wrist, even as she abruptly fell asleep on trains as a result of a childhood head injury or perhaps narcolepsy. She also kept her reticule at her side when she made abolitionist speeches in the 1850s.[78] Such evidence suggests that while enslaved women relied on sacks, reticules—often perceived as the purview of upper-class white women—were striking in the hands of Black women like Tubman.

What did Tubman carry inside her reticule? After her escape from enslavement, Tubman used her reticule to carry *cartes de visite* wherever she went. Because she was unable to read or write, Tubman used these small photographs as a litmus test to determine if people who claimed to be anti-slavery activists could identify familiar faces within the anti-slavery movement. Her aim was to distinguish activists from fugitive slave catchers, an incredibly important distinction that meant the difference between freedom or a return to slavery. According to Tubman's biographer, "[W]hen she made contact with persons she had never met before, Tubman's treasured pack of *cartes de visites* became her insurance policy. She showed these persons her images and asked them to name the people in the pictures to test their credentials."[79] Without a reticule by her side, Tubman would not have been able to access these images at a moment's notice and thereby secure her safety. While Tubman carried a reticule after escaping slavery, free women in abolitionist societies in both Great Britain and the United States formed sewing circles where they designed reticules that featured anti-slavery images and messages.[80] These and other objects were distributed or sold to raise awareness and funds for the abolitionist cause and could also be stuffed with abolitionist pamphlets.

"THIS SACK SO FULL"   33

HARRIET TUBMAN.

Figure 1.3. Sarah H. Bradford used this illustration of Harriet Tubman (born Araminta Ross) to highlight her role as a spy in the Civil War for the frontispiece of *Scenes in the Life of Harriet Tubman.* Tubman carries both a large rifle and haversack. Bradford credited Mr. J. C. Darby with creating the woodcut. (W.J. Moses, Auburn, Alabama, 1869, Vol. 2, 6.)

Perhaps the most famous illustrated depiction of Harriet Tubman features her carrying a bag much larger than a reticule. In 1869, the American writer and historian Sarah H. Bradford used a woodcut illustration of Tubman in *Scenes in the Life of Harriet Tubman.* The image shows Tubman carrying a large bag, perhaps a haversack, over her shoulder. Bradford used this text to raise funds for Tubman after the U.S. government refused to pay the pension she earned as a spy and nurse during the Civil War.[81] This image of Tubman with a rifle and haversack bag became iconic and was later featured in *The Woman's Era*, a newspaper run by Black women in the late 1800s. The illustration was the inspiration for several later works, including both William Johnson's 1945 painting of Tubman and Romare Beard's 1963 adaptation, "Harriet Tubman with Rifle."[82] To the modern eye, the most conspicuous component of these images is likely Tubman's long rifle, which is nearly as tall as she is. In fact, Tubman did carry a rifle, according to one of her biographers.[83] In these images, the rifle represents the courage and militarism she showed during repeated journeys through the Underground Railroad, as well as her service in the Civil War. However, in the context of the history of sacks, bags, and purses, Tubman's shoulder bag is just as important as her rifle.

After the Civil War, Tubman became the victim of a purse-snatching when she was lured into the woods under the pretense of buying buried gold. Instead, she was attacked by thieves who chloroformed her and stole her purse.[84] Marking Tubman's life by these multiple purse-related incidents (her reticule, haversack, and stolen purse) suggests the shifting but consistent importance of portable containers across one woman's remarkable lifetime. Despite having been robbed, Tubman's access to a portable bag across multiple decades enhanced her ability to successfully negotiate spaces specifically designed to disempower her.

The fundamental objective of slavery was to contain the movement of enslaved bodies within prescribed spaces in the dogged pursuit of maximum profits. Though men and women were both bound by this "geography of containment," enslaved women "in greater numbers and in greater consistency were confined to southern plantations; as a group they enjoyed far less mobility than did men."[85] Indeed, many historians have noted that women were routinely sexually assaulted, and forced to give birth to children who would automatically inherit their enslaved status. After the constitutional ban on the importation of enslaved Africans went into effect in 1808, the survival of the institution of slavery depended on enslaved women producing more generations of enslaved people.[86]

Perhaps Harriet Jacobs was right when she argued that "slavery is terrible for men, but it is far more terrible for women."[87] If slavery was indeed more terrible for women, women were perhaps more resourceful and imaginative in turning textiles into tools that could be used to circumvent its most invasive cruelties. Exploring the ways in which enslaved women used textiles to carve out secret spaces alongside their bodies renders visible the social, psychological, and political value of a sack—an otherwise seemingly mundane artifact. In fact, the ways in which enslaved women used sacks as instruments in their own fight for liberation parallel how Black women in America would use purses in later decades. Indeed, between World War I and World War II, Black women migrants saw special purpose in the pocketbooks and suitcases they took aboard trains during the Great Migration; some even referred to these containers as "freedom bags."[88] And in the Civil Rights Movement a few decades later, Black women used purses to conceal guns, enter segregated spaces, and prepare for sit-ins. Taken together, these stories reveal the creative and versatile ways in which Black women used material culture, and movable containers in particular, to improve their lives in the antebellum period and throughout American history.

2

Purses and Pathbreaking Women at the Turn of the Century

In the late 1880s, Nellie Bly (born Elizabeth Cochrane) was the literal picture of the plucky, brave New Woman in modern America. By the time she planned a trip around the world, Bly had sealed her reputation as a muckraking young journalist who dared to do what others would not. For ten days, she lived undercover at Blackwell's Insane Asylum to expose the brutal conditions in which patients were forced to live. Her newspaper articles and subsequent book, *Ten Days in a Madhouse* (1887), made her a household name. But when she proposed her next idea—traveling around the world at record speed—she knew she would face some skepticism.

Bly recalled approaching her editor at the *New York World*, "afraid that he would think the idea too wild and visionary."[1] She had been inspired by the fictional character Phileas Fogg in Jules Verne's *Around the World in Eighty Days* (1872). Fogg undertook his trip around the world on a bet and carried a carpetbag, but Bly wanted to beat Fogg's fictional record. She explained to readers that her office "had thought of this same idea before and the intention was to send a man."[2] "It is impossible for you to do it," Bly recalled hearing. "You are a woman and would need a protector, and even if it were possible for you to travel alone you would need to carry so much baggage that it would detain you in making rapid changes."[3]

After first being rebuffed, Bly was later called back to the office and informed that she would depart for her trip the next day. In a hurry, she prepared that night, focused on taking a smaller bag than the fictional Phileas Fogg. After ordering a custom dress and coat, she "bought one hand-bag with the determination to confine my baggage." As she recalled in *Around the World in Seventy-Two Days* (1890), that "one piece of hand luggage no bigger than a gripsack, sixteen inches wide and only seven inches tall" would sustain her throughout her trip.[4]

Yet Bly recalled, perhaps hyperbolically, that "packing that bag was the most difficult undertaking of my life; there was so much to go into such little space."[5] Inside that small bag, she claimed, she was able to fit a large collection of items. Bly kept her most critical item, her passport, "down in the bottom of my hand-bag," where many women kept their most important possessions and where it was least likely to get pickpocketed. She told readers that she considered taking a revolver, but ultimately decided not to, even though she claimed someone proffered that it "would be a good companion piece for the passport."[6] Ever the optimist, Bly believed that she would be met with kindness and hospitality during her travels, and a gun would therefore be unnecessary.

In addition to her leather satchel, Bly wore a "chamois-skin bag, which I tied around my neck."[7] Necklace bags helped offset the lack of integrated pockets in women's clothing; because they rested on the chest and had to be lifted over the head, they were harder to steal than a purse hanging from one's hand. Dressed for departure, Nellie Bly posed for a photographer and her portrait became iconic. Adorned in her traveling coat, cap, and gloves, Bly stood tall, carrying her small satchel and looking determinedly into the distance. Her photograph would appear on newspaper covers, advertisements, and even board games over the next several years. The image emphasized Bly's ability to take very little with her, and this detail became one of the most celebrated anecdotes about her trip. Since Bly went alone and had only one small handbag as her companion, she carried that bag herself.

When Bly departed for her trip near the end of the nineteenth century, American women had entered the workforce in larger numbers. Married women were also gaining access to new rights, which (in at least some cases) legally allowed them to keep their own wages, pursue a divorce, and eventually open their own bank accounts.[8] In the Victorian era, home and work had been positioned as opposites of one another. Although many white middle-class Americans still believed that a woman's place was in the home, in the late nineteenth century, seismic shifts in acceptable styles, behavior, and sexual mores were unfolding.[9]

As more American women like Bly traversed city streets and state lines, crossed national borders and engaged in activism, purses and bags took on new cultural significance.[10] Because they were necessary for leaving the home as more and more women sought to do just that, purses and bags became symbols of women's new public roles. While they provided privacy in public, purses also became a critical way in which women fashioned and (re)created themselves as public figures.

Figure 2.1. Nellie Bly appears in a hat, dark gloves, and full-length plaid coat while holding her 16- by 7-inch "gripsack" in her left hand. (Circa 1890, the Miriam and Ira D. Wallach Division of Art, Prints and Photographs: Print Collection, The New York Public Library.)

From the 1870s to the 1910s, women successfully challenged old ideologies that they did not belong in public. In these later decades, they claimed city spaces as their own, bumping elbows with men on crowded sidewalks, streets, and streetcars.[11] In doing so, they confronted older stereotypes that they were immoral and promiscuous. Window shopping, studio portraits, vaudeville performers, and early silent films simultaneously created a culture of visual display centered around women.[12] These images reveal tensions over women's autonomy and vulnerability and the central role purses played in this story. Though Nellie Bly was exceptional in many ways, working-class women of all different races and regions could make or buy purses to emphasize their identities as consumers, waged workers, and travelers who valued mobility and independence. While purses did serve ornamental purposes, in this era, they became highly functional. As early women's ready-made clothing did not often include pockets, women used purses to hold money, keys, important papers, writing utensils, and many other essential items.

During these transitional decades, women like Nellie Bly increasingly pictured themselves as active participants in public life. They wrapped up a petite portable version of the domestic sphere in their purses and bags, and stepped out, heading to work outside their immediate neighborhoods.[13] In doing so, they also rubbed shoulders with strangers and navigated cityscapes supposedly replete with purse-snatchers and pickpockets. Crime columnists increasingly wrote about purse-snatchings, framing them as an intimate violation. Some newspapers sensationalized and coded these "snatchings" as a form of sexual assault, especially in the cases of white middle-class women who claimed the assailants were Black. In fact, many male-to-female interactions centering around purses highlight sexual and racial tensions at the turn-of-the century. Media coverage disproportionately focused on stories about white women who were alternatively portrayed as active agents and vulnerable victims.

The potent symbolism of purses is especially evident in turn-of-the-century studio portraits of women. These portraits illustrate the fraught tensions surrounding women's relatively new and contentious place in turn-of-the-century America. Photographs produced from the 1880s to the 1910s illustrate the significant social, legal, and economic changes in the lives of American women. Viewing these images both in isolation and as a constellation allows us to contextualize not just who is pictured in each image but what she is doing, wearing, and holding, and to at least speculate why.

In analyzing photographs, we must attempt to separate the photographer's intentions from those of the subject.[14] For the most part, female subjects co-created photographic portraits with (almost entirely) male photographers. As women sought to gain control over their lives, they simultaneously sought to control their own image too.[15] By commissioning others to photograph their dressed bodies in portraits, however, women affirmed their ideal sense of themselves. They also asserted their right to be seen.[16]

Studio portraits were, by definition, a commodification of one's own body. In the late nineteenth century, they often featured women wearing mass-produced clothing, jewelry, shoes, hats, and purses. Thus, they represented a doubly commodified product.[17] But this does not mean that women were unwitting victims of exploitative forces. Instead, they used time spent in studios to perform, document, and later distribute "visual autobiographies" of themselves as they wanted to be seen.[18] Rather than position women as passive subjects, turn-of-the-century studio portraits locate women as authors of their own visual narratives.[19]

While the professional photographer framed the scope of vision and perhaps positioned women's bodies before the camera, it was the women themselves who paid photographers and decided what to wear. Women's sartorial choices gave them the opportunity to distinguish themselves amid standardized backgrounds of pedestals, chairs, and pillars. Although the possibilities and reverberations of women's choices varied depending on their class, race, religion, age, and marital status, female subjects of portraits knew accessories could be used to make a particularly bold statement.[20] As a result, they chose their attire carefully.

Americans who could afford to do so had long relied on portraiture to demonstrate their sense of self and status. Paintings, daguerreotypes, and ambrotypes allowed them to visually secure their spot in existing social hierarchies.[21] Starting in the 1840s and 1850s, other forms of illustration began to play a central role in American life.[22] Photographic studio portraits became accessible to working- and middle-class Americans beginning in the 1860s with the creation of *cartes de visite,* which translated into English means "visiting card."[23] These were 2.5- by 4-inch mechanically produced photographs, the perfect size to fit inside a small handheld purse. Consumers typically purchased several copies for as little as a dollar a dozen.[24]

In many *cartes de visite,* women were photographed holding emblems of femininity (often flowers) or doing appropriately gendered tasks, including arranging a vase, reading a letter, or holding a child. Such images fit contemporary gender norms suggesting that women were delicate, selfless creatures.[25] However, studio portraits also reveal the changing ways in which a variety of women used accessories to create more modern identities as they visually entered the public realm.[26] In the 1890s and early 1900s, more women began carrying purses and they gradually appear more frequently in photographs. Unlike flowers, purses represented visibility outside the home, mobility, and the (admittedly meager) wages many women were now independently earning.

In this milieu, studio portraits enabled American women to produce and distribute visual evidence of their class, gender, and racial status.[27] Yet, the mass reproduction and distribution of images of women made some particularly anxious. In the same way that many critics worried that white women would be robbed, kidnapped, and generally harassed on city streets if left to their own devices, some argued that mechanically reproducing a woman's body over and over again, only to have the final product passed out and shared among many, constituted a kind of "prostitution."[28] They cringed at the thought of women's bodies being "bought and sold and handled in card format" in an era when women were still largely expected to avoid the public eye.[29] In the mid-nineteenth century, other widely circulated illustrations suggested that women who dared to become public figures were "manly" women who wore pants and smoked cigars.[30] Political cartoons and postcards especially satirized suffragists in this way. However, abolitionists, suffragists, women like Nellie Bly, and seemingly ordinary women could use photographs to assert their own stories and styles.[31]

Black women with the means to do so also seized on the opportunity to fight insidious stereotypes by creating their own visual autobiographies. One of the earliest advocates for women's suffrage, Sojourner Truth, was strategic about circulating and selling her image. Born Isabella Van Wagenen sometime between 1797 and 1800, Truth renamed herself and took ownership of her image, sitting for her photograph at least seven times between 1863 and 1875.[32] Rather than selling the rights to a photographer, Truth copyrighted her own image, sold her own photographs, and managed the profits.[33]

Most of these images featured Truth in traditionally feminine poses, sitting next to a vase of flowers or knitting. However, one of these images shows Truth, who stood nearly 6 feet tall, standing upright.[34] She holds her cane with her right hand, while a large purse rests on her left forearm. The purse is unusual, appearing to be a cross between an oversized reticule and a small carpetbag. This image suggests that Truth wanted others to know she carried a purse. In fact, in her narrative, Truth told others that she carried her *cartes de visite* in a bag when she traveled, in lieu of food, clothing, or copies of her book *The Narrative of Sojourner Truth* (1850). In 1867, Truth told the *New York World*, "I do not carry 'rations' in my bag. I keep my shadow there," by which she meant her portrait. "I don't want my shadow even to be dogging about here and there and everywhere, so I keep it in this bag."[35] Truth controlled and used her image strategically, just as Harriet Tubman did. Because Tubman was unable to read or write, she used *cartes de visite* to determine if those who claimed to be abolitionists could identify familiar faces within the anti-slavery movement. Clearly, formerly enslaved women like Tubman and Truth carefully chose what to include in the small space of privacy that a reticule provided.

Figure 2.2. Sojourner Truth stands for her portrait wearing a bonnet, scarf, and glasses. Perhaps a hybrid of a small carpet bag or large reticule hangs from her left forearm. It features a plaid print, flower motif, a drawstring closing, and appears to contain several exterior pockets. (Circa 1860s, Women's Rights Collection, Series II Biographical Materials, Photograph SSC-MS-00397, Sophia Smith Collection, Smith College, Northampton, MA.)

Sojourner Truth sold copies of her own *cartes de visite* on the lecture circuit when she made speeches. At the bottom of this and other *cartes de visite*, Truth inscribed the motto, "I Sell the Shadow to Support the Substance."[36] She acknowledged the transgressive nature of selling her own image (her shadow) but framed her choice to do so as an ethical and effective one that served a higher purpose. She managed to live off the profits from sales of her book and

Figure 2.3. Jessie Tarbox Beals, one of the first successful female photojournalists, took this portrait of Mary M. Cunningham around 1910. Cunningham arranges both of her gloved hands around the handle of a very small purse. (Cunningham Gelatin silver print, Library of Congress Prints and Photographs Division, Washington, DC, LC-DIG-ds-00022.)

photograph, selling 21 dollars' worth of her *cartes de visite* at a single event.[37] This would amount to approximately 700 dollars today.

Decades later, younger Black women continued to use their image to push back against negative stereotypes and write their own visual stories. Taken around 1910 by one of the first successful female photojournalists, Jessie Tarbox Beals, Mary M. Cunningham, a young Black woman who was likely a member of the National Urban League in New York City, posed for a portrait.[38] This photograph captures Cunningham looking away from the camera, in a relatively plain outfit (a skirt and a white shirtwaist) with no coat, hat, and minimal jewelry. Yet, Cunningham appears to be wearing white gloves, a sign of her literal and figurative purity and cleanliness. She holds a small purse with both hands, perhaps so that she has a designated space for them to be. While men could shove their hands in integrated pockets, women had no such opportunity (and this gesture would have been considered rude if they had). Thus, purses gave women like Mary Cunningham a place to put their hands, enhance their access to private space, and take on a defensive posture. Cunningham hugs her purse close to the front of her body as if to protect both her possessions and herself. Her purse also creates a barrier between the most vulnerable part of her body and the photographer and viewer. One cannot help but won-

Figure 2.4. The cover of sheet music for the score of "Hannah! (I Want My Hannah)," composed by E. H. Pendleton in 1899, features a Black woman leaving a small rural home. She is mockingly adorned with outsized accessories, including a purse, gigantic bow, bonnet, and handkerchief. (M. Witmark and Sons, New York Public Library Digital Collections.)

der what Cunningham placed inside this purse; certainly, *cartes de visite* would have fit neatly.

Performing a middle-class ideal of respectability was particularly important for African American women, who were told by mainstream popular culture that they were inherently promiscuous, deficient, and subservient.[39] The cover illustration for the 1899 song "Hannah! (I Want My Hannah)" illustrates what kinds of stereotypes Black women faced in this regard. The cover illustration lampoons Black women for attempting (and failing) to look like respectable ladies. While the lyrics of the song are written in dialect, the woman on the cover is wearing an oversized bonnet and bow, as she very conspicuously dangles a purse and handkerchief. The accessories she dons typically connote femininity, but in this case, they do not fit her body and she holds them awkwardly. The image suggests that Black women who attempted to fashion themselves as respectable modern women did so to the amusement of whites. This image is one of many in circulation that featured racist and sexist caricatures of Black women in the late nineteenth century.[40]

Early suffragists used purses in their activism and, in later decades, would make more explicit use of bags in their campaign for the vote. In 1853, one of the most famous suffragists, Susan B. Anthony, wrote in her diary that "every woman must have a purse of her own."[41] Though in this instance, Anthony was likely speaking of women's property rights, she knew that purses were powerful beyond their potent symbolism. She used her own dark red alligator bag to hold both her speeches and the transcript of her trial after she was arrested in 1872 for illegally voting. Anthony took her large purse everywhere and became so associated with it that a jump-rope rhyme dubbed her "the lady with the alligator purse." The Susan B. Anthony Museum and House in Rochester, New York, even sells 250-dollar modern replicas of Anthony's purse; visitors can view Anthony's own bag under a glass box on the first floor of her home.[42]

In the last two decades of the suffrage movement, suffragists claimed ownership of their images, suggesting how bags and purses could be displayed and deployed. Activists used shop windows to display pro-suffrage messages and images. Some attempted to reach working-class women by stamping paper grocery bags with suffrage propaganda. In 1910, suffragists in Brooklyn printed and distributed 30,000 grocery bags with suffrage information. In 1911, the *San Francisco Chronicle* reported that retail store managers promised to stick suffrage propaganda in the pay envelopes of their workers. Others tucked these messages inside napkins at cafés and in the pockets of clothing delivered by tailors.[43]

As the ranks of suffrage organizations multiplied exponentially in the last ten years of the movement, the National Woman's Party proved adept at garnering publicity and portraying a particular visual narrative.[44] Nina Allender, who worked as an illustrator for the new National Woman's Party, created political cartoons that visualized suffragists' hopes for a Nineteenth Amendment.

In several cartoons, Allender used purses to represent women's votes and wages. The political cartoon "Carry Your Luggage, Lady!" demonstrates the significance of women carrying their own bags, as Nellie Bly did on her trip around the world. In this image, four men appear eager to compete to carry the luggage of a fashionable young woman stepping off a train. Her suitcase is labeled "Woman's Party," but a closer look reveals that each of her two smaller bags is labeled "Votes." The woman holds her own small purse labeled "Votes" close to her body, much as Mary M. Cunningham did when posing for Jessie Tarbox Beals. Carrying one's own purse clearly had symbolic political meaning at this time. In Allender's cartoon, while one man specifically reaches for her small purse (labeled "Votes"), the woman's gaze drifts in the opposite direction, and she does not relinquish her grip. In the last decade of the suffrage movement, political cartoons like this one depicted women's purses as the key to their vote and symbols of their agency.

In the case of suffrage bags, photographs reveal that suffragists used canvas tote bags to contain and distribute suffrage newspapers like *Woman's Journal* and *The Suffragist*. A 1913 photograph of suffragist Margaret Foley and an unidentified woman illustrates the practical utility of purses and tote bags among suffragists, who carried essentials with them as they spent their days in the streets. Next to Foley, a smaller woman carries a leather purse with a locking mechanism on the left side of her body. Ungloved, behatted, and sporting a racoon fur stole, the woman carries a small black leather purse typical of the times. A canvas bag on her right side (emblazoned with the suffrage slogan "VOTES FOR WOMEN") was likely meant to hold additional copies of the *Woman's Journal*, though those copies are piled up in the crook of this woman's left elbow. Here, the woman's purse and canvas bag literally carry her political beliefs as they free up her hands to pass out political texts.

In the first decade of the twentieth century, popular culture also played a significant role in portraying purse-wielding women as independent actors and individuals. Perhaps more than any other star of the vaudeville stage, in the first decade of the twentieth century, Eva Tanguay dazzled audiences with her bold costumes and brazen behavior. Known alternatively as "The I Don't Care Girl" and "Egotistical Eva," Tanguay quickly rose to stardom as a symbol of the irreverent modern woman who did not care if she undermined men. In 1909, 31-year-old Tanguay stepped out on stage in a short heavy dress and

Figure 2.5. Aided by an unidentified woman, suffragist Margaret Foley (right) helps distribute copies of *Woman's Journal and Suffrage News*. (November/December, 1913, G.V. Buck Studios, Washington DC, Folder, Margaret Foley, Box I: 150, Records of the National Woman's Party, Manuscript Division, Library of Congress.)

matching purse she claimed to have made herself out of 4,000 pennies. The costume was created for a number she called "Oh, You Money." During her performance, Tanguay reached into her penny purse and threw the coins at her audience as she sang. Her fan mail included a telegram from a man who proudly reported that one of her pennies "struck me on top of the nose when you performed."[45]

Tanguay stood just 5 foot 1 inch tall, but she was an expert at taking up space. According to the press, performing this song was not the only occasion on which Tanguay used a purse to brazenly boast about her self-made fortune. Newspaper columns breathlessly covered her personal life. Though they likely took liberties in making her appear more outrageous than she was, columnists were especially interested in how much money Tanguay carried with her. According to one source, "[I]t was a famous Tanguay gesture that she often carried five to fifteen thousand-dollar bills in her purse and to settle [a] dispute, she simply peeled one off her roll."[46]

Tanguay's purse served as a powerful reminder of the fact that, in the first decade of the twentieth century, more women were earning wages working outside the home than ever before, and some of them were outearning men by large margins. As a well-paid star, Tanguay was not typical by any means. But her outsized reputation and ubiquitous presence in popular culture hint at her influence as an icon. Although most working-class women were obliged to turn their paltry paychecks over to their fathers or husbands, they could at least sing along to Tanguay's songs and occasionally spare a dime to catch a vaudeville show where they could watch her reach into her purse and throw money in the faces of her fans. On other occasions, they could save up dimes to buy a new purse for themselves.

In the early 1900s, advertisements demonstrate that some men were still carrying their money in items called "pocketbooks" and "purses." Many of these items were functionally and aesthetically similar to "ladies'" pocketbooks and purses. Thus, the exclusive association of purses and pocketbooks with women was not yet fully complete during these decades. Nonetheless, manufacturers and advertisers were paying close attention to gender.

Silent films released in the 1910s also commented on the place of the purse as a point of tension in modern America, portraying men swinging their wives' purses to get a laugh out of viewers. In 1915, Keystone Pictures released *Mabel and Fatty's Wash Day*, a silent film starring Fatty Arbuckle and Mabel Normand.[47] At the time of its release, Arbuckle was a comedy legend and one of the highest-paid actors of his era. Many of Arbuckle's films offered a comedic take on domestic discord, and this film was no exception. In the film, Arbuckle is forced to do stereotypical women's work. As signs of his subservience, he wears an ill-fitting women's apron while scrubbing the family clothes as his vain wife looks on. As the beleaguered husband, Arbuckle then goes outside to hang the laundry in the backyard at the same time as his neighbor, played by Mabel Normand.

Normand is similarly neglected by her good-for-nothing husband and is left to do all the housework herself, although in her case this situation was common rather than comedic. As both Arbuckle and Normand's characters proceed to hang their undergarments on a shared clothesline, they laugh at confusing their linens and eventually decide to sneak away from their spouses and head out to a soda shop together. Once Arbuckle's character arrives at the shop, however, he realizes that his pockets are empty, and he cannot pay for a soda. Not only is he doing "women's work," but he has no money of his own either. Because his date Mabel also forgot her purse, Arbuckle must sneak back to his wife. Instead of grabbing some money out of her purse, he steals her entire purse, gingerly carrying it back to the soda shop. When he hands money from a small purse to the waiter, the waiter seems to laugh at the sight of a large

Figure 2.6. This screenshot comes from *Mabel and Fatty's Wash Day*, a short silent film produced in 1915. The man on the left (possibly actor Harry McCoy) and right (Roscoe "Fatty" Arbuckle) discover themselves both holding other women's diminutive purses. (Library of Congress.)

man with a dainty purse. Meanwhile, Normand's husband is left holding a very similar purse she abandoned to go out with Fatty. A case of the mistaken purse unfolds as the police are called and all sorts of hijinks ensue. Not only is it comical that Mabel's husband is left holding her purse, but it is laughable that Arbuckle does not have any money of his own. In both cases, women control the family's spending and men have been feminized through their proximity to small purses. In the midst of attempting to woo another woman, an already emasculated Arbuckle must steal money from his henpecking wife. Perhaps unsurprisingly, at the end of the film, both women end up beating their useless husbands with their purses.

Arbuckle's films often provided comic relief about beleaguered American men. The theme of the feckless husband who has no money of his own appears in multiple Arbuckle films, and purses became a way for actors and directors of silent films to depict this theme without saying a word.[48] In *Fatty's Chance Acquaintance* (1915), Arbuckle's character again wanders away from his wife, played by actress Billie Bennett, to flirt with another woman (Minta Durfee, who was Arbuckle's actual wife). Durfee's boyfriend steals Bennett's purse, confusion ensues, the police arrive, and a high-speed chase follows.[49] In *Coney Island* (1917), Arbuckle once again steals away from his nit-picking wife who treats him more like a child than a husband. When she goes searching for him, she uses her purse as a weapon, whacking a security guard over the head to gain admission to Coney Island's Luna Park.

The male characters in these films are a source of derision and comedic relief. As a symbol, the purse could be used to signify changing power relations between men and women. Studio portraits of real women coupled with actors' stage and screen performances made it easier for women to visualize themselves in particular ways at the turn of the century. Dressed in modern ready-made clothes, American women carried purses containing money that not only seemed to function as a passport to modern public life but also could be used to undermine men. Beginning in the 1880s, the growth of ready-made clothing for women, the cosmetics industry, the popularity of department store window shopping, the rise of professional actresses in vaudeville and silent film, and the marked expansion of the suffrage movement all conspired to create this new culture of display centering women. While this visual culture brought some women exciting new levels of visibility, fame, and even fortune, it also caused concern over women's vulnerability as independent actors in public life.

Throughout the nineteenth century, American cities were largely perceived as masculine spaces of danger to women. Spaces exclusively designated for women—like ladies shopping counters, doors, cars, and eventually comfort stations (public restrooms)—were created to keep women segregated from strange men, though these spaces were often racially segregated and excluded women of color.[50] Meanwhile, actresses who called attention to themselves on stage were considered "public women" who risked their reputations. Among white middle-class reformers, their reputations ranked only slightly higher than prostitutes, who were regarded as "fallen women."[51] At the same time that women's visibility was increasing, fears over "white slavery" reached new heights. In 1910, the "White Slave Traffic Act" (also known as the Mann Act) was enacted in response to growing (and mostly ill-founded) concerns that young white women were being abducted and forced into prostitution.[52] Some believed that women were to blame for making themselves too accessible to white slavers and thieves.[53] According to some critics, by the first decade of the twentieth century, women had become too visible, a change that rendered them vulnerable and worthy of special surveillance.

Both middle-class and working women were warned of the dangers that cities posed to them. Crowded streetcars and sidewalks were of particular concern, to say little of places of commercial leisure like dance halls and saloons.[54] Purses were both part of the problem and part of the solution. In 1916, the *Los Angeles Times* noted that "every girl has need·of a coin purse...it really is not safe to venture forth without one's carfare home even if attended by the most trustworthy of men or the most reliable of autos." The article then described a series of steps that would enable "any girl" to construct such a "simple purse" in a "spare hour" by reusing an 8-inch by 3-inch piece of silk or leather.[55] Having a purse that was small enough to fit into the palm of one's hand became a matter of safety as much as style, though these purses could not be as effectively used as weapons with which to whack men.

According to historian Georgina Hickey, "[I]f nineteenth century gender segregation aimed to lock women away, the twentieth century version tried to scare them away."[56] Dark evenings were seen as the most dangerous, far more so than mornings and afternoons.[57] Some advocated that women learn self-defense, an effort that coalesced into a movement during the Progressive Era.[58] In 1909, members of the Boston Equal Suffrage and Good Government Association asked for the appointment of a "police matron" who could "watch and care for the girls on the streets" at night where they might be "exposed to grave moral danger."[59] But "the girls" almost always meant white girls. However, the average American Black woman had long worked outside her home and had to traverse city streets and public transportation at night when returning from working long days in white homes.[60] And she was often denied access to ladies' cars and rooms. Because she was Black, intrepid teacher and anti-lynching activist Ida B. Wells was forcibly removed from a ladies' car en route to Memphis in 1883. She responded by biting the man who was attempting to remove her.[61] But because most white Americans already viewed Black women as hypersexual and unclean, most mainstream discussions narrowly focused on protecting young white women.

Etiquette books and advice manuals warned women to think strategically about their safety. In the 1880s and 1890s, American-born British writer Lillias Campbell Davidson attempted to advise women how to make the most out of new opportunities for adventure.[62] In her book *Hints to Lady Travelers: At Home and Abroad* (1889), she noted that increasing numbers of women were now traveling farther "from the security of her own roof-tree."[63] Indeed, with the invention of the bicycle, the expansion of railroads in Europe and the United States, and the availability of efficient ocean liners, middle-class women had more opportunities to explore previously masculine spaces than ever before. And because it was not always practical to do so with a "maid" or a man, Davidson offered "some practical hints and advice upon the wide subject of wanderings abroad."[64] She covered the mundane logistics, featuring chapters on "Hotels," "Luggage," "Night journeys," "Watering places," and, of course, "Hand-bags." She recommended that women carry courier bags, "round leather bags with a strong lock which may be slung over the shoulder by the leather strap...and worn under the arm." She added that they "have the advantage of being safe" and were "not likely to be either lost or mislaid."[65] Like Nellie Bly, Davidson hoped to set an example for independent women who sought to travel the world on their own.

With an eye on the working woman, Davidson recommended a British firm from which women could purchase "neat little hand-bags specifically fitted up for ladies with writing and work materials." For short trips to and from home, she recommended handbags with a "square frame and wide-opening mouth...as they hold more."[66] Davidson suggested that the safest choice for traveling women might be smaller "waist bags," which lay flat and close to the body and were presumably harder for a thief to snatch than a purse.

Davidson's focus on safety and security as the most important features of a handbag were not unique. Her advice reflects the same elements that purse sellers sought to promote in their advertisements. "To be really useful," Davidson concluded, "a bag should always be provided with a lock and key, in addition to the little snap catch which secures it."[67] Finally, she encouraged discerning women to carefully test the strength of a lock before purchasing any handbag.

Purse makers picked up on and perhaps profited from anxieties about traveling women's vulnerabilities. In 1894, *Harper's Weekly* advertised a "burglar-proof" bag that contained an "automatic" metal mouth for fastening. The advertisement boasted that the purse was "the hardest thing on earth to open and close unless you know how, then simple as breathing."[68] Whereas in previous decades purses like the small reticule functioned as ornamental accessories, over time purses expanded in size and were constructed of more durable materials. Some purses even began to include zippers and locks that were intended to protect both the money and privacy of its owners.[69]

Advertisements for small purses boasted about their safety features. In 1916, a "ladies" silver-plated purse with vanity box (powder-puff and mirror included) measured only 3 inches long but was "finished [with] a ring to slip over the finger to carry Purse safely when shopping." In addition, the "mesh and chain of the bag are both very strong, making this Purse a safe receptacle for money."[70] The ring attachment purportedly made the purse harder to drop in a crowd, forget on a store counter, or be ripped from one's hand.

Six years later, an Italian immigrant named Salvatore Picciotto filed a patent for a vanity case that was designed to look like a revolver. In his patent filing, Picciotto argued that the shape of the case simulates "a revolver for the purpose of affording a certain degree of protection for the owner."[71] However, once the trigger is pulled, perfume is emitted from the muzzle of the gun. Many more women would carry personal hygiene products in their purses in the 1920s, but Picciotto's invention allowed them to simultaneously carry what appeared to be a deadly weapon that would help protect the owner from attackers and purse-snatchers.[72]

In the same year that *Harper's Weekly* advertised a "burglar-proof purse," a reporter for *The New York Observer* speculated as to "whether [a] woman was predestined by nature to carry her pocketbook in her hand." The reporter concluded that a woman was not and further noted that it was curious that women's clothing failed to feature pockets because "the female form should be better adapted to the support of pockets than the male." Without elaborating on why he believed this to be the case, the writer next acknowledged a theory that claimed "the persistence of woman in carrying her pocketbook in her

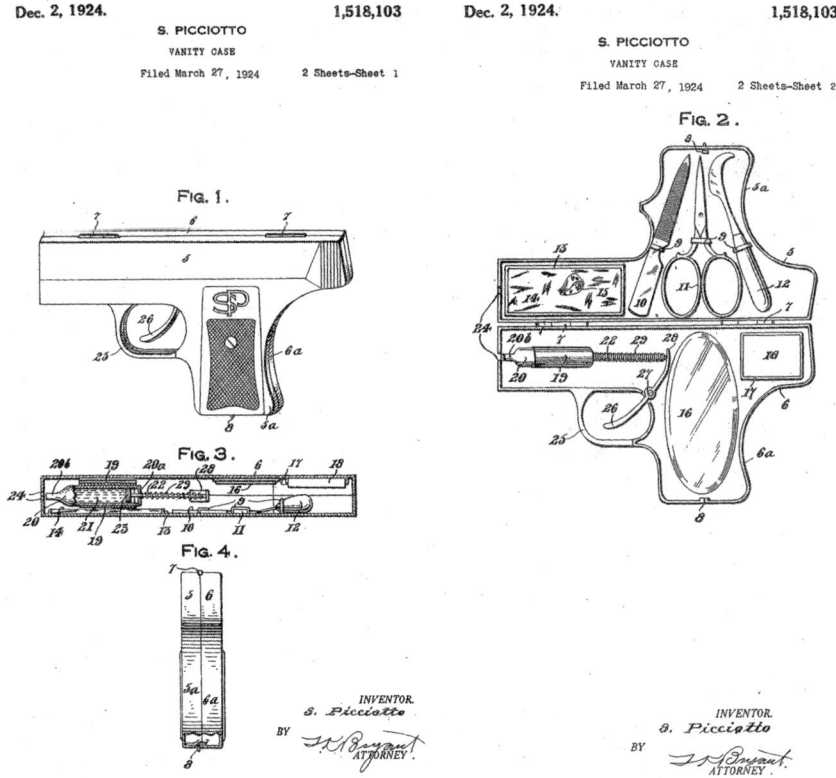

Figure 2.7. Filed on March 27, 1924, Salvatore Picciotto received a patent for his submission of this blueprint for a vanity case designed to look like a gun. (US1518103A, Google Patent Image.)

hand" is evidence of her "lack of thrift and inability to care for property. It is urged that the way she carries her purse tends directly to its loss, and that her negligence in matters of finance is so innate that even if she had pockets all over her, she would still use a separate receptacle for money."[73] Though this critic acknowledged that women did not have "pockets all over," he failed to see that women had little choice in how to hold purses with short handles either. Purses with long straps designed to hang from one's shoulder would not become widely available until World War II.

Some women called attention to the sartorial injustice of not having integrated pockets. The American Ladies Tailor Association recognized the problem, designing a "suffragette suit" that featured up to eight pockets.[74] In 1905, feminist writer Charlotte Perkins Gilman began criticizing this inequity in her nonfiction. Though she called men's trousers "ugly," "heavy and hot," she bemoaned the fact that only men had access to integrated pockets; she saw purses as an inferior substitute.[75] She also dedicated pages of her fiction to imagining a world in which women had access to integrated pockets. In 1914, Gilman published a striking story called "If I Were a Man." In it a woman named Mollie suddenly finds herself to be Gerald, who sees his pockets as a "revelation" that provided "armored assurance."[76] The next year Gilman published her famous utopian novel *Herland*, in which all women wore the same comfortable clothing with plenty of pockets. When three American men stumble upon these women, they were impressed by the women's pockets: "As to pockets, they left nothing to be desired...They were most ingeniously arranged, so as to be convenient to the hand and not inconvenient to the body, and were so placed as at once to strengthen the garment and add decorative lines of stitching."[77]

Yet functional integrated pockets did not exist in American women's clothing so the focus remained on purses. One of the other problems posed by the growing presence of purses was maintaining control of them. Discussion of purses continued to provide unending opportunities for assessing women's flaws and strengths. Although some critics blamed women for their purported absent-mindedness, others asserted that such assumptions were wholly unfounded because women were "naturally more cautious than the man, and quicker to imagine danger." Thus, she "carries her purse in her hand in order that possession may always be assured by the sense of touch."[78] As evidence of women's cautiousness and business acumen, this unknown author asserted that women knew how to find the best deals and ultimately balance the family budget, concluding that "*his* ability to save depends largely on *her* care and thrift."[79]

Indeed, a spirited debate emerged about women losing their pocketbooks at the turn of the century. The central issue seemed to be women's intelligence, vigilance, and memory. In November 1913, *The Chicago Defender* asserted that carrying purses had made women's minds "retentive." A shop manager who had just discovered an unattended purse on a counter proposed that years of carrying a purse instead of using built-in pockets had "strengthened the feminine memory." The manager acknowledged that women were likely to set their purses down in the millinery and costume departments of their stores, yet they infrequently forgot them altogether. "The manufacturers help them to remember. There are bags that dangle from the little finger and bags with hand straps, bags that go around the neck, and here is a bag that is part of a shoe, a little pocket, in fact, that will hold a few sovereigns." He concluded, however, that "women as a rule, prefer to trust their memories."[80]

Some male contemporaries believed that a purse was the key to a woman's inner character. In 1897, *The Chicago Tribune* published a lengthy article entitled, "Found: A Purse—What was the Character and Appearance of the Woman Who Lost It?" Perhaps inspired by the popularity of Arthur Conan Doyle's detective series starring Sherlock Holmes, the article was penned by a (likely fictitious) "handsome young gentleman" who seemed intent on determining the character of the owner of a seal-skinned women's purse with a pearl snap button. Based on a "thorough examination of the purse and its contents," he concluded that the woman's character could be ascertained. After sifting through all the pockets of the purse like an archaeologist, he shared his findings one by one with his readers. The purse contained a number of bills from milliners and a receipt for toilet goods. In describing these effects, the author attempted to both titillate his readers and embarrass the purse's owner; he suggested that her feet were calloused and corned because of a receipt for a "perfumed bath and pedicuring."[81]

He then surmised that the woman "is young and fair...trustful and clinging...she is philosophical, has a buoyant personality, a big bump of humor, and is interested in art." The presence of a "lucky penny" in her purse was thought to be evidence of her romantic nature, and a "lawyer's card shows that she is a woman of spirit and intends to have her rights." Membership tickets to "various institutions and clubs show that she is...perhaps a 'new woman'... though it is hoped that she is not a 'women's rights' speaker."[82]

This writer's ideal woman was modern enough to consult professionals but not to the disappointing degree of insisting on her political rights. Timecards and commuter tickets were thought to show that she was a working woman on the move. A set of visiting cards and a small photograph found in the back of the purse supposedly revealed that she is not "an old maid" but a beautiful young widow.[83] Though the writer did not belabor the material characteristics of the purse itself, he saw this woman's purse as the key to her identity, a window into her soul, and a clear indicator of her age and level of attractiveness.

Many Americans in the late nineteenth century believed that clothing and appearance were revealing indicators of a person's inner character. For example, clean, pressed clothing was thought to represent a pure, organized mind. But purses were a particularly revealing item because of their capacity to conceal. Observers believed that women's purses could be read like wordless autobiographies. *The Chicago Tribune* article suggests not just the awareness that women carried their most important possessions, but a sneaking suspicion that they carried secrets in their purses. Purses were a charged and deeply intimate space in which a "handsome man" could rummage and expose a woman for her private insecurities. Likewise, readers of *The Chicago Daily Tribune* were expected to be ensnared by the prospect of reading a story that relished exposing a woman's privacy.

Cultural anxieties about women's independence inspired newspaper articles about more than misplacing purses. They also conveyed rising concerns over "purse-snatching" and shoplifting. Hundreds of advertisements, illustrations, and newspaper articles confirm that purses operated as a central metaphor in precarious interactions between single women and strange men, especially when racial lines were crossed.[84] The largest circulating Black-owned newspaper at the time, *The Chicago Defender*, frequently published articles covering the activities of thieves who attempted to steal purses from women on the street. Such purses sometimes contained large sums of money, jewels, and other high-value items. In 1909, *The Defender* reported that one woman allegedly left a handbag containing 30,000 dollars' worth of jewels behind on a train.[85] For Black newspapers publishing stories like these, part of the point was to celebrate Black wealth during the nadir of race relations in the United States. At a time when rates of lynching remained high and Jim Crow segregation was fiercely enforced, these stories highlight Black success during deeply oppressive conditions. Because *The Chicago Defender* was circulated throughout the country, Black Southerners who were considering moving north or west would have taken note of these stories, seeing them as signs of both the opportunities and dangers cities like Chicago, Detroit, New York, and Philadelphia could offer Southern migrants. Whether or not they were reading accurate or sensationalized stories—and perhaps some of them simply made good copy—newspapers seemed to delight in reporting stories that provided a peek inside the intimate space of a woman's purse.

Purses offered women a space that was both deeply public and private. Unlike undergarments, worn directly on the body underneath clothing, women carried purses outside the body. And they nearly always took their purses with them when they left home. While purses provide women with a space to hide their most intimate objects, compared to integrated pockets, they also offered interlopers opportunities to separate a woman from the contents of her purse. Despite some of the more sensational stories, on average, most newspaper articles on snatching purses at the turn of the century suggest that thieves typically yielded a rather low profit from the crime. The most common sum reported was 2 dollars (or approximately 65 dollars in 2025).[86]

While thieves in general did not necessarily target women, purse-snatchers (who sometimes alternatively identified themselves as "moll-buzzers") usually did.[87] Items marketed as purses and pocketbooks were still occasionally carried by men at the end of the nineteenth century, but they were slowly becoming feminized objects. It is not surprising that purse-snatching increasingly became a crime perpetrated in public spaces by boys and men against women. One study showed 95 percent of child pickpockets were male and 73 percent of thefts occurred on streets.[88]

As the term suggests, "snatching" a purse was a different and perhaps more violent kind of crime than picking a pocket. While boys and men typically picked the integrated pockets of other men, male snatchers invaded and stole women's purses. In 1894, the white-owned *Atlanta Constitution* published an article about a "snatch thief," with the subtitle "The Queer Conduct of a Queer Darky." The article described a woman who was walking alone with an alligator skin purse when a young male thief who was hiding in an alley jumped out. He tugged at her purse, and despite the woman's screams, the thief managed to make a quick get-away.[89]

Press coverage of these incidents distracted readers from the daily violence against women occurring in American homes, but they also belied anxieties about race, particularly concerning interracial encounters between white women and Black men and boys. W. E. B. Du Bois wrote about this phenomenon in his 1899 essay "The Negro Criminal." "So frequent have these crimes become," he argued, "that sometimes Negroes are wrongfully suspected; whoever snatches a pocketbook on a dark night is supposed to be black."[90] Though Black-owned newspapers seem to have printed these stories as often as white-owned ones did, Black journalists explicitly critiqued how such crimes were sensationalized and racialized in the mainstream press. *The Chicago Defender* argued that when committed by Black males, purse-snatchings were described as "attacks on white women" and the "nature of these attacks have been...left to inference." Indeed, because a purse was considered a highly personal space, even Black-owned newspapers described women whose purses were "snatched" as having been "molested."

A reporter for *The Chicago Defender* suggested, "If some Negro miscreant snatches the purse of a white woman, or some member of our group jostles some white woman, the cry is immediately raised that an attack has been made on a white woman...the public is left to believe another sort of crime has been committed.... The word 'attack' is deliberately confused wherever colored and white are concerned." *The Defender* referred to these articles as "yellow journalism"; in other words, they contained bias and seemed intent on inflaming existing racial tensions by suggesting that purse-snatchings were similar to cross-racial sexual assault.[91] And they did so at a moment when many states were passing laws outlawing interracial marriages and record numbers of Black men were being lynched under the pretense of violating white women.

The Defender critiqued the presumption of Black male guilt regarding purse-snatchings and highlighted the fact that some white purse-snatchers exploited this assumption. In October 1914, a reporter for *The Defender* "discovered one of the old tricks that are usually pulled off down south by white criminals and brutes. With a blackened face crimes of all kinds are committed and laid at the door of an innocent Afro-American." One week earlier, the reporter alleged to have witnessed a purse-snatching near the police station. He was alerted to the ongoing crime when he heard a voice yell "Catch the n*gger." When the man was finally chased down, he was not only found with a pocketbook, but "much to the surprise of the pursuers, the man was white, with his face blackened." Finally, the column bemoaned the fact that "many such cases will be like this in the winter."[92]

Purse-snatchers of all races were sometimes surprised by how young working women fought back to maintain control of their purses. In 1912, Margaret Dixon, a young, "plucky" working woman from Altoona, Pennsylvania, was "held up by a bold highway man while on her way home with half a month's pay in her purse." When the would-be-thief attempted to steal her handbag, Dixon "courageously repelled the insolent fellow...bravely beating him over the head" with a closed umbrella.[93]

Starting in the late nineteenth century, more Americans defined their success by their ability to accumulate things and they hoped to advertise their wealth through public display. Yet, they also needed to protect their bodies and their possessions. At the same time, more people in congested cities saw purse-snatching and shoplifting as a potential means of upward mobility. The ways in which these crimes were written about—even fixated on—and the ways in which purse manufacturers responded to the concerns they elicited reflect changing views and values about women as visible pedestrians, consumers, and independent agents in public spaces.

Purses played a dually disruptive role because they did not simply make women vulnerable; they also gave women a convenient vessel for committing their own crimes. Department store managers knew that purses could conceal shoplifted goods. A satirical illustration published in *Puck* in 1910 illustrates the fact that these concerns permeated popular culture. As horrified men look on in the upper left corner, unruly ladies bedecked in high hats and white gloves load silverware into their purses and sleeves.

In fact, kleptomania was thought to be a disease unique to women, a theory that persisted into the twentieth century. In 1953, sociologist Henry Angelino wrote a critical review of the literature on shoplifting and concluded that "the greatest number of amateur shoplifters are women, from 70 to 99 percent."[94] Both shoplifting and purse-snatching were crimes thought to be committed largely by young people. In each case, the purse played a critical role. Both

Figure 2.8. Illustrated by Gordon Grant and published in *Puck* magazine in 1910, this image shows women outnumbering men and stealing everything they can fit into their purses. In a circle located in the upper left corner of this image, a group of men observe in horror. ("Ladies' Day at the Club," *Puck* 68, no. 1750, September 14, 1910, Library of Congress, LC-DIG-ppmsca-27667.)

kinds of crime involved crossing gender, class, and race-based categories to enhance the thief's status. While purse-snatching necessitated abrupt, intimate contact with a victim, which could result in an extended tug of war, shoplifting was, by contrast, a more impersonal and often undetected crime, which most often occurred indoors.

The trade journal *Women's Wear Daily* was aware of the problem of purse theft in department stores. While most "purse-snatchers" were men stealing from women, in the white middle-class, feminized space of department stores, over the course of two days two "women thieves" in St. Louis allegedly stole thousands in jewels and cash by stealing purses from other women. "Their method, according to reports from the stores, was to wait until a shopper put her purse on the counter while trying on a garment."[95]

Some women used the power of the purse against each other. But for most, purses were a symbol of women crossing boundaries. They provided women with a vehicle to transition from the private to the public sphere, as they stood before cameras, on stages, and in the streets holding their proud purses. They could alternately mark women as victims but also serve as women's weapons in a culture oriented around being seen. In the late nineteenth and early twentieth century, purses took on heightened roles in visual narratives women used their own images to tell. As the next chapter demonstrates, purses also helped women to pack up a miniature and mobile version of the home and head out to work, preserving a particular image along the way.

3

Space, Privacy, and the Pocketbooks of Working Women

According to the weekly magazine *Outlook*, on March 24, 1911, sisters Becky and Gussie Koppelman punched their timecards at the Triangle Shirtwaist Factory in New York City. It was Friday night and they had spent a long day hunched over noisy machines making women's blouses as their bosses barked over their shoulders to move faster. However, each sister had to stand in a single-file line before she could go home. There, she would wait to have her pocketbook inspected by the watchman (indeed, it was always a man). He was posted at the only unlocked exit, which was just 30 inches wide. Hundreds of women would have to pass him before they were able to leave the factory.[1] After he looked inside their pocketbooks and was satisfied that they had not stolen any fabric, thread, or lace, the sisters headed home to the room they rented on New York City's east side.[2] Their landlady claimed she overheard them bitterly complain about how their boss "searches our pocketbooks and bags to see that we don't carry any goods or trimmings away. Oh, you would think you are in Russia again!"[3]

For Becky and Gussie, who had been in the United States for only a year, having a strange man peer into their purses made them feel as though they were living under the oppressive regime of a tsar.[4] Indeed, for many working-class immigrant women from Europe, their purses were the only private spaces over which they could generally claim control. Though upper-class "ladies" had the luxury of occupying more capacious domestic spaces and had servants and porters to carry their money and baggage, working immigrant women had little privacy.[5]

At work the next day, a deadly fire broke out on the eighth floor of the Triangle Shirtwaist Factory as the bell rang to indicate it was quitting time. At that moment, many women were already waiting in line to have their pocketbooks inspected. Beckie Rothstein recalled that after the closing bell had rung and she grabbed her coat and hat from the dressing room, "I was just going to give my pocketbook to him [the watchman] to open it, and just as I opened it, I heard him say 'Fire.'"[6] At 4:45 P.M., the fire began to spread throughout the factory, forcing many women to the edges of the walls and the windows of the building. Soon the glass from the windows began to burst open. The women faced a terrible but imminent choice: be burned alive or jump at least eight stories to certain death.

On that day, 146 Triangle Shirtwaist Factory workers would burn, asphyxiate, or jump to their deaths when fire erupted. Gussie Koppleman would survive; her sister Becky, age 16, would not.[7] Although the disaster happened more than a century ago, it remains notorious because of its high death toll and profound impact on the American labor movement. It is clear now, as was the case then, that if the factory owners had shown less interest in what was inside their employees' purses and more regard for their safety, there would likely have been no deaths at all.

In the context of this massive loss of life, the daily indignity of having a hired male guard stop each woman to peer inside her purse might seem insignificant. On its face, this purse inspection seemingly merits just a small footnote—a moment—in the lives of working women, many of whom would perish in what would become one of the most significant workplace disasters in American history. Yet, American women alive today know that this interaction was anything but insignificant.

Boyfriends, husbands, psychologists, journalists, watchmen, and especially employers sought to control women's purses in the first two decades of the twentieth century. At best, they viewed women's pocketbooks and bags with curiosity. Sometimes they trivialized them as reminders of women's frivolity and vanity, though at others they cast a suspicious eye on them. It was as if they thought women had no right to an autonomous physical existence. Indeed, men sought to stare into and ultimately control women's pocketbooks, believing that they provided vital information about the women who carried them. They were not wrong on this account. But there was much more to purses than how men perceived them. Purses offer direct access to the most private dimensions of working women's lives. Analyzing the pocketbooks of working-class women reveals their anxieties, hopes, and fears, ultimately illuminating a great deal about their lived experiences.[8]

The women who worked at the Triangle Shirtwaist Factory were in the center of dramatic cultural, economic, demographic, and political shifts. In the context of so much change, the purse became a central site of transition, a toolkit, and passport with which to leave the Victorian era behind and step into modernity. Because women were revising their roles in nearly every aspect of American culture at the same time urban landscapes were rapidly changing, in the first two decades of the twentieth century, pocketbooks helped women leave the home. They provided young immigrant women with a female-controlled private space in which to store whatever they pleased, including a change of clothes for after work—perhaps for a date or an opportunity to discard the degradation of the workday and walk home in their favorite dress.[9] They offered women a place to keep their timecards and their pay envelopes, lunch, photos of loved ones, jewelry, mementos, cosmetics, and the keys to shared and private domestic spaces. In short, turn-of-the-century pocketbooks (sometimes referred to as "purses" or "bags") both facilitated and accelerated working women's departure from the home.

As the size and style of pocketbooks began to change in the late nineteenth century, so, too, did the American labor force. The number of waged working women increased from 18 percent in 1890 to 24 percent in 1920.[10] Yet, most women were funneled into sex-segregated, low-paying work.[11] In some cities, by 1920, over 40 percent of women worked for wages and increasingly left their neighborhoods to do so. Some were newly able to access higher education and obtain employment in nursing, teaching, or social work. Although some gained clerical positions, many others worked as domestic servants (a job that was reviled by almost all women) or in factories making ready-to-wear garments.[12] In New York City, immigrant working women were especially likely to find employment in a garment factory. By 1909, the number of garment factories in New York City rose to 2,995, an increase of 86 percent over the previous decade. By the same year, the number of New Yorkers who earned a living working in a garment factory numbered nearly 95,000.[13] The pay was low, the hours were long, and the work was often irregular, especially in slow seasons during winter and summer.[14]

At the same time employment conditions were changing, immigration continued to increase as women arrived at Ellis Island with bags containing their entire lives. For most of the nineteenth century, women had come to the United States from northern and western Europe. But by 1900, they increasingly arrived from southern and eastern European nations, including Russia, Poland, and Italy. These were "undesirable" countries, as many of their populations were Jewish or Catholic. They either did not speak English or spoke it with a heavy accent. These women lived in cramped tenement buildings and competed for jobs that few others wanted.[15]

The generation of émigrés of which Becky and Gussie Koppleman were a part also ushered in radical changes in sexual mores. When away from the watchful eyes of their parents, young women enthusiastically participated in commercialized leisure activities that allowed them to socialize with young men. When they could afford it (or a date would treat them with an admission ticket), they spent their Friday and Saturday nights watching vaudeville shows, riding roller coasters at amusement parks, or doing the "Grizzly Bear" or the "Monkey Glide" at dance halls.[16] They also rode bikes and jumped onto crowded electric streetcars across the city. Still others were hoping to make an impression by saving their paltry pay envelopes to purchase their own ready-made clothing, especially French heels, wide-brimmed hats, and black leather pocketbooks in which they could carry their hard-earned money. Young women worked hard to purchase these accessories, believing they deserved to adorn their bodies with the fruits of their labor.[17] These young women had already abandoned petticoats and bustles, and as they spent more money on eye-catching accessories, they were more likely to leave their corsets in the closet, too. Increasing numbers of women were also delaying marriage and having fewer children. In such a rapidly changing environment, pocketbooks offered expanding numbers of women workers a private space with which to help navigate a shifting but still ultimately white male world.

In the early 1900s, women carried a variety of vessels on their arms and wrists. These containers were made of various materials and might take up a little or a lot of space. Fabric bags offered a cheaper alternative to leather but, for women who worked in factories, they were less likely to withstand everyday use. Contemporary advertisements from Sears, Roebuck and Co. catalogues reveal that leather bags ranged in price from as little as 8 cents for a small leather coin purse to 4 dollars for an alligator-skin bag. Typically, the larger the purse, the more it cost the consumer because of the increased costs of materials and labor. Depending on their age and responsibilities, the girls and women who worked at the Triangle Factory made as little as a dollar and a half and as much as 7 dollars a week, though many made closer to 3 dollars. However, most had deductions taken out of their salaries for mistakes and slow seasons.[18] Clearly, they would have had to scrimp and save to purchase a purse that cost around 50 cents.[19]

Yet, purse and pocketbook manufacturers began providing women who could afford them with more product options. New purses featured multiple interior compartments, and some even came with accessories such as built-in mirrors, card cases, and a coin purse. Specialty pocketbooks and purses were

Figure 3.1. The exteriors of many affordable bags sold around 1910 were constructed of black seal grain leather, reputed to be of "good" or the "finest" quality. Lined interiors often featured a silky moiré cloth and featured interior pockets for additional storage and privacy. Many of these bags also had metal frames with a "fancy gilt snap catch" or double short leather handles. At the time of the factory fire, the average purse cost between 50 cents and 1 dollar. Garment workers likely would have owned purses costing about 50 cents. The largest bag for sale in this issue of Sears, Roebuck and Co. was 11 inches wide. (From "Spring Features in Women's Apparel," Sears, Roebuck and Co. Catalogue, Spring 1909, 26.)

Figure 3.2. Both advertisements refer to these objects as purses, though the top one is categorized as a man's purse and the purse beneath it is marketed for "ladies." The purses are very similar in size, identical in materials and color, both featuring nickel-plated brass frames and a two-ball clasp. Both items sold for the bargain price of 8 cents due to their small size. The purse marketed for women is three-quarters of an inch longer, shaped like a trapezoid and is explicitly identified as featuring a lining. Otherwise, the two objects are remarkably similar. (From Sears, Roebuck and Co. Catalogue, Spring 1911, 9.)

advertised to students, workers, and shoppers in the early 1900s. This specialization enabled manufacturers to sell more types of pocketbooks to more people.

Advertisements suggest that some men were still carrying items called "purses" and "pocketbooks" at this time, but when marketed to male consumers, advertisers typically used the term to describe coin purses and leather-bound envelopes that contained folders, paper, and a place to carry money. For example, in 1910, a children's magazine named *A Youth's Companion* published a full-page advertisement for Perry Mason's "pocketbooks and bags." Sample items included several bags made out of seal and calf skin, marketed as a "ladies' handbag," "bill book and coin purse," "gentleman's one-piece pocketbook," and a commodious and apparently gender-neutral "envelope bag" and "leather shopping bag."[20] Sears, Roebuck and Co. also featured advertisements for objects called purses for both men and women. The shared use of the terms "purse" and "pocketbook" is noteworthy, given that most straight American men today would shrink from using either term to refer to any of their possessions. Unlike women's pocketbooks, however, men's pocketbooks and purses during this time almost never featured a large, cavernous space that afforded them significant privacy in public. (The many pockets in their suits and the right to traverse the city alone already provided that.) Indeed, the feminizing of purses and pocketbooks as both objects and terms was underway but not yet complete in the first decade of the twentieth century.

Many of the women who died on March 25, 1911, were purse-carrying members of the International Ladies' Garment Workers' Union. Some leaders of the union were concerned that factory workers cared too much about their clothing and not enough about their working conditions. These concerns, however, were not mutually exclusive. One study of female factory workers contends that working women invested financially and psychologically in their hats, purses, and heels.[21] Indeed, accessorizing their bodies allowed working-class immigrant women who lived in difficult circumstances to experiment with their identities.[22] Women factory workers simultaneously saw themselves as legitimate workers and as political actors, even though both of those labels had historically almost exclusively been applied to white men.[23] Because purses held the wages women earned and were themselves a symbol of their purchasing power, of all dimensions of their dress, the purse most clearly represented both their productive and consumptive power.

Some middle-class settlement workers concerned themselves with the dress of working women. Lillian Wald, founder of a settlement house on Henry Street in New York City, pointed out the "exaggerated raiment" that rendered such women conspicuous.[24] As the founder of Hull House and innovator of social work in Chicago, Jane Addams was also concerned about overworked young women who some believed spent their money frivolously on clothing. In 1909, the same year that Triangle Shirtwaist factory workers and thousands of other New York garment workers went on strike in the "Uprising of the 20,000," Addams published *The Spirit of Youth and the City Streets*. She noted that although "these overworked girls stream along the street, the rest of us see only the self-conscious walk, the giggling speech, the preposterous clothing. And yet through the huge hat, with its wilderness of bedraggled feathers, the girl announces to the world that she is here." Addams concluded that a woman garbed in "preposterous clothing" demands "attention to the fact of her existence, she states that she is ready to live, to take her place in the world."[25] Two years later, Addams would experience embarrassment over her own dress when Leo Tolstoy commented on her "monstrous" sleeves, which he noted contained enough extraneous material to make an entire girl's dress. Addams defended herself by saying that factory girls wore even bigger sleeves and that they would not see her as legitimate if she dressed like a "peasant."[26] Like many middle-class women who came of age in the Victorian era, Jane Addams made allowances for working women but believed that clothing represented one's inner character and she justified her own fashionable attire as a matter of political expediency. She understood that young working women's accessories meant much more than an outsider's first glance would suggest.

Of all their possessions, purses were especially meaningful to the women who worked at the Triangle Shirtwaist Factory. Survivor Pauline Pepe felt similarly about her pocketbook and the money she kept inside it. Pepe was a machine operator working on the eighth floor on the day of the fire. When interviewed at the age of 95, almost seventy-five years after the tragedy, Pepe recalled that when the fire first broke out, "I left the pocketbook, everything; coat and everything." Seven decades later, she still seemed shocked that she had left her pocketbook behind, because inside it she had "twelve dollars, my God."[27]

Although Pepe had witnessed incredible trauma that day and likely lost friends who died in the fire, her mind kept coming back to that lost pocketbook. Many decades later, the detail of having lost her bag with 12 dollars in it had become engrained in the Pepe family narrative. Pauline's daughter knew the story so well that she recounted how often her mother had bemoaned that "I left my pocketbook there." Pepe must have echoed this refrain many times during the course of her children's and grandchildren's lives. Her daughter used to tell her, "They'll give it to you, Ma, don't worry."[28] They never did.

Other women insisted on leaving the factory with their pocketbooks in hand, even as they faced down flames. According to the *Chicago Sunday Tribune*, one woman "climbed to the sill, stood in black against the light, hesitating, then, with a last touch of futile thrift, slipped her chatelaine bag over her wrist and jumped." What the *Tribune* reporter saw as simply a "touch of futile thrift" was just as likely an effort to escape with an item that held great meaning for her and on which she counted for her very survival. This woman's bag would have provided her with a means for exerting a small degree of control over her life.[29] Her "chatelaine" (a specific type of small purse that was often belted or pinned to a woman's dress) was not simply an inert container for money. Instead, as women increasingly would do in the coming decades, she likely viewed the purse as if it was a part of her own body. Her chatelaine was her passport to whatever came after she jumped. At the least, it would not be burned to ashes with everything else left in the building. Perhaps its contents might even prove useful in identifying her remains.

During her attempt to escape the fire, Kate Alterman, who had worked at the factory for just four months, recalled that her "pocketbook began to burn... but I pressed it to my heart to extinguish the fire."[30] Alterman did not follow what must have been an instinct to drop the enflamed purse as it began to burn her hands. Instead of parting with her pocketbook, she pressed it to her heart, using her own chest to extinguish the flame. Alterman's unwillingness to let go of her pocketbook also suggests that the object was meaningful beyond its monetary value.[31] To Becky, Gussie, Pauline, Kate, and others, their purses were a source of comfort, a toolkit; they held the promise of a better future.

Of the workers who died that day, 84 percent were women or girls.[32] After the fire was extinguished, police began the grim work of sending bodies to the morgue for identification. In many cases, the bodies were burned beyond recognition. At a historical moment when photojournalism had become an established feature of newspapers, vivid images of helpless police standing next to mangled women's bodies and broken nets were published across the nation.[33] The policemen who scoured the personal effects of the victims of the fire would face a daunting task. Because so many bodies were unidentifiable, the objects in their purses, hands, and around their necks were brought to the police station in hopes that they could help families identify the victims.[34] The precinct record noted "one lady's handbag containing rosary beads, elevated railroad ticket, small pin with picture, pocket knife, one small purse containing $1.68 in cash, handkerchiefs, a small mirror, pair of gloves, two thimbles, a Spanish comb, one yellow metal ring, five keys, one fancy glove button."[35] These items suggested the owner's faith (Catholicism) and the distinct possibility that she was an Irish, Italian, or Polish immigrant. They also suggest that the purse's owner had thought of her bag as a toolkit, even carrying a pocketknife that could have been used for protection. Yet, this woman also traveled and sought to do so while looking her best (the mirror may have been built into the purse). Finally, she carried five keys with her. This fact suggested that not only was her purse a private space, but it gave her access to at least five other spaces as well.

Those who had to comb through the wreckage to search for signs of life continued to find objects that hinted at the contours of working women's lives cut short. Fire Chief Ed Croker found another "lady's handbag containing one gent's watch... and a $1 bill, one half-dozen postal cards, a button hook, a

Figure 3.3. After the fire, police officers carried baskets containing the personal effects of Triangle Shirtwaist Factory fire victims to the 26th Street pier morgue. The basket on the left appears to contain several black pocketbooks. Thirteen months earlier, policemen were involved in brutally suppressing the Triangle Shirtwaist strikers in their nearly three-month protest against unsafe working conditions. (Photographer unknown, March 25, 1911, Photo ID 5780PB39F16BP400G, International Ladies' Garment Workers' Union Photographs [1885–1985], Cornell University, Kheel Center for Labor-Management Documentation and Archives.)

man's photo, a man's garter, a man's razor strap."[36] Both of these women's purses contained less than 2 dollars, an amount that helps us understand why Pauline Pepe was still so upset about losing 12 dollars more than seven decades later. The interior of each purse gave each owner a space in which they could keep material evidence of their intimate connections to a web of other loved ones. Since most of the young working women at the factory were immigrants from Europe, the postcards in this purse suggest that the owner intended to correspond with relatives she left behind. Just as many American women do today, this woman also carried more than just her own belongings in her purse. A man's razor strop, garter, and wristwatch (a relatively new convenience at the time) suggest her connection to a man with whom she was quite familiar.[37] Perhaps the man in the photograph, whose picture she snuck a peak at while at work, was the owner of these items.

When a reporter for *The New York Times* was granted permission to tour the ruins of the Triangle Shirtwaist Factory, he witnessed "almost a bushel of pocketbooks and handbags . . . taken out of the debris."[38] Indeed, it is likely that each of the 123 women who died brought a pocketbook with her to work that day. At a vigil held that night, when shock and anger reverberated through the crowds, a reporter claimed have seen an "old woman . . . take a small phial [*sic*] from her pocketbook. It had death's head on it."[39] Implying that the woman was carrying a vial of cyanide, the reporter expected that women would use their purses to avenge the loss of their loved ones. In such cases, purses were potential vessels for punishment.

Eight months after the fire, the factory's owners, Isaac Harris and Max Blanck, were tried for manslaughter in the first and second degree. Though the 2,200-page transcript of *People of the State of New York v. Isaac Harris and Max Blanck* was believed to have been lost for many decades, 900 surviving pages of the transcript reveal extensive discussions about the significance of the women's pocketbooks, as well as a dramatic prosecutorial demonstration centering on what women kept inside them. The transcript ultimately illuminates the contrast between how the women viewed their purses and how their bosses, the prosecutor, and the all-male jury perceived them.[40] It also tells us how deeply violated the women felt when male interlopers looked inside their pocketbooks. As survivors attested, the "watchmen" who checked the women's pocketbooks at the factory blocked the one usable exit door so that no workers could leave without going through this inspection process.[41]

According to Mary Domsky-Abrams, a blouse machine operator who worked on the ninth floor, "the bosses wanted to save the expense of having another watchman at the front" so "they allowed only one exit to be used for all three floors."[42] When it was each woman's turn to unclasp and open the mouth of her purse, the watchman would look inside to ensure she was not stealing any "goods, embroidery, or lace."[43] If he felt like it, he might poke around a little further to see if he could deduce how much money she had or if she had a photograph of a boyfriend. The purses the women had to submit for inspection were the same containers in which they kept their lunch, timecards, personal effects, and pay envelopes as well.[44] Like many of her peers, employee Mary Bucelli found this process particularly burdensome; she recalled that opening her purse "was compulsory. He wouldn't let us pass unless we did so."[45]

Although Harris and Blanck both conceded that they had ordered the watchmen to inspect the women's purses, they did not admit to locking the doors during working hours, which was a violation of Article 6, Section 80, of

New York State labor law.⁴⁶ Nonetheless, countless women testified that the Washington Place exit was nearly always locked. It is perhaps fitting then that the workers commonly referred to the factory as "the prison."⁴⁷

Two years before the fire broke out, in November 1909, the Triangle Shirtwaist Factory workers had joined the largest strike of women workers to date. In what now looks like a precursor to modern-day social justice movements, many more thousand garment workers struck than expected and they were brutalized by the police who sometimes hurled clubs and slurs at them during the protest. On December 3, 1909, one photographer captured six women locking arms; labor reformers and suffragists marched with hats on their heads and purses in hand to City Hall to register their complaints about the abuse they endured from the police.

One of the leaders of the "Uprising of the 20,000," Clara Lemlich, told a reporter for the *New York Evening Journal* that most of the women workers

Figure 3.4. During the "Uprising of the 20,000," striking factory workers locked arms with other activists and more famous benefactors as they marched toward City Hall to protest police violence against the striking workers. On this cold December day, at least three of the women carried small purses, all six wore wide-brimmed hats, three wore gloves, and one wore a heart-shaped necklace. Ida Rauh (pictured third from the left) was an American actress and suffragist who was associated with Margaret Sanger and Emma Goldman. (Photographer unknown, December 3, 1909, Photo ID 5780PB32F27B, International Ladies' Garment Workers' Union Photographs [1885–1985] Cornell University, Kheel Center for Labor-Management Documentation and Archives, Ithaca, NY.)

put in thirteen-hour days, six days a week, typically earning from 3 to 7 dollars each week. After adjusting for inflation, this sum would be roughly equivalent to slightly over 200 dollars a week or approximately 10,400 dollars per year today, well below the poverty line in most states at the time of this writing. In addition to requesting formal recognition of their labor union, shorter hours, and safer working conditions, the women demanded access to dressing rooms in which they could keep their coats and hats. Lemlich noted, "[T]here are no dressing rooms for the girls in the shops. They have to hang up their coats and hats . . . on hooks along the walls." Nonetheless, she noted, "Sometimes a girl has a new hat. It is never much to look at because it never costs more than fifty cents but it's pretty likely to be spoiled after it's been at the shop. . . . And if one of us gets a new one, that means that we have gone for weeks on two-cent lunches—dry cake and nothing else."[48]

Their demand for dressing rooms was important to workers who did not want the clothing in which they invested both psychologically and financially to be ruined on the factory floor. They succeeded in getting dressing rooms but not much else. More than two years after the strike, most women workers who testified in the criminal trial following the fire recalled keeping their hats and coats in the new dressing rooms. However, none of their testimonies mention retrieving their purses from the dressing rooms. Even at the risk of having them ruined, the women made sure their purses were never more than an arm's length away. Most often, they kept their purses right next to them at their workstations.[49]

Though she no longer worked at the factory at the time of the fire, Pauline Newman's experiences as a Triangle employee provide important insight into the young working women's experiences. Newman immigrated to the United States at the age of 10 and got a job at the Triangle Shirtwaist factory in 1903 when she was 12.[50] Newman, who often wore masculine attire and kept her hair short, worked at the factory for seven years and would become a pioneering organizer for the International Ladies' Garment Workers' Union.[51] Decades later, she recalled that she left home at 6:40 A.M. each day and paid a nickel to ride "the horse car" and the electric trolley to the factory.[52] While there, she resented having no privacy and being under constant surveillance: "You were watched when you went to the lavatory, and if in the opinion of the forelady you stayed a minute or two longer than she thought you should have you were threatened with being fired."[53] There was also no drinking water available, and the girls and women were not permitted to talk during working hours.[54] Most nights, Newman worked until 9 o'clock as her employers paced the aisles and perched themselves over her shoulders to make sure she never paused in her work.⁵⁵ In this environment, the 20 to 50 square inches of privacy a pocketbook afforded was vital. Because she was initially only paid a $1.50 a week for six to seven days of work, Newman would have had to work approximately eighty hours before she could buy herself a 1 dollar pocketbook like those for sale in Sears, Roebuck and Co. catalogues.⁵⁶

Survivor Beckie Rothstein's testimony confirms the importance of keeping her pocketbook close by. As soon as the closing bell rang, "I took my pocketbook and the paper [timecard] and went away from my machine."⁵⁷ Like others, Rothstein kept her pocketbook at her workstation, not in the dressing room. Samuel Bernstein, brother-in-law of one of the owners, also testified that once the fire broke out, "I seen [*sic*] a girl going back after her pocketbook; she said, 'I have got my pocketbook by my machine' and I just *made* her go along without it."⁵⁸ The workers were defiant when it came to being separated from their purses. Only in the case of a deadly fire could some be persuaded to leave their purses behind.

Becky Bursky was different from her coworkers on this account. She testified that she took her coat and not her pocketbook when "once in a while I used to go downstairs" for lunch. Like Ida Singer, Bursky made the sacrifice of leaving her pocketbook behind at lunch because she wanted to avoid the embarrassment of having it inspected by strange men. Singer testified that she kept her money in her stocking rather than her pocketbook: "I was ashamed because they looked into the pocketbooks."⁵⁹ Commercially made disposable sanitary napkins were not yet widely available in 1911, so Bursky and others may also have carried a rag or a piece of cotton cloth for menstruation. With the knowledge that their purses would be inspected by the prying eyes of men, women like Becky had to weigh the balance between need and embarrassment when they decided what to place inside their purses. In this context, purses that featured hidden interior pockets would have been particularly appealing.⁶⁰

Indeed, it is likely that these women considered their purses their most valuable possession and they hoped to prevent both being separated from their purses and the invasion of prying eyes. Their bosses, however, were keenly aware of the trouble-making potential of purses. In fact, they accused their workers of stealing up to 25 dollars of merchandise from March 1910 to 1911.⁶¹ In one case, they claimed a worker stole two shirtwaists that she "hid in her rat."⁶² "Rats" were padded hairpieces that women hid inside their natural hair in order to add volume to the popular upswept styles of the time. Though hiding two shirtwaists inside one's hair seems improbable, the accusation itself made the women appear both greedy and bold.⁶³

Given how important they were to the women involved, it is not surprising that purses also played an important role in the ensuing criminal trial. Max Steuer, who had once worked in a garment factory himself, was the owners' defense attorney. He argued that the owners were not responsible for the locked doors. Steuer claimed that, even if the doors had been unlocked, the rapid path of the fire would have made them unusable. However, at the same time, Steuer also attempted to undermine the credibility of the young women who survived the fire and offered eyewitness testimonies of the event. He did so by repeatedly asking survivors about their pocketbooks, portraying the young women as untrustworthy thieves whose behavior would have made locking the doors a reasonable choice.

Steuer interrogated multiple witnesses about whether or not they had to physically hand the watchmen their pocketbooks, or just open them so they could look inside. When questioning Rose Mayers, for example, Steuer accused her of lying: "Do you say that you handed the man your pocketbook?" When Mayers answered in the affirmative, Steuer did not relent: "Isn't it the fact that as you walked by you opened it?... And you didn't mean that you handed that man your pocketbook?"[64] Mayers clarified that, indeed, she held her own bag as the watchman looked inside. The point was not a moot one. Since pocketbooks were becoming gendered, private spaces in which women kept their most important possessions, physically grabbing and opening a young woman's purse would have been a far more egregious violation then simply peeking inside an already opened purse. Steuer was keenly aware of the fact that his clients were being portrayed as callous monsters who saw their employees as cogs, rather than sisters and daughters. Nearly admitting that forcibly touching a woman's purse would have been tantamount to an assault, Steuer tried to convince the jury that his clients never touched the women's purses.

At the trial, several survivors brought their pocketbooks with them to the stand as they rose to testify. When Rose Mayers explained that she was required to show her pocketbook to the watchman, Steuer asked her to clarify what she meant by pocketbook: "You call that a pocketbook, which you now have? May we stipulate the size of that?" Steuer then chose a particularly dramatic way to demonstrate the exact size of the bag for the jury.[65] Notes taken during the trial indicate that Steuer pulled out a ruler and measured Mayer's bag, noting that it was 8.5 by 12 inches.[66] He then moved on to other subjects.

Steuer had done something similar with other eyewitnesses. When cross-examining Becky Bursky, for example, he asked if she, too, carried a pocketbook at the factory like the one she took with her to the stand. "When you say a pocketbook, you mean one like that you have now?" He then asked prosecutor Charles Bostwick if Bursky's pocketbook was a similar size to "the one that was measured this morning."[67]

Steuer sought to convince the all-male jury that the women had the means to steal from their employers. Purses were the key players in such a scenario; the bigger they were, the greater the threat they posed. Thus, the men needed to inspect the women's purses and keep the doors locked. In order to dramatically illustrate this point, Steuer did something odd. He had asked an assistant to purchase a large pocketbook during the recess. The bag was supposedly a similar size to the one whose dimensions he had measured earlier, though its exact measurements and cost remain unclear. He then threw the bag at Assistant District Attorney Robert Rubin and said, "Just open it and see for yourself how big it is."[68] Naively, Rubin complied and pulled four shirtwaists out of the bag in front of the jury. One imagines whispers and gasps could be heard across the courtroom at this moment. Indeed, it appears to have been a turning point in the trial. Even Bostwick admitted that the pocketbooks were large enough to steal multiple shirtwaists, though he refused to concede that this gave the owners the right to lock the doors, a fact that led directly to the women's deaths. Nonetheless, the demonstration vividly showed the jury the dangers women's purses presented in the workplace, implying exactly how much the women could be stealing from their bosses on a daily basis.

For their part, the surviving women found these accusations insulting. "They should be ashamed of spreading such slanders," a ninth-floor operator later argued. "The fact was that, even if the workers had wanted to steal anything, it would have been impossible, because when bundles of work were distributed, every item was counted and listed on the tickets. And when the work was completed, everything was counted again."[69] Upon discovery, the women would certainly have been charged for any missing materials or dismissed altogether. In fact, the owners made regular deductions from the women's wages for the most minor infractions, including being just five minutes late to work because of a delay on the trolley.[70]

Despite compelling consistencies in the testimonies of more than 100 witnesses, many of whom verified that the exits were locked, Harris and Blanck were acquitted of the charges of manslaughter. Steuer had raised reasonable doubt about the owners' knowledge of the locked doors and the pocketbook demonstration had the desired effect of swaying the all-male jury against the women. Although most reporters were sympathetic to the victims of the fire, the jury took just two hours to determine that the women were essentially culpable for their own deaths.[71] After being found not guilty, Harris and Blanck were eventually able to reopen their factory, though they continued to violate existing labor law after they went back into business. Most of the women who survived the fire could not bring themselves to go back to work where they had experienced tremendous trauma. But the women who worked at the reopened factory still toiled long days with low pay and went home to cramped tenements at night.

Unlike the crowded factory floor, in the nineteenth and early twentieth centuries, the white, middle-class Victorian home was idealized as a feminine space that offered male workers a private refuge from a cruel world. Yet for many working-class women, the urban home was not a refuge. On the contrary, it often provided little to no privacy, quiet, or rest. Particularly during periods of financial hardship, the average household size rose because fewer relatives could afford to live independently. At night, mothers had their children help them earn extra income by sewing piecework. To make ends meet, families living in tenement housing were forced to take in boarders. In tenement buildings, they often placed mattresses in hallways and on the kitchen floor in order to accommodate extra guests who could help pay the rent. Privies were shared by dozens of people and fresh air, light, and quiet restorative sleep were hard to come by. In this context, the control that working women usually had over the private spaces inside their purses was deeply meaningful.

Both inside and outside the home, American women and their bodies were rarely afforded the space and privacy they desired and deserved.[72] Until the late nineteenth century, women were expected to circulate in the city only with chaperones. Public space, especially at night, was considered inappropriate for lone women who did not want to be mistaken for "streetwalkers."[73] In such a context, pocketbooks provided immigrant working women with a small but sacred piece of privacy. They afforded women a rare refuge in which they could conceal their savings, pictures of loved ones, money, keys, and other talismans. Indeed, many women treated purses as portable safety deposit boxes, using them to maintain access to their most prized possessions. A close examination of the lives of women marginalized by their ethnicity and class in addition to their sex reveals that purses offered women privacy in public. When they lost that privacy, it was painful.

In growing cities, purses challenged existing hierarchies by facilitating women's transition from the private to the public sphere. In fact, in the early 1900s, American cities were still largely perceived as masculine spaces. Actresses who called attention to themselves on stage were also considered "public women" who ranked only slightly higher than "prostitutes." Indeed, many working-class women occasionally performed sex work in order to keep the family afloat during difficult times. Other women who saw themselves as superior to sex workers called themselves "charity girls" because they never accepted money directly. Instead, they exchanged companionship and sexual favors for "treats" from men who paid for their tickets and drinks at dance halls and theaters.[74]

Some Americans were especially concerned about young "women adrift" who walked city streets alone and lived outside of nuclear households.[75] Instead of being the subject of condemnation, however, in the early 1900s, such women became a point of intrigue, and their purses were one of their most revealing components. In 1900, Theodore Dreiser published his first novel, *Sister Carrie*. Now considered one of the most influential American novels of all time, the plot loosely followed the path trod by Dreiser's own sister, Emma.[76] In the first line of the novel, readers learn that the main character, Carrie, carries "a cheap imitation alligator-skin satchel . . . and a yellow leather snap purse, containing her ticket, a scrap of paper with her sister's address on Van Buren Street, and four dollars in money."[77] Just as a writer for *The Chicago Tribune* believed that the contents of a woman's purse could be used to reconstruct her personality and a veritable biography of her life, Dreiser used Carrie's purse to reveal a great deal about her character.

Readers find Carrie, at the age of 18, sitting on a train with her shabby purse. She is a country girl en route to "the great city" of Chicago, "ambitious to gain in material things."[78] Lurching closer to the city, she was observably out of her element and vulnerable. She knew no one aboard the train and had no companion or chaperone to see her to her destination. In the nineteenth century, travelers' experiences were deeply shaped by gender, race, and class. For example, when traveling by rail, only white women enjoyed the privilege of traveling in "ladies' cars," which were cleaner, quieter, more comfortable, and more private than smoking cars filled with men.[79] By the early twentieth century, ladies' cars were disappearing and working-class women like Carrie had to contend with man-spreading men on trains and streetcars.[80] Before Dreiser's main character even arrived at her destination, then, he concisely conveys just how ill-equipped Carrie was to live in the city by taking the reader directly inside her train with her cheap satchel and yellow snap purse.

Before stepping off the train in Chicago, Carrie met Charles Drouet, a well-dressed man who sat behind her. Drouet's dress made Carrie keenly aware of the shabbiness of her "plain blue dress" and the "worn state of her shoes."[81] When she fumbled through her purse looking for her sister's address, Drouet "reached down in his hip pocket and took out a fat purse. It was filled with slips of paper, some mileage books, a roll of greenbacks. It impressed her deeply. Such a purse had never been carried by anyone attentive to her."[82] Dreiser's use of the term "purse" in reference to Drouet's personal container provides further evidence that the term had not yet been fully feminized in 1900. And Dreiser's deliberate contrast between the two purses—one skinny and one fat—demonstrates the significance of the purse in conveying one's socioeconomic status and experience.

When she was about to disembark from the train, Carrie gathered "up her poor little grip and closed her hand firmly upon her purse."[83] Perhaps she was worried about losing her purse or having it snatched from her; those few dollars were not much, but they were her lifeline. The act of carrying one's own purse and luggage suggested independence. Though having a servant carry one's bag could be a symbol of a woman's high socioeconomic status, having a strange man carry one's purse or baggage suggested a physical intimacy and familiarity with a strange man that Carrie could not yet risk letting her waiting sister see. If purses represented women's bodies, as they increasingly would in the coming decades, refusing to let a man hold one's purse could also be a statement of sexual purity.[84] Although Drouet offered to carry her "poor little grip," Carrie quickly and curtly responded, "Oh no, I'd rather you wouldn't."[85]

Just as the two purses establish the distance between the two main characters on the very first page, purses play a central role throughout the novel. Over time, Carrie loosens her grip on her purse both literally and figuratively. After a brief stint working in the oppressive conditions of a shoe factory, she eventually leaves her sister, Minnie, in order to live with Drouet as a "kept woman." Carrie no longer worries about Drouet touching her purse, but instead regularly accepts money from his "fat purse." Drouet provides her with money to buy the expensive clothing and furniture she desires and establishes her in her own apartment. He takes her shopping for a new wardrobe, where the "shine and rustle of new things . . . immediately lay hold of Carrie's heart."[86] After buying her a coat and shoes, Drouet bought her a new purse to replace her shabby yellow one.

As her purse and ambitions mutually grow in size, Carrie leaves Drouet for Hurstwood, an older married man who promises to finance her new lifestyle. Hurstwood subsequently leaves his wife, marries Carrie, and slowly begins to lose his wealth. Before long, Hurstwood starts begging for coins from Carrie's purse, which she has now filled by working as a chorus girl. Both Drouet and Hurstwood follow a downward spiral, but Carrie rises to fame as an actress, eventually leaving Hurstwood behind as a homeless beggar. Although the vast majority of women never realized such dreams, by the first decade of the twentieth century, the number of actresses in America had grown exponentially.[87] And the pay envelopes of female stars could be astronomical.[88]

It is perhaps not surprising that Dreiser's novel was controversial at the time of its publication. In fact, it almost did not get published because it was perceived as immoral. This was in large part because Carrie, a kept woman obsessed by a material world, is never punished for her misdeeds. At the end of the book, Drouet has been humiliated and Hurstwood has committed suicide, but Carrie has been rewarded with fame and fortune. Unlike many Victorian novels, the book offers no moral lesson and does not reinforce traditional gender roles. Carrie starts with a cheap satchel and lean purse, and her first job in the shoe factory nets her 4 dollars and 50 cents a week, a size similar to the paychecks of women who worked in the Triangle Shirtwaist Factory. At the end of the novel, however, she is single and has just earned her own 150 dollar paycheck from a show in which she starred.[89]

Most women who dreamt of becoming celebrity actresses woke up to factory work. But purses offered women like the fictional Carrie and the real Triangle Shirtwaist Factory workers a private autonomous space in a contested landscape. This was particularly true in cities in the first two decades of the twentieth century. Working women themselves turned purses into spaces that were full of possibility in modern cities. Purses provided limited square footage but a much-needed place to store their objects and aspirations. Thus, women nearly always took purses with them when they left home. And in the early 1900s, women stayed away from home for far longer than their mothers and grandmothers had.

4

The Bag and the Body
Purses and Personal Hygiene, 1920s–1940s

For many Americans, what distinguished the 1920s from previous decades was the presence and possibilities of new products. From refrigerators and phonographs to cars and electrified homes with indoor plumbing, new technologies were within reach for the first time.[1] But it was not just powerful time-saving appliances that were newly accessible. A wide range of personal products offered to improve Americans' social and material lives. To be convinced, one need only to examine the advertisements of magazines and newspapers proclaiming to help consumers, especially women, achieve social acceptance, self-confidence, a trim and youthful appearance, and perhaps, find a husband.

Americans learned about these new products through a variety of media, but newspapers and magazines played a particularly important role in disseminating this information. For much of the 1800s, most newspapers had been regionally focused and few magazines had national circulations. But this changed drastically by the early 1900s, when magazines specifically aimed at women expanded.[2] By 1923, the aggregate circulation of magazines had doubled to 65 million since the early 1900s; by 1939, it nearly doubled again.[3] Subscribers to women's magazines like *Good Housekeeping* increased significantly, and *Red Book Magazine* reached a circulation of 1 million in 1937. By then, the average American had a radio in their home, but print media could graphically illustrate what new products looked like and how to use them in ways that radio could not. As the number of magazines, their circulation, and their frequency of publication increased, the amount of money that advertisers spent also increased 10-fold from 1914 to 1929.[4] Many magazines targeted middle-class white women, but newspapers and catalogues like Sears, Roebuck and Co. reached wider audiences.

Alongside the increasing pervasiveness of print media, in the 1920s, the daily patterns of many Americans also began to shift. A few decades earlier, most

Americans only bathed on Saturdays, washed their hair once a month, and did not use deodorant.[5] But by 1925, advertising for toiletries outpaced advertising for every other category besides food.[6] In women's magazines, the content of these advertisements often communicated the idea that women's bodies were problems that only commercial products could solve. Colgate toothpaste and Listerine mouthwash offered to fix Americans' bad breath, "reducing" regimens promised women weight loss, and deodorizing products guaranteed women that they would not offend anyone's nose. Women became the primary targets as the purchasers and users of many of these household products.[7]

Purses were not new in the 1920s, but they were both manufactured and purchased much more frequently than in previous years. Though these numbers decreased in 1919 and 1920, between 1921 and 1923, the number of establishments manufacturing leather purses nearly doubled. Likewise, the amount of workers earning a wage by making leather purses also more than doubled.[8] A report commissioned by President Herbert Hoover in 1933 confirms these data, establishing that the per capita output of "pocketbooks" increased rapidly starting in 1921.[9] It then increased 2.5-fold by 1923, and nearly quintupled by 1927, increasing even further by 1929.

These numbers were not just a result of a general boom in the economy, or an increase in the production and sales of clothing and accessories. During this same time period, the number of establishments manufacturing other leather goods such as trunks, suitcases, and gloves stayed the same or decreased.[10] Although both men and women carried items called purses and pocketbooks in previous years, in the 1920s and 1930s, these objects became more pervasive at the same time they became the sole cultural property of women. And this process continued to further crystallize in the 1940s. Why would this be the case? What prompted more women to buy and carry pocketbooks, while seemingly discouraging men from doing so?

In 1918, World War I ended and the influenza epidemic began, prompting a nationwide obsession with cleanliness. The burden of cleanliness (closely linked to daintiness) fell disproportionately on women as douching products, deodorants, and miniature perfume misters became more popular.[11] Gender norms continued to change in discernible ways, but at a more rapid pace than in the Victorian era. Just as the production and sales of purses and standards of personal hygiene were increasing, more women were publicly visible as waged workers, leisure seekers, shoppers, students, and eventually, voters, jurists, and soldiers. The 1920 census also indicated that for the first time more than half of Americans lived in urban areas and were therefore more likely to traverse city streets, shop in department stores, and ride public transportation. Meanwhile, the numbers of women who smoked cigarettes and drove cars also increased.

The privacy that purses afforded women was not a new benefit of purses in the 1920s. But as the personal hygiene market expanded at the same time that more women were stepping out for longer periods of time, women needed a portable place to put more and more stuff. Purses offered them the opportunity (and burden) of taking a personal hygiene kit everywhere they went, enabling them to continually monitor and manage their bodies. Personal products specifically marketed to fit inside of a woman's purse forged a close and seemingly organic relationship between women's bodies and their bags. This association made it less palatable for men to carry purses. Women could dip into their purses to freshen their makeup, reapply perfume, reach for a Midol tablet to dull their period pain, and even grab a new disposable sanitary napkin. Although employers and other authority figures continued their attempts to regulate the ways in which women workers used purses, advertisers used bags to sell purse-sized commodities that offered to liberate modern female consumers from their burdensome bodies. In doing so, they transformed the purse into a specifically feminine site for bodily maintenance. And by the 1930s, purses had become proxies for women's bodies.

The year 1920 is widely known as a watershed year in American women's history because it was the year the Nineteenth Amendment, which guaranteed white women the right to vote, was ratified. However, 1921 was also a consequential, if underexamined, year. In addition to the dramatic rise in the production and sales of purses in 1921, several events unfolded that changed the lives of Americans.[12] On the political front, Warren G. Harding became president, promising a "return to normalcy," while Adolf Hitler assumed leadership of the Nazi Party in Germany. The Tulsa Race Massacre brutally destroyed a large and prosperous Black neighborhood in Oklahoma, and white hostility continued to push the northward and westward migration of African Americans out of rural areas of the South.[13] On a federal level, the Sheppard Towner Act brought new attention to maternal and infant mortality rates, infusing states with federal funds to improve infant and maternal healthcare. The act expanded federal welfare legislation and medicalized the birthing experiences of many American women, ultimately edging Black midwives who carried folk remedies in their bags out of the business through new licensing procedures.[14] That same year, Margaret Sanger founded the American Birth Control League, Coco Chanel released her first perfume, and 16-year-old Margaret Gorman won the first Miss America Pageant.[15]

Less famously, in 1921, Kotex began its campaign to sell disposable sanitary napkins, a revolution in menstruation technology for those who could afford them. Carrying menstrual products inside one's purse became even more practical when Tampax began producing purse-sized tampons in 1936.[16] And as the Great Depression hit American families the hardest in the 1930s, women began carrying douching products, cervical caps, condoms, and purse-sized "female hygiene" pamphlets that purportedly explained how to limit the number of children they had. In the 1940s, they joined the military as soldiers for the first time and fit these products into brown leather purses issued by the army.

These developments collectively altered how women cared for their bodies, transforming purses and pocketbooks into fully feminized objects at a transitional moment shaped by a variety of cultural, social, and political changes. Indeed, a new variety of purse-sized products raised societal expectations of bodily management for women. Despite these pressures and double standards, purses provided new opportunities for women to at least attempt to control their work lives and their bodies, leaving the home more often and for longer than ever before.

Though they kept tools of bodily maintenance in their bags in the 1920s and 1930s, many women knew very little about their own reproductive systems. For decades, legislation such as the Comstock Act of 1873, which deemed discussions of contraception "obscene," systematically kept girls and women from accessing literature that candidly and accurately discussed the most intimate inner workings of their bodies.[17] Before the 1940s, most American girls had no formal sexual education that taught them about menstruation. Girls who did receive instruction often got it from companies like Kotex, which mailed booklets like "Marjorie May's Twelfth Birthday" and "Marjorie May Learns About Life."[18] Outside the confines of married women's friendships, decades of silence and shame shrouded issues like puberty, menstruation, sex, reproduction, and contraception. Caches of desperate letters written to birth control advocate Margaret Sanger demonstrate that women were eager to learn the basics of menstruation and contraceptive care.[19]

In the first few decades of the twentieth century, many women hid signs of menstruation from everyone but themselves. Even mothers attempted to shield evidence of menstruation from their daughters and other immediate family members.[20] Born around 1910, Onnie Lee Logan recalled, "Nobody hadn't told me how to take care of myself. I don't know why mothers in those days wouldn't tell you. . . . Naturally we wouldn't go buy a sanitary pad. There weren't sanitary pads to be bought."[21] Though commercial sanitary pads were, in fact, available by the time Logan was an adolescent, they were likely inaccessible and unaffordable to her as a young Black girl in rural Alabama.[22]

Instead, girls like Logan relied on their own ingenuity. Without the ability to purchase sanitary products, she explained, "[W]e had to make em. I worried about that day and night." Before her period arrived for the first time, Logan prepared by making her own sanitary pads using a needle, thread, buttons, a safety pin, and unbleached mesh fabric. "Nobody told me one iota thing. It come to me and I made it and wrapped it up in a lot of paper and then stuck it up under the house until that time come."[23] Just as Rose had prepared a sack for her enslaved daughter Ashley in mid-nineteenth-century South Carolina, Black women in succeeding generations prepared for emergencies in ways that many middle-class white women did not have to. They were particularly creative in crafting the objects and securing the knowledge they needed to manage the challenging circumstances in which they found themselves.

When girls were given even rudimentary advice or instruction, they were often told to improvise with what they could find within the home. This left those less enterprising than Logan feeling woefully unprepared for their periods. One woman recalled that her mother curtly told her to "go find a cloth, and pin it inside your pants," but she did not elaborate further.[24] Ida Smithson explained that, before her adoption of disposable pads, "we used, just, old sheets, old things you had around the house." If they were told anything, girls tended to learn about menstruation from each other. One woman taught her sister how to use Kotex and "explained to her that she would have it every month. And that's another way she was getting rid of her bad blood. That's what they used to tell us."[25] The ambiguous phrasing "bad blood" emphasized the shameful nature of menstruation but offered no real insight to girls and women about what was happening with their bodies and why.

Young women also had to navigate a wide variety of myths about menstruation. Many Americans believed that women and girls were particularly vulnerable and weak during menstruation; some were instructed to stay away from baths so they did not catch pneumonia.[26] Others believed that women were volatile and unpredictable during menstruation. Some sociologists claimed that kleptomania was a disease unique to women and a form of sexual perversion; other so-called experts argued that thefts correlated with menstruation, menopause, and pregnancy.[27]

The significance of the arrival of disposable sanitary napkins and tampons can be fully appreciated only when one considers earlier menstruation myths and practices. In fact, women who could afford sanitary products were released from the enormous burden of creating, wearing, and—worst of all—cleaning menstrual "rags." Cleaning menstrual cloths was tedious, unpleasant work that literally caused girls and women to lose sleep. Since they were pressured to hide evidence that they were menstruating, this work was often done in the middle of the night when no brothers, fathers, or boarders were likely to see or smell the process. One woman explained that "you had to soak them and wash them and cleanse them . . . and hang them up so no one would see them."[28] For those who had interior plumbing, this often meant boiling rags and hanging them in bathrooms overnight instead of on outdoor clothing lines, which would have proved too embarrassing. Even those with plumbing had to hurriedly hide the rags in the morning before the rest of the household awoke.[29] Women who did not have access to plumbing or who could no longer get rags clean enough after several uses just threw the used cloths in outdoor privies with the rest of the trash.[30] In this context, the disposability of sanitary napkins and later tampons constituted a significant upgrade. Their availability meant there was no need to hide the cleaning process because there was no need to engage in the cleaning process altogether. And the vehicle on which the successful use of these personal hygiene products relied was the purse.

Early advertisements for sanitary products in the 1920s and 1930s spoke to women's concerns about mobility, cleanliness, and health. Advertisers shrewdly framed menstruation as an unfair burden that women alone carried. To live more like men, they argued that women needed feminine hygiene products. Alongside sanitary napkins and, later, tampons, advertisers for sanitary products suggested purses were one of the tools that could help women bridge this gap. Women needed their purses to maintain access to a fresh supply of these products outside the home. With new commercially available menstrual products, women could leave the home for as long as men without having to worry about embarrassing stains or odors. In short, ads promised that sanitary napkins could allow women to live without fear.

Kotex, the first main manufacturer of sanitary pads in the United States, faced the challenge of informing readers about the advantages of its new product. In addition to doing so without offending contemporary sensibilities, the biggest problem that Kotex had to conquer was getting women to purchase the product, a potentially embarrassing endeavor. In 1922, Kotex aimed straight at middle-class white women when it placed several advertisements for its new disposable sanitary napkins in *Vogue* magazine (in 1925, each issue of *Vogue* cost 55 cents, approximately 10 dollars in 2025). These ads promised customers that the napkins were discreetly packaged to save "embarrassment in several ways."[31]

Kotex reassured women that their privacy would be preserved because the labeling on Kotex boxes was discreet. The pads were packaged inside a blue box with no text besides the word "Kotex."

Kotex also tried to relieve women of the dreaded task of having to explicitly ask a drugstore or dry goods clerk for sanitary pads. Advertisements told women they need only ask for its product brand: "Kotex—ask for it by name!"[32] Though a single Kotex pad was 9 inches long and 3.5 inches wide, the product came in a gauze envelope that was a much more conspicuous 22 inches long.[33] In 1921, one box included twelve Kotex pads and cost 65 cents (nearly 11 dollars in 2025).[34] Upon request, clerks took out each sizable box from behind the counter and then brought out plain brown wrapping paper to disguise the box further. Though intended to be helpful and ensure privacy, this process may have exacerbated the ordeal for women standing in line with other customers waiting behind them.[35]

Like tissues and the brand Kleenex, Kotex and the blue boxes in which its menstrual products came quickly became synonymous with sanitary pads in general.[36] As Kotex boxes became recognizable, they became less discreet and having a commodious purse or shopping bag in which to quickly stash the box became even more important. Ida Smithson remembered being thoroughly embarrassed when she entered a dime store and had to ask for sanitary pads since they were hidden from view, usually behind the counter. Once she was handed the box, "I would just take a look around, and see if anybody sees you ask for it, and you kind of slip it in the bag."[37] Cellucotton Products Co., which manufactured Kotex, encouraged this connection by urging women to "keep Kotex always on hand" because a "supply can be carried easily in a lady's handbag."[38]

Advertisements for Kotex in the 1920s rarely, if ever, pictured the pads themselves. Instead, they showed women arranged in attractive poses.[39] In May 1923 and in several other issues printed over the next three years, *Ladies Home Journal* featured essentially the same advertisement as those that appeared in *Vogue*. In these ads, Kotex again boasted that a "supply can be carried easily in a lady's handbag."[40] Many of these early advertisements feature illustrations of fully clothed white women reading, being aided by maids, or engaged in other activities but almost none show the product itself.[41] Advertisers for Kotex faced a conundrum: How could they market a product that they could neither explicitly show nor candidly discuss?[42] The answer was not packaging, but purses.

Purses allowed women to carry a variety of products linked to menstruation besides sanitary pads. By the 1920s, purses had become so linked with privacy and intimacy, advertisers used them as a cipher for a range of products they suspected readers would be squeamish about looking at and reading about. Purses featured prominently in advertising for several products, including cosmetics, the painkiller Midol, and women's deodorizing products such as Kurb and Per-stik, which collectively cemented the link between purses and women even further.

First created in 1875, Lydia Pinkham's Vegetable Compound was a precursor to Midol, marketed to treat discomfort associated with menstruation, and it was enormously popular. Made primarily of herbs and alcohol, it became a best-selling but likely ineffective patent drug for women's reproductive problems.[43] In the late 1800s and early 1900s, advertisements for Pinkham's compound did not mention its portability or recommend that consumers carry it in their purses. Instead, they highlighted how the compound could help ailing women complete their household chores.[44] Such advertisements emphasized that Pinkham's product could also help "tired mothers" cure any "derangement of the uterine system."[45]

Previous iterations of the compound only came in liquid form, and advertisements did not mention purses or pocketbooks. By 1930, however, the new vegetable compound could be purchased in tablet form especially "for the convenience of busy women." Tablets were far lighter, neater, and fit more easily inside a purse of any size than a glass bottle full of liquid. Liquids were also more prone to leak, stain, and ruin a perfectly good purse. In the middle of the Great Depression, most women needed to extend the lives of their personal belongings, including purses. Readers of the *Maryland Independent* were instructed to "slip a package in your handbag. Take your medicine regularly, wherever you are—shopping, traveling, at the theater, or at your desk in the office."[46] Both purses and Lydia Pinkham's Vegetable Compound could be taken everywhere.

In the 1930s, advertisers sought to appeal to "busy women" who spent much of their time outside the home and had few chances to pause for rest during their periods. Advertisements for Pinkham's compound featured an illustration of a woman's hand slipping a small box into the mouth of her open, lined purse. Each box contained seventy tablets (thirty-five doses) and the medicine claimed to be "particularly valuable during the three trying periods of maturity, maternity, and middle age."[47] In other words, advertisers of Pinkham's Vegetable Compound attempted to lock in female consumers for several decades.

Advertisers used vivid language when describing how women should place items in their purse. In 1931, advertisers for Pinkham's Vegetable Compound (still in tablet form) again encouraged readers of the *Bismarck Tribune* to "slip a

—Now you can
Carry your medicine with you!

FOR THE convenience of busy women, Lydia E. Pinkham's Vegetable Compound is now sold in tablet form. These tablets are chocolate coated, easy to swallow and are just as effective as the liquid Compound. Each package contains 70 tablets or 35 doses, the same number of doses contained in a bottle of liquid medicine. Slip a package into your handbag. Take your medicine regularly, wherever you are—shopping, traveling, at the theater, or at your desk in the office.

LIQUID — TABLETS — EQUALLY EFFECTIVE

Lydia E. Pinkham's
Vegetable Compound
Lydia E. Pinkham Medicine Co., Lynn, Mass.

Figure 4.1. This advertisement for Lydia Pinkham's Vegetable Compound was designed to appeal to "busy women." Users were encouraged to "slip a package" into their handbags. (*Cincinatti Enquirer*, April 25, 1930.)

box of the new tablets in your handbag...."[48] The word "slip" followed by an ellipsis suggested this act could be stealthily done without any friction or anyone noticing.[49] Just as advertisers instructed women to "slip" a supply of Kotex pads in their purse, Lydia Pinkham's Vegetable Compound encouraged readers of *The Washington Times* to "tuck the little box in your purse and be ready."[50]

Increasingly, advertisers for products like Lydia Pinkham's Vegetable Compound and Kotex's sanitary pads also emphasized the sense of safety and preparedness their products could offer, and they explicitly linked those qualities to purses. But so did other personal hygiene products aimed at women. In the early 1930s, advertisements for a deodorizing product called MUM appeared in several issues of *Ladies Home Journal*. These ads encouraged women to "keep it in the purse, just to be ready for any occasion." Prospective users were also advised to take advantage of MUM's special function: "[S]pread a little on your sanitary napkin and you will be serenely sure of yourself; confident of perfect daintiness at all times." In italics, the advertisement assured women that applying MUM will ensure "*you are safe for hours.*"[51] A 1931 advertisement for MUM in *Ladies Home Journal* featured a white woman sitting at a dressing table while reaching into her purse for a small jar of MUM. This time women who wore makeup were encouraged to "carry MUM in your purse" but were again reminded of the special use of MUM on sanitary napkins.[52] The name "MUM" also emphasized the privacy its product purported to provide, seemingly referring to "Mum's the word," a centuries-old idiomatic expression that meant to keep something a secret.[53]

In December 1910, a New York–based company trademarked Midol as a remedy for headaches.[54] Unlike Lydia Pinkham's compound and later iterations of Midol, the drug was initially marketed to "businessmen" as a solution for headaches, eye strain, and toothaches.[55] An advertisement from 1922 still appears to have been aimed at men; however, by 1929, Midol was touted as a solution for menstrual and "febrile pain particular to women."[56] Advertisements for the product targeted working women, featuring an illustration of a perplexed woman above this text: "A book full of dictation and she must go home; what can she tell her employer?"[57] These ads regularly mentioned the portability of Midol for working women. Depending on the specific advertisement, the product came packaged in a "purse-size metal case," "handy aluminum purse-size container," or "little purse-size container."[58]

In 1937 and 1938, several advertisements for "Kurb," a Kotex product similar to Midol that was "designed to lessen discomfort with menstruation," appeared in *Cosmopolitan* magazine.[59] These advertisements noted that twelve tablets fit inside "a purse-size container."[60] Though some newspaper articles from this time period revealed anxieties that vulnerable women would struggle to remain safe while carrying purses that could be "snatched" by thieves, these ads suggested that purses were key to making women feel safe. Here, the threat was internal and the danger was public humiliation, but Kurb promised to help women reliably manage their own bodies.

The market for personal and feminine hygiene products kept getting more crowded in the 1930s. In 1935, *Ladies Home Journal* printed a large advertisement for Per-stik, a purse-sized personal deodorant product, which retailed for the relatively high price of 50 cents. The subheading of the advertisement claimed that the product was "easy to fit in your purse." An accompanying illustration demonstrated a hand delicately dropping a product the size of a tube of lipstick into a small strapless clutch, a style of purse that was particularly popular in the 1930s. More frequent applications of Per-stik meant that women would need to buy this product more frequently. "If you have ever—even for a moment—suspected the presence of under-arm odor when away from your boudoir, you will appreciate having a Per-stik with you at all times."[61]

In 1935, Kotex advertised its own brand of deodorizing powder called Quest. "Evolved primarily for use in sanitary napkins," *Vogue* marketed Quest as a general deodorizer that came in a "practical little purse container, a well-devised contrivance that doesn't let the powder spill out."[62]

As more women purchased purses and carried personal hygiene products inside them in the 1920 and 1930s, many also began to wear makeup in more pronounced ways. Advertisements for feminine hygiene and cosmetic products went hand-in-hand with purses. A 1931 advertisement for MUM explicitly instructed women to carry its product alongside a compact in their purses.[63] Cosmetics such as lipstick and rouge—once thought to be the purview of sex workers—called "painted women"—were now accepted and even expected to be worn on the face of the average American woman. More women paired whitening powders with lipstick to offer a striking contrast. They were also more likely to dye their hair, paint their nails, and wear perfume than previous generations.[64]

Like lipsticks, perfumes and powders did not last throughout the day; women on-the-go were encouraged to carry these items in their purses for further applications. In 1932, *Good Housekeeping* featured an advertisement for "Ambrosia Flask," which promised a one-minute facial that could fit inside a "purse or weekend-bag." The solution came in a flask that was designed to be flat "so it could be tucked lightly into your purse."[65] For the price of 50 cents, *Red Book Magazine* also offered women a "purse-size box" of Carmen Complexion Powder and a "handsome purse mirror."[66] Increasingly, manufacturers integrated small mirrors into purses to help women manage their appearance and apply their makeup with precision. And many cosmetics products, including lipstick, perfume, rouge, eye shadow, and powders, were specifically designed to neatly fit inside a small purse so they could always be accessible.

It is possible that makeup became more acceptable to the average American at this time because it feminized women and emphasized visible gender distinctions at a time when men's and women's "spheres" seemed to be colliding.[67] In the nineteenth century, most Americans felt that political affairs, a formal education, and working outside the home were the exclusive purview of men. But by 1930, much of that had changed. Not only were (white) women now able to vote, but they were also more likely to live in a city, serve on a jury, and work outside the home than ever before. For example, by 1930, 67 percent of women were working for wages in Chicago.[68] These changes did not happen overnight; they unfolded unevenly on a city-by-city and state-by-state basis.[69] Yet, more and more white women encountered these opportunities as they took jobs in

Figure 4.2. A stylish white flapper wears a small, brimmed hat and beaded necklace while carrying an open leather handbag and looking into a purse-sized vanity mirror. (Circa 1924, Hulton Archive, Getty Images.)

offices and factories. In this context, perhaps makeup helped assuage fears that women were turning into men, at the same time that more men were likely to work indoors in clerical jobs. Although men and women were increasingly doing similar things, when women managed their faces and carried objects in visually distinct ways, perhaps they reminded men that they were, in fact, constitutionally different.[70]

However, such a perspective centers men's motivations and discounts the many reasons women had for wearing makeup and carrying purses. The growing number of advertisements for cosmetics and a whole host of new personal hygiene products likely made this generation of women more self-conscious about their faces and bodies. Nonetheless, many purchased and applied makeup because they saw it as a way to self-create new identities in public life.[71] Such entrepreneurs as Madame C. J. Walker, Annie Turnbo Malone, Estée Lauder, and Elizabeth Arden were also major innovators and powerbrokers in the cosmetic industry. In fact, the most successful of these cosmetics entrepreneurs were working-class immigrants or women of color.[72] So, if makeup became more acceptable in public spaces for a variety of reasons, so, too, by the 1920s and 1930s, purses visually and publicly marked women as different from men. In fact, purses became so exclusively associated with women in the following decades that men who dared to carry purses were often met with harassment and violence.

In addition to wearing visible makeup, more American women also began to smoke cigarettes. Without sufficient integrated pockets, women needed an alternative place to carry cigarettes. An article published in *Ladies Home Journal* in 1922 asserted that "women smokers, young and old, are increasing in legions," and they were smoking "men's brands" of cigarettes.[73] Advertisements for "ladies' cigarette cases" also expanded during this decade.[74] One 1922 advertisement in Washington, DC's *Evening Star* revealed the expectation that women felt ashamed of their smoking habit. Yet, this ad for a lined cigarette case promised to help women hide the habit. "Smoke, do you?" the tagline read. "Well, you needn't confess it if you don't want to, but just the same you will love to have one of these little smoking sets tucked away in a safe corner of your handbag."[75]

Though ostensibly designed to sell a cigarette case, this advertisement extolled the virtues of the modern handbag by pointing out that purses offered a secure space for the storage of private items. Indeed, in the 1920s and 1930s, more handbags integrated secure closing mechanisms in the form of buttons, snaps, and, increasingly, zippers. Whitcomb Judson had patented "slide fasteners," later called zippers, in August 1893 for use in shoes, but it was not until 1925 that *Women's Wear Daily* mentioned the arrival of "zipper bags."[76] Zippered closures allowed women to feel that their belongings would not spill out and betray their secrets.

By the mid-1930s, the notion of women smoking became less scandalous, though purses still played a key part in maintaining the habit. In 1935, Isabel Sheldon of *The Los Angeles Times* published an article praising a new "tricky handbag" which helped a woman satisfy "her immediate whim. . . . All she needs to do is turn the ornamental dial-like knob on her bag and presto! . . . out pops a cigarette." Aiming right at the "collegian or the active young businesswoman" who regularly multitasks, Sheldon wrote that the new bag eliminates the need for rooting around in a purse "especially when she's driving. Then there are those other moments afoot when she is trying for a puff or two and possibly has a book or package to manage."[77]

This new "trick" purse dispensed up to ten cigarettes from the dial. It also included a built-in mirror and change purse. Sheldon suggested this purse could help young women achieve the increasingly important qualities of efficiency and organization. In other articles, Sheldon noted the necessity of having a purse that offered separate compartments to help "businesswomen or travelers" stay organized. In 1937, she hailed a "fifteen-compartment model made of genuine seal in a smartly conservative envelope style." She praised the purse's ability to offer "well-ordered segregation," a curious choice of words given the racial politics of the time period.[78] Such purses could provide a clear structure to a potentially chaotic, dark space. As more women used their purses to hide personal products, advertisements and newspaper articles amplified concerns that unsecured and unorganized purses could be a source of shame. Retailers of such purses claimed that they could help women avoid such shame by appearing organized when retrieving important items in front of others.

Although women's roles in American life were continuing to expand in the 1920s and 1930s, the most popular styles of purses were still relatively small envelope-shaped purses in dark colors. In 1925, *Women's Wear Daily* noted that leather envelope purses—sometimes called "underarm bags"—were selling well and several stores sold them outfitted with a special pocket for passports.[79] Far smaller than the large "Boston bags" popular in the late nineteenth century, these purses opened and closed securely with a snapping feature and offered zippered pockets for extra privacy.

Durability was also important and, in the midst of the Great Depression, Vachelle handbags guaranteed that its bags—available for just 1 dollar—would last at least six months. Women were also urged to keep their purses looking clean and new; a woman's purse was expected to be as hygienic as her body. In 1929, Sears, Roebuck and Co. advertised its purses in *Good Housekeeping*, showcasing models ranging in price from 5 dollars to an exorbitant 19 dollars. A full-page advertisement noted how "a woman's whole appearance is judged by her gloves, her hat.... And her purse. Probably her hardest problem is how to keep her purse from becoming shabby, for many of them soon begin to look worn and unattractive."[80] Like women's bodies, purses could betray unflattering signs of aging.

Such comments pressured women to own the newest fashions in purses and that pressure only continued to grow. Though it is hard to know how often the average American woman bought a new purse, and the frequency likely varied widely across class and race, in addition to differences in materials and size, advertisers presented the latest spring and fall fashions as necessities. Though they were constantly exposed to the outdoors, purses likely lasted longer than items of apparel like shoes that touched the ground and undergarments that directly touched the skin. Clothing that came in various sizes would no longer fit when women gained or lost weight, but a purse would always fit.

Figure 4.3. Advertisements for Vachelle bags boasted about their "developed handbag material," which they guaranteed would last longer than other products. (Sears, Roebuck and Co. Catalogue, Golden Jubilee Edition, 1936, 6.)

A well-made leather purse could be kept and carried for years. And because they did not require a personal fitting, purses also made particularly good gifts.

In the 1930s, envelope purses or clutches remained popular. However, they had no handle or strap and therefore largely rendered one arm or hand useless.

These bags were less functional than larger bags with straps that freed both hands, but they offered expanding numbers of pockets. Companies producing purse-sized products had to shrink them in order to accommodate tools the modern woman wanted to have with her at all times. In *The Los Angeles Times'* recurring column "What's in Fashion Now," Amos Parrish asked, "Is there anything more exasperating than a handbag which won't accommodate all the things a woman wants to put in it!" One perk of the new spring handbags of 1934, according to Parrish, was their "willingness to open up and devour" items like cigarette cases and cosmetics. "Surely," he argued, "these are legitimate luggage for any woman bound about her everyday affairs."[81]

In an era of small, flat bags, advertisers began to boast about how super-small their products were. Ronson's Perfu-mist claimed to be "the perfect purse-size perfume spray." An advertisement published in *Cosmopolitan* in 1929 promised: "Dainty, decorative, and diminutive, the Perfu-mist fits inside your tiniest purse, instantly ready to renew your perfume, as handily and as often as your compact renews your complexion!"[82] The 5-dollar product (equal to more than 90 dollars in 2025) was just a very small empty bottle, to be filled by the consumer's favorite brand of perfume.

Though *Ladies Home Journal, Red Book Magazine, Cosmopolitan,* and *Good Housekeeping* focused their marketing on white women consumers, far fewer magazines with lasting nationwide circulation were owned by or specifically aimed at Black women.[83] Two exceptions that targeted middle-class Black women include *Ringwood's Afro-American Journal of Fashion* (1891–1894) and *Half-Century Magazine for the Colored Woman and Homemaker* (1916–1925).[84] Nonetheless, small advertisements appeared for similar products in Black-owned newspapers, of which 500 existed between 1865 and 1889. Unlike women's magazines, these newspapers were read by both men and women, so the advertisements aimed at women's bodily management are fewer, shorter, and lack images or details. However, advertisements that mentioned products like Kotex were typically part of larger ads for sales at Black-owned pharmacies and dry goods stores. These stores noted that they carried products such as Kotex, but ads rarely featured much more information than the price of the product.

Very few of the advertisements published in Black-owned newspapers contained images or specific details on how the product worked or might be carried. For example, *The Philadelphia Tribune* featured a small advertisement for "Wood's Cut Rate" store, which devoted one line of text to Kotex, offering three pads for the high price of 50 cents (approximately 11 dollars in 2025).[85] Similarly, the *New Journal and Guide*, published in Norfolk, Virginia, featured a small ad for "Very Special! Kotex" in 1934, though the ad provided no details on what made the product special and did not include any images. It revealed only the price of the product and the address at which it could be purchased.[86] Another ad published in *The Atlanta World* noted that J.M. High Company sold Kotex, adding only that customers were limited to eight boxes each.[87] Advertisements aimed at Black women often listed Kotex alongside products and brands like Kleenex, Colgate toothpaste, Midol, Lydia Pinkham's Vegetable Compound, and various deodorizing products. However, unlike advertising aimed at white women, Kotex was also paired with products specifically marketed to Black women, such as hair-growing products, straightening combs, talcum powders, and bleaching creams.[88] Though Black women were clearly carrying purses in large numbers in the 1920s and 1930s, with some exceptions, advertisements in Black-owned newspapers aimed at both men and women largely promoted Black-owned businesses over mainstream brands of feminine hygiene products.

Carrying products related to menstruation inside one's purse became even more practical for women of all races when, in 1936, Tampax began selling tampons. Tampons were an innovation that dramatically changed the market and consumer experience. Just as Kotex needed to navigate how to sell sanitary napkins in the 1920s, early advertisers of tampons had the unenviable job of explaining what tampons were and how they worked, without featuring explicit illustrations that might have been deemed indecorous. This was particularly important when the product was new, but remained so, especially for girls whose mothers never taught them about periods or menstruation technologies. Early advertisements for Tampax explained that the product was made of "surgical cotton, compressed, highly absorbent" and whispered the tagline, *"Tampax is worn internally."*[89]

Because so many women had been taught that any sign of menstruation was potentially humiliating, it was exceedingly important that purses could securely store tampons so that they would not fall out. In its advertisements, Tampax eagerly emphasized how small its product was, frequently mentioning that customers could fit "a *month's* supply in their purse." Advertisements in 1937 and 1938 in *Good Housekeeping* and *Red Book* claimed that a "month's supply" of tampons "comes in a purse-size package."[90] By contrast, Kotex customers were told "[A] supply can be easily carried in a lady's handbag."[91] While a few tampons could fit in stylish small clutches, larger bags could have held many more and, in the 1940s, purses would grow in size. The fact that a month's supply of tampons purportedly fit inside a woman's purse meant not only that she could stay away from home longer, but also she could be prepared in the event of an emergency and be able to help a friend, coworker, or daughter in need. Since many women felt the need to hide these products in their own homes where children and spouses would not find them, purses may also have given some women a place to privately store their entire supply.[92] Even as Tampax began to show its product in 1939, advertisements continued to highlight how tampons were "compact" enough to "carry in your purse."[93]

In the *Evening Star*, Tampax published advertisements designed to appeal directly to women's feelings of inequality. One Tampax ad led with the eye-catching headline, "There's One Less Disadvantage in Being a WOMAN," and another published in *Good Housekeeping* touted the "unbelievable freedom" Tampax provided customers.[94] Published in 1936, the advertisement featured an illustration of a fashionable young white woman from the collarbone up. However, the bottom of the ad featured a drawing of a woman's fingertips slipping a box of Tampax into her purse. This image, in either photograph or illustrated form, would be featured in many more Tampax advertisements published that year. Once again, the ad claimed that "a month's supply came in a purse-size package."[95] Both the purse and tampons were explicitly framed as complementary liberatory tools.

As these examples illustrate, early advertisements for Tampax used the purse as a proxy for a woman's body. In fact, purses were critical in helping Tampax advertise a product that was otherwise unshowable in its first few years of existence. Many early advertisements for Tampax featured white well-manicured fingers gently parting the mouth of an envelope purse, while slipping in a small box of Tampax. For those already inclined to see the opening of a woman's purse as a material metaphor for her vulva, this image visually approximated the process of a woman inserting a tampon into her own body. Through these illustrations, the company was perhaps stealthily instructing women how to insert a tampon in a way that was palatable enough for publication.

By the 1920s and 1930s, purses had become associated with the most intimate, vulnerable parts of women's bodies, a process that further feminized purses and made them untouchable to American men. Sigmund Freud was not the first or the last person to make an explicit link between women's bodies and their bags. Many speakers and writers did so linguistically. The *Oxford English Dictionary* notes that the derogatory slang term "bag" was used to disparage "sexually promiscuous women" starting in 1924.[96] And the term "old bag" had been used to disparage aging women at least as early as 1947; it is still used in that manner today.[97]

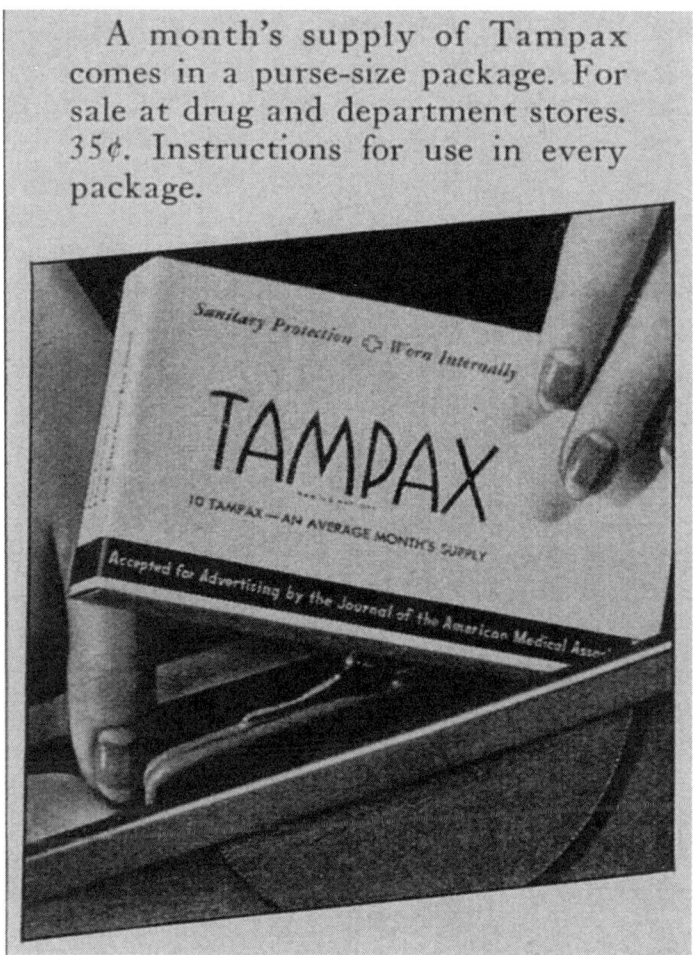

Figure 4.4. This image, featuring a white woman's fingers slipping a small box of tampons inside her purse, appeared in several Tampax advertisements in women's magazines. (*Good Housekeeping* 104, is. 4 [April 1937], 190.)

These terms also carried specific sexualized meanings across regions and among various demographics. In 1942, Harlem Renaissance writer Zora Neale Hurston used the term "pocketbook" to refer to a woman's genitalia in a short story published in *American Mercury*. In "Story in Harlem Slang," she described how an unnamed female character accused a man of "trying to snatch my pocketbook." She then attempted to slash him while threatening to "spread my lungs all over New York and call the law. . . . And I'll holler like a pretty white woman!"[98] Poet and memoirist Maya Angelou used this term in a similar manner in her first autobiography published more than two decades later. Angelou recalled that "Momma had drilled into my head: 'Keep your legs closed, and don't let nobody see your pocketbook.' "[99] In this coded language, Black Southern young girls were urged to remain modest virgins. Later in *I Know Why the Caged Bird Sings*, however, when "Ritie" refers to her "pocketbook," her mother responds by saying "Ritie, do you mean your vagina? Don't use those Southern terms. There's nothing wrong with the word vagina."[100] For Hurston and Angelou, the term "pocketbook" carried a sexualized, regionally specific meaning. Given these linguistic changes, some readers of advertisements for Tampax likely saw multiple meanings in images of fingers slipping a tampon inside a pocketbook.

After Tampax released its line of tampons, other companies followed suit. The Kimberly Clark Corporation, which produced Kotex pads, chose a revealing name for its first tampon, choosing to call its product "Fibs."[101] Just as the brand name Kotex was a play on the words cotton and texture (hence the abbreviated form, "co-tex"), "Fibs" was short for fiber but also carried a second meaning. Because tampons (and purses) allowed women to hide evidence that they were menstruating, the brand winked at the fact that tampons allowed women to function as if they were not having their periods. In other words, they could *fib* about their menstrual status.

Other than coats, in the 1920s and 1930s, ready-made women's clothing was not generally manufactured with functional integrated pockets, as clothing for boys and men had been for several decades. Thus, girls and women who did not carry purses were at a disadvantage.[102] Those who attended school without purses or bookbags in the 1930s were forced to hide sanitary napkins and tampons inside their notebooks or stuffed inside their shirts, from which they might fall out.[103] Sanitary napkins required unwieldy pins and belts and could even peek out under clothing, thereby betraying that a woman was "on her period."[104] But together, tampons and purses rendered periods invisible. These purses did not just hold what women needed to carry—they carried what they needed to hide.

In the Great Depression, American women were using their purses not just to be prepared for their periods, but for preventing pregnancy, too. Indeed, it is no accident that the term "birth control" came into its most popular use in the 1930s. In the United States, the average birth rate dipped in 1935 to what was then an all-time low of 2.1 children per woman.[105] But in reality, only wealthy women had access to personal doctors who might be willing and able to help them control the size of their families. Though a variety of products purported to help regulate women's periods, most consumers were not educated about reproduction so they could not effectively evaluate advertisers' claims to provide them with "safety" and "protection."

After the passage of the Comstock Law in 1873, advertisements for contraceptives did not disappear, but this legislation explicitly deemed literature discussing contraception "obscene," so advertisers had to be creative. Advertisements for such products used euphemisms to refer to their wares as "feminine hygiene" or "marriage hygiene" products. "Birth control" was officially banned, but advertisements for products that offered to "restore menstruation" and "eliminate germs" proliferated. It is difficult to determine how many Americans were using specific contraceptives at any given time.[106] When trying to determine how often women used their purses to purchase, transport, and carry contraceptives, that challenge is compounded by the fact that the entire purpose of keeping condoms, douches, or diaphragms inside purses was to ensure these products remained hidden from view. Thus, they have largely remained hidden from historians as well.

Nevertheless, some archival records document the connections between purses and contraception. In the 1930s, the American Birth Control League distributed promotional literature designed to be safely stored inside a woman's purse. In May 1935, the board of the Planned Parenthood Federation of America issued a report highlighting achievements of the year. The report detailed the federation's growing list of allies and affiliated clinics but also noted the forthcoming publication of a "purse-size" pamphlet.[107] Since discussions of birth control were verboten, it was critically important that literature discussing birth control be easy to hide; in this case, inside a woman's purse. Indeed, women, birth control advocates, and advertisers seemed to implicitly understand that the purse had become an extension of the woman's body and was perhaps the only private place she could control.

American companies that sold "feminine hygiene" products knew that they could market a parade of products to desperate women, whether or not they were effective as contraceptives. For example, Lenori Laboratories exhibited a "little booklet" that purported to explain "just what Feminine Hygiene is and why it has become the practice of millions of married women."[108] Inside its pages, the company promoted the virtues of its own product, Bir-Con-Jel. What supposedly made Bir-Con-Jel stand apart from its competitors was its patented new applicator. Women were instructed to fill the applicator with Bir-Con-Jel and take it with them, dropping it "into the week-end bag or the purse."[109] Bir-Con-Jel was not alone in praising the portability of both its pamphlet and its birth control product. In the 1930s and 1940s, Sears, Roebuck and Co. also featured purse-sized feminine hygiene products such as portable douches.[110]

Though mail order catalogues helped supply many Americans with items like feminine syringes, condoms, and vaginal suppositories, most Americans purchased their contraceptive products in person at small shops and pharmacies.[111] Much like buying Kotex sanitary pads, this intimate interaction could prove embarrassing. It necessitated asking a clerk for a particular product, paying for the product, carrying it out of the store, bringing it home, and finding a safe place to keep it. Men could purchase condoms in fake cigarette cases and small tin boxes that could be stashed inside one of their copious pockets.[112] Women, however, had no such luck without a purse.

In addition to manufacturers looking to sell their contraceptive products, the Birth Control Federation of America (BCFA) undertook a national campaign to engage public health officials and medical leaders about birth control.[113] The BCFA considered the use of purses in this process. Between 1939 and 1941, the BCFA sent officials in every state a letter contextualizing their outreach in terms of "the reduction of infant and maternal mortality rates." It then highlighted the health benefits of child spacing and "a medically directed contraceptive service program for indigent women."[114]

One report on the BCFA's outreach to public health officials noted the response of a medical leader named C. A. Armstrong of Prairie du Chien, Wisconsin. Though the BCFA was encouraging medical leaders across the country to take a more proactive role in teaching young people about birth control, Armstrong reported, "With most of the schoolgirls carrying 'condems' [*sic*] in their purse—birth control is doing fine."[115] Teen pregnancy, in his estimation, was not a problem because girls had ready access to contraceptives in their purses wherever they went.

What is the significance of Armstrong's comment? Without question, it is challenging to determine what girls and women were carrying inside their most private possession nearly a century ago. However, Armstrong's statement indicates that, in addition to carrying personal hygiene products like pads, Perstiks, and douching products, at least some "schoolgirls" likely attempted to maintain control of contraception by carrying condoms in their purses. One wonders how Armstrong learned of this information and whether, like other men had before him, he invaded and probed the girls' purses himself. Unfortunately, the BCFA report gives us no indication.

In contrast to women's clothing, men's waistcoats (essentially vests worn under blazers), trousers, and suit coats sometimes contained up to forty pockets. But with few exceptions, including bicycle bloomers in 1890s and some coats, ready-made women's clothing largely lacked consistently integrated pockets in the 1940s.[116] And while Hollywood began featuring a few women like Katherine Hepburn, Greta Garbo, and Marlene Dietrich wearing pants on film in the 1930s, pants were still verboten for the average American woman.[117] During World War II, however, functionality became fashionable. For women working at home, more practical dresses became popular. In 1941, designer Claire McCardell began manufacturing a "pop-over" dress, the front of which contained a large, quilted pocket, big enough to hold "matches, cigarettes, the morning mail, and the duster."[118] When women began working in the war industry during World War II, previous prohibitions against women wearing pants would sometimes be cast aside for safety reasons.

Prior to World War II, women had been able to join the military only as nurses. In 1941, however, women were able to enlist in the newly created Women's Auxiliary Army Corps (WAAC), which was renamed the Women's Army Corps (WAC) in 1943.[119] The following year, President Franklin D. Roosevelt signed a bill creating a women's branch of the Navy called the WAVES (a.k.a. Women Accepted for Volunteer Emergency Service). The SPARS (Coast Guard) and the WASPS (Air Force) soon followed.[120] Uniforms for women in these groups had to be functional and standardized. Wearers needed to look like soldiers but, most of all, the uniforms needed to make male and female soldiers look different from each other. A woman's dress had to delicately balance a woman's femininity with her new role as a soldier, which many Americans considered masculine.[121] This combination of function and femininity was a tall order.[122]

Attempting to avoid concerns about masculinization and lesbianism, women in the WAC were not given pants but were issued winter and summer versions of olive drab jackets and skirts.[123] They were also encouraged to style their hair and wear cosmetics within certain parameters.[124] Company officers also gave WAC members instructions in "personal hygiene."[125] Women stored both cosmetics and menstrual products in their purses, which were sometimes called "utility bags."[126] In fact, women who joined the WAC in World War II were issued standardized brown leather shoulder bags. Though shoulder bags were relatively uncommon in civilian life before World War II, these items kept women's hands free for tasks like typing, driving, photography, cryptography, cartography, and radio operation.[127] Indeed, women's ability to work with both hands free was exceptionally important in these new military roles. One commander of an all-female artillery brigade praised women for their efficiency in "manual dexterity," which he proclaimed was superior to men's.[128]

WAC handbooks instructed members to wear their bags (shaped like the bottom half of a circle) on their right shoulder, "crossing the body diagonally to the left."[129] Featuring a lined olive-colored interior, these bags had at least eight interior compartments, providing a wide variety of organizing options. The bags also featured two leather straps, a short one on the back to slip a hand through and a longer adjustable leather strap that stretched to at least 21 inches. Lacking zippers, these bags closed with a simple flap and single button. One surviving example of a WAC leather purse contains a matching brown hairnet hidden inside an interior pocket. The bag's owner, Katherine Mildred Keene, was born in 1919 and earned her bachelor's degree at the University of Washington in 1940. In December 1942, exactly one year after the attack on Pearl Harbor, she joined the WAAC.[130]

Figure 4.5. The brown leather bags issued by the Women's Army Corps in the early 1940s contained eight different compartments. These bags were 10.5 inches wide, 8.5 inches tall, and 2.5 inches deep while empty, though the mouth of the purse could open to 8.5 inches when stretched. In 1942, this purse was issued to Katherine Keene, who spent most of the next three years in London. Her bag is worn from use near the fastening button and at the corners. In the left-most pocket of the olive interior compartments, Keene tucked a matching hairnet made of brown string and kept two pins at the top of the middle section dividing the two main compartments. (Author's photograph, 2015. Katherine Keene Papers, 1941–1977, Box 5, MC 817, 5CB.1m, Schlesinger Library.)

Only women between the ages of 20 and 50, three decades of life during which most women were regularly menstruating, were eligible to join the WAC.¹³¹ Thus, women soldiers needed to be assured that they could access menstrual products during the war. Kotex sought to eliminate such worries by featuring illustrations of women in military and nursing uniforms in its ads. In 1942, Kotex published two advertisements in *McCall's*, each of which featured a smiling blonde, white woman in uniform carrying a purse over her right shoulder. "Who would have dreamed that you would be in uniform?" one ad asked. Another noted that Kotex would "keep your secret safe whether you're wearing a uniform or your favorite formal." The ads encouraged women readers to "keep going—everyday!" regardless of whether they were menstruating.¹³²

Slacks for women were not consistently available in stores in the 1940s, but even when they were, they never threatened to replace purses. Instead, purses

Figure 4.6. Born in Nebraska in 1906, Helen Sagl earned her bachelor's and master's degrees, a pedigree that likely improved her chances of being chosen for the highly competitive Women's Auxiliary Army Corps (WAAC). She was working as a teacher in Lincoln when she joined the WAAC in 1942. In this photograph taken in Texas in 1943, she appears with other members of WAC in her winter uniform. She holds the brown bag hanging down from her left shoulder instead of diagonally across the body from the right shoulder, as the WAC handbook dictated. (Courtesy of Nebraska State Historical Society, history.nebraska.gov.)

simply evolved alongside women's changing roles as consumers, workers, and soldiers. Especially as purses grew in size and durability, they offered more space and security than the average integrated pocket ever could. Even after the war, women still needed a place to keep their tampons, and advertisements for Tampax gradually became more candid. In addition to showcasing that women could "go swimming" and "sit on the beach" while using tampons, Tampax continued to boast that a "month's supply" could fit inside a woman's purse.[133] And the association between tampons, sanitary pads, and purses only deepened over time. It was so strong by the late 1950s that the Campana Corporation produced a line of tampons called "Pursettes." Indeed, these tampons were "tiny," with the entire box measuring just .55 inches wide and 2.4 inches high. The tampons themselves had a prelubricated tip and no applicator, which was intended to make them particularly appealing to girls and young women, some of whom were concerned that inserting a tampon could break their hymen.[134] More than any other personal hygiene product, the name Pursettes emphasized that the product intrinsically belonged inside a purse.

In the 1950s, junior high and high school girls regularly carried tampons and pads to school in their pocketbooks. Though having such supplies on hand was helpful, Mary Olsen remembered that this could simultaneously make girls vulnerable on the playground. She described one unforgettable day when "one of the boys grabbed one of my friend's pocketbooks. And the boys went running with the bag. And she was hysterical because she had a pad in there. 'Oh my God, they're going to see it," Olson recalled thinking, "is that why he took her bag? Does he want to see what's in there?"[135] The prospect of a boy touching a young woman's purse, never mind wresting control of it and potentially pouring out its contents in front of his friends, was horrifying. Just as the women who worked in the Triangle Shirtwaist Factory felt that mandatory purse inspections were a highly personal violation of their autonomy, Olson described a similar feeling of horror watching a young boy running around with a stolen bag that he threatened to open.

Menstrual products, personal hygiene products, and carrying a purse each became linked to womanhood and femininity, even more so when they were combined. One man recalled how when his wife asked him to run to the drugstore to purchase menstrual products for her, he thought, "That's like carrying a purse down the street [Laughter]. Oh no! . . . Even if that's all we needed, I'd get milk, or something else to go around it."[136] He was afraid to be seen with either a purse or a menstrual product, both of which seemed to serve as proxies for a woman's body.

As his comment demonstrates, the feminization of purses and their association with women's bodies in general and with menstruation, vulvas, and vaginas in particular were thoroughly complete by the 1950s. Though his wife was either comfortable or desperate enough to ask her husband to purchase sanitary products on her behalf, he balked at the request, equating carrying a box of menstrual products to carrying a purse "down the street" in full view of others. It was as if he feared that carrying a purse or menstrual product would irreparably feminize him or even turn him into a woman. His anticipation of public humiliation indicates that purses and period products were simultaneously untouchable for the American man, though they remained vital for the American woman.

In the 1920s, 1930s, and 1940s, purses were a literal "mixed bag" for women. They held feminine and personal hygiene products that offered girls and women new levels of mobility and novel ways to manage their bodies. New menstrual technologies enabled women to work long shifts and even go off to war. However, these changes also increased the standards by which women were supposed to discipline the supposedly shameful parts of their bodies and spend their meager wages in doing so.

5

Pickets, Protests, and Purses in the Civil Rights Movement

When Rosa Parks boarded a city bus in Montgomery, Alabama, in 1943, James Blake was behind the wheel. After Parks paid her fare, Blake ordered her to get off the bus and then board again at the back, as was the custom. When Parks refused, Blake attempted to drag her off the bus. Thinking quickly, Parks recalled, "I dropped my purse. Rather than stoop or bend over to get it, I sat right down in the front seat and from a sitting position I picked up my purse."[1] Parks knew that strategically "dropping" her purse could give her an opening to reach into and enter a space in which she was otherwise not welcome.[2] Once sitting, she warned Blake, "You better not hit me" and he didn't.[3] More than a decade before she became one of the most recognizable faces of the Civil Rights Movement, Rosa Parks understood that purses could function as powerful political tools. Understanding this purse-centered prelude to Parks's 1955 arrest highlights the fact that she was not simply an "old" woman too tired to stand up. At 42 years old, she had already been pushing back against segregation for years and, on at least this one important occasion, used her purse as a tool to negotiate space, wedging her way into the white section of the bus.

In carrying their purses in the 1950s and 1960s, civil rights activists like Parks appeared to simply follow prevailing trends about how "respectable" Black women should dress. Yet, they consciously used purses to prepare to face harassment and assault while they rode public transportation, attended political events, sat-in at restaurants, and tried to register to vote.[4] In fact, Black and white civil rights activists both deployed purses as political tools.[5] Oral histories, memoirs, diaries, monuments, and photographs reveal how they used purses in clever and creative ways to challenge existing power structures. Purses helped Black women protect themselves in a racist, sexist climate that fundamentally denied them their value and dignity. And although they have largely been left out of the history of Black armed self-defense, they also used purses to shield their bodies and discreetly arm themselves.

White women often faced different kinds of risks than Black women, but they, too, used purses to achieve political ends. However, white women were more often able to use the advantages of their skin color to maintain direct control of and access to their purses. Most importantly, white female activists strategically prepared the contents of their purses to help them endure lengthy sit-ins and prison sentences.

By the 1950s, purses, bags, sacks, and suitcases had been closely associated with women's work and travel for many decades. Black women in the early twentieth century attached special meaning to the bags they packed when they boarded segregated trains to migrate North. Oral histories reveal that some Black women who migrated to Washington, DC, in the 1920s referred to the bags they took on northbound trains as "freedom bags."[6] During the Great Depression, Black domestic workers gathered on the street corners in the Bronx (dubbed the "Bronx Slave Markets") clutching their bags. As they waited for white women to select them for a day's work, they huddled on benches or leaned against walls holding their purses and paper bags containing their uniforms.[7] Black reformers like Ella Baker and Marvel Cooke referred to the "invariable paper bundles" the workers carried as "disreputable"; they appear to have been concerned that these working women were on display and could be picked up by men for nefarious purposes.[8] But the women themselves lovingly called the bags in which they carried their uniforms "freedom bags."[9] Because they no longer "lived in" the homes of white families as domestic servants, the bags allowed them to walk or ride to work with pride, adorned in their own clothing instead of a uniform that indicated the subservient nature of their employment.[10]

Since the end of enslavement, keeping up appearances had been of particular political import for Black women. Indeed, Black women have historically been viewed by whites as unclean and licentious and therefore undeserving of protection.[11] But at the end of the nineteenth century, Black women developed a "politics of respectability" that had a strong visual component.[12] Many self-consciously dressed and groomed themselves in order to undermine white claims that they were uncivilized, promiscuous, and unkempt.[13]

However, Black conceptions of respectability were neither unchanging nor monolithic; indeed, they varied across class and region and did not go unchallenged. In different contexts and historical moments, many working-class Black women carved out their own notions of what it meant to be "respectable."[14] Yet, in the context of the Civil Rights Movement in which photographers created countless visual records of protests, many Black activists in the 1950s and 1960s continued to emphasize the importance of looking respectable. Impeccably clean and demure dress was particularly important where Black women were regularly subject to white surveillance.[15] Dressing up was also a strategy that many Black women used to enhance their own sense of dignity. Black fashion designer Reginald Thomas described growing up in Chicago as the son of a maid in the early 1960s. Thomas's mother "always pride [sic] herself she always made sure that her hair was in place. Back in those days women had gloves, purse, hat. That was the most important thing for them." Thomas noted that he "grew up in a[n] era where women were polished as far as you wouldn't walk out the house without your hair being combed. You always had to have a purse, gloves, hat. Everyone had to be groomed. . . . Even if [the men] were unemployed, they would have . . . groom[ed] themselves a certain way." In the 1950s and 1960s, Thomas said, "[T]here were dos and don'ts and rules and regulations of appearance."[16]

Because dress had long been thought to reveal one's inner character, these accessories were an important arena for Black women attempting to overcome deeply entrenched racist stereotypes that they were hypersexual. In addition to hats, hosiery, and purses, in the 1950s a woman's gloves helped avoid inadvertent intimacy with men.[17] Indeed, short white gloves were particularly popular when gender roles contracted during this decade. They also indicated that the women who wore them did not do dirty work. It is not surprising, then, that a virtuous woman was expected to wear a girdle and gloves. When they were not being worn, white gloves could be kept clean inside a compartment of a tidy, organized purse. It is no coincidence that, in the mid-twentieth century, the term "pocketbook" was being used as a euphemism for women's genitalia.[18] Though gloves communicated a particular message by themselves, the combination of a clean, matching pair of gloves, hat, and purse suggested an organized, polished, pure woman.

Historically, Black women have disproportionately faced related charges of being physically and biologically unclean. Historian Tera Hunter has persuasively argued that, in the late nineteenth and early twentieth centuries, many white families believed Black domestic workers were "pathological agents of contamination" who might sicken the whole family by passing on deadly diseases like tuberculosis.[19] This hyper-focus on the sexual and hygienic cleanliness of Black girls' and women's bodies provided a rationale for some whites to continuously violate their bodies in search of signs of uncleanliness. For example, in the 1930s, a young Mabel Williams, whose mother was a maid for one of the wealthiest families in North Carolina, had her skirts lifted by white women who did not trust her to wear clean underwear.[20]

In such a context, Black women who coordinated their gloves, hat, and purse and kept them all clean guarded themselves against such accusations. Student Nonviolent Coordinating Committee (SNCC) activist Roberta "Bobbi" Yancy described this as "the church lady look."[21]

Figure 5.1. Three unidentified Black women pose for a photographer in Greenville, Mississippi. Each wears heels, earrings, and a modest dress cut slightly above the ankles. The woman on the right manages to showcase her purse even though she is likely right-handed. (Photographed by Rev. Henry Clay Anderson, circa 1955, Smithsonian National Museum of African American History and Culture, Object Number 2007.1.69.21.45.D.)

Yet, Black women carrying purses did more than just follow the rules and regulations of appearance. Since the police and judicial system refused to protect Black women's and children's bodies, Black women used their purses to protect themselves. In the late 1950s, Daisy Bates, who was a local leader of the National Association for the Advancement of Colored People (NAACP), faced considerable danger when she escorted the Little Rock Nine to Central High School during Arkansas's desegregation crisis. Bates was always impeccably dressed and ready to meet the media; she often wore matching earrings and a necklace, donned short black gloves, and carried a structured black leather purse shaped like a trapezoid, which was particularly popular at the time. But Bates knew firsthand how white men could violate Black women's bodies without facing legal consequences. When she was 8 years old, Bates discovered that, while she was still a baby, her biological mother had been raped and murdered by three white men.[22] Bates vowed that "someday I would get the men who killed my mother."[23]

Bates channeled her anger over this trauma into her efforts to protect the Little Rock Nine. She knew that students and their families who attempted to integrate all-white schools could face a wide range of potentially devastating consequences—from job loss and eviction to school closures, harassment, physical assault, and even death. For these reasons, the Little Rock Nine met at Bates's house every morning, and she personally escorted them to school throughout the crisis.[24] But Bates, who was the only woman permitted to speak during the main program of the March on Washington in 1963, did not exclusively rely on her husband and male friends to keep herself safe.[25] She carried her own .32-caliber pistol, which she kept in her purse.[26]

At the height of the school desegregation crisis, young Black girls and women also used purses to protect themselves as they gained new access to formerly all-white spaces. Bobbie Steele remembered that in the mid-1960s her mother, Mary Laney Hodges, was one of the first Black students to integrate Mississippi's Delta State Teachers College. Steele recalled that upon starting school, her mother purchased a gun: "I think it was a .32 . . . to protect herself." Fearful of being assaulted, Hodges took her gun with her and "as she would ride to school she'd put it on the seat of her car. And when she got out, of course she'd take it out and take it in the school with her and put her purse up."[27] Hodges knew that in the mid-1960s, where schools remained racial battlegrounds, a young Black woman could not openly carry a gun. But a purse offered her privacy in public, and hiding a gun inside her purse provided her with powerful protection even though she appeared to be alone, unarmed, and otherwise unassuming.

By the 1950s, leather purses fashioned in trapezoid or hexagonal shapes outfitted with short handles supplanted the clutches of the 1930s and shoulder bags of the 1940s. Steele's mother most likely carried a small, structured leather bag typical of the decade. Though these bags were not especially large, they could accommodate a .32-caliber pistol, often referred to as a "pocket pistol," which was designed for men to carry in the pocket of their coat or trousers. However, in the hands of women whose clothing lacked integrated pockets, these guns became purse pistols. Despite the widespread (and largely incorrect) belief that Black women were in less physical danger than Black men during the movement, when white men sexually assaulted Black women, they were rarely investigated, let alone prosecuted for such crimes. In such circumstances, purse pistols could easily prove life-saving.

Fighting the desegregation of schools was one way in which white Southerners could maintain white supremacy. But keeping Black men and women from voting in the South was perhaps the surest way to safeguard the existing racial hierarchy. White Southerners often leaned hard on aggressive tactics when trying to intimidate Black voters. White employers threatened Black domestic workers with firing if they were seen attempting to register or vote. Tenant farmers and sharecroppers could also be forced out of their homes on short notice. As SNCC began its voter registration drives in the early 1960s, terrorist threats grew alongside the lists of registered Black voters. In his memoir *Ready for Revolution*, Stokely Carmichael recalled that in Alabama "these terrorists put it out there that they'd shoot the entire place up before they'd let that [Black voting] happen. But our people simply refused to be run off.... They made what preparations they could."[28] Those preparations often involved being ready to physically defend oneself, and Black men were not the only ones to take this approach.

Though there were laws against bringing firearms to polling places on election day, Black Southerners who believed in self-defense sometimes ignored them. When Stokely Carmichael was in his early twenties, he helped an elderly woman in Lowndes County Alabama to vote: "She had to be eighty years old," he recalled, "all proud and determined-looking, dressed for church and going to vote for the first time in her life." The woman must have carried a generously proportioned purse that day because "[t]hat ol' lady came up to us, went into her bag and produced this enormous, rusty, Civil War-looking old pistol. 'Best you hol' this for me, son. I'ma go cast my vote now.'"[29] The woman's age made the moment particularly memorable, but it is also noteworthy that, in front of Carmichael's eyes, she chose to remove the gun from the private space in which she kept it hidden and to entrust it to him. Perhaps she was hoping to avoid getting searched at the polls, but the gesture meant that Carmichael, a young Black man, knew she carried a gun in her purse. Carmichael stated that this was not uncommon. "They would come, these old church sisters, bring their pistols and stuff, put it right there, and step on up to the polls."[30] Whether or not this Alabamian woman ever fired her pistol, carrying it and showing it to others communicated that she wanted observers to know she was armed.

Carmichael was emboldened by witnessing elderly Black women reject white supremacy in such a stark and unapologetic way. But he also recalled how Black women used their purses to stand up to Black men like himself as well. After Carmichael and Cleveland Sellers had recruited two young activists in DC to go to Mississippi, they were relaxing on their front porch when "all of a sudden, these two grim-faced, well-dressed black ladies came marching up the block." As the mothers of the two new recruits approached them, one of them "went into her purse, pulled out a high-heeled shoe and measured my nappy head, with some sho-nuff bad intentions."[31] She hoped to protect her daughter using a spare shoe as an improvised weapon that fit snugly inside a purse.

Even though SNCC was a nonviolent organization, some members did not just witness and record Black women carrying guns inside their purses; they did so themselves. While a student at George Washington University in 1963, Cynthia Washington became a member of SNCC. In the sweltering summer of 1964, she joined approximately 1,000 students who entered the Mississippi Delta to register Black voters during "Freedom Summer."[32] But she soon found herself questioning the group's pacifist philosophy when three of the volunteers were brutally murdered.[33] After learning the horrific details of how Black activist James Chaney was beaten to death before being shot in Mississippi on June 21, 1964, Washington reconsidered the strategic value of nonviolence: "The thought of being beaten to death without being able to fight back put the fear of God in me.... So I acquired an automatic handgun to sit in the top of that outstanding black patent and tan handbag that I carried."[34] Washington recalled both the "outstanding" handbag and automatic handgun with equal reverence.[35] As a project director, she often drove a truck alone, with only her handbag to keep her company.[36] Keeping an automatic gun at the very top of a stylish patent leather handbag meant that Washington could appear relatively unthreatening yet be able to grasp and discharge a weapon in a matter of seconds. In fact, Washington was following in the footsteps of generations of Black women who understood the political value of purses and used them as portable arsenals.

In the 1950s and 1960s, patent leather was a glossy, waterproof material that was particularly popular for making women's purses and shoes. Women often paired matching patent leather purses and shoes with gloves and a hat on Sunday mornings at church. Yet, Washington also wore denim pants and overalls, a style adopted by many SNCC activists who were attempting to register sharecroppers to vote in the rural South in the early 1960s.[37] Sharecroppers wore denim for its durability, and SNCC activists mixed politics with pragmatism when they adopted similar attire.

Denim also helped middle-class college students blend in with rural sharecroppers. At the same time, overalls gave them access to pockets in which they could keep flyers and leaflets.[38] However, a gun would leave a conspicuous bulge inside a denim pocket. Although respectable dresses, gloves, hats, and heels did not necessarily protect Black women from violence, the guns they carried in their purses could.[39] For Washington, who had grown up in a middle-class Black family, keeping an automatic gun at the top of a patent leather handbag meant that she could work among sharecroppers yet still carry an accessory that allowed her to hide, grasp, and discharge a weapon in a matter of seconds.[40] While there is no evidence that Washington ever shot anyone, the presence of a gun was key to maintaining her feeling of safety. And when Washington was interviewed in 1976, she made sure the historical record would reflect that she was armed.

The fact that so many Black women appear to have carried guns inside their purses (and did so without getting caught) is particularly meaningful given long-standing white anxiety about Black access to guns. As early as 1680, the Virginia General Assembly passed a law making it illegal for "any negroe or other slave to carry or arme himselfe with any club, staffe, gunn, sword or any other weapon of defence or offence." Violators of this ordinance would be punished with "twenty lashes."[41] Nearly 200 years later in the aftermath of the Civil War, many Southern states passed highly repressive laws known as Black Codes, which often forbade Black people from owning firearms.

White fears of Black gun ownership did not dissipate with time. In 1943, sociologist Howard Odum documented widespread rumors among whites that Black people were stockpiling guns and hiding them in coffins in segregated Black cemeteries. Odum also noted stories that Black North Carolinians were mail-ordering large amounts of guns and ammunition from Sears, Roebuck and Co.[42] Two decades later in Louisiana, members of the Ku Klux Klan told police that Black residents were using the Mississippi River to smuggle guns and bullets into Washington County, thereafter, hiding them in coffins inside a segregated cemetery. The Klan even convinced the police to "exhume the grave of one elderly Black man."[43] Needless to say, as arsenals, purses were more convenient, discreet, and portable than coffins. Even in patriarchal organizations like the Black Panther Party, women like Tareka Lewis "carried a gun in her purse" after joining the group in 1967.[44] Women's participation in armed resistance has largely been ignored in favor of nonviolent approaches.[45] However, examining the activities of Black women through the eyes of one object—the purse—illuminates how some Black women carried portable arsenals while they engaged in activism. Such findings suggest that Black women were prepared to play a much more significant role in armed self-defense than we have previously appreciated.

Women activists celebrated for their nonviolent approach also strategically used their purses to defend their bodies and civil rights. It is noteworthy that the most favored female figure in the pantheon of popular civil rights icons, Rosa Parks, has been memorialized in several monuments that emphasize the passive nature of her resistance and her demure femininity.[46] In each case, the artists prominently featured Parks's purse, though the size and shape of the purse vary. The bronze statue erected in the U.S. Capitol shows her carrying the most quintessentially feminine bag of all. It depicts Parks primly seated with her ankles crossed, holding a small handbag with a short strap draped across her lap.[47] Her hands are also crossed, shielding the most vulnerable part of her body. She wears a dress, glasses, and a pillbox hat, all signs of a finely curated midcentury feminine respectability. Parks's purse is much smaller here than in other memorials, and it has the added feminine embellishment of ruching near the top as well. In fact, most photographs from the 1950s and 1960s depict Parks carrying a variety of medium-sized black leather bags, all larger than the one depicted in the memorial of Parks displayed in the Capitol.[48] This purse and its placement indicate her virtue and respectability, both revered as irreproachable inside Montgomery's Black community.[49]

This statue and others freeze Parks at the age of 42 and memorialize a specific vision of what transpired on Thursday, December 1, 1955. That day, Parks was returning home from her job as a tailor at the Montgomery Fair department store. In addition to the 10-cent bus fare, she likely carried some sewing implements in her purse. In the Jim Crow South, Black women were the least likely demographic to own a car and constituted the largest portion of bus patrons in many areas. Montgomery, Alabama, was no exception. Because the boycott lasted more than a year, it was essential that women remain mobile, and a purse or "freedom bag" allowed them easy access to daily essentials and a

Figure 5.2. Erected in the U.S. Capitol Building in 2013, this memorial shows Rosa Parks seated with her ankles primly crossed and her small, snap-close purse dangling from her fingers. She has her coat closed and wears a pillbox hat, short Oxford heels, and glasses. (Photograph courtesy of Wikimedia Commons.)

place to keep their wages. Black women like Parks were especially vulnerable when walking or riding alone on public transportation. Parks recalled that, even before her arrest, "I could leave home feeling that anything could happen at any time."[50] In such situations, purses and bags functioned as resourceful toolkits containing money, weapons, a change of clothes, or simply a bodily shield to keep white men from getting too close.[51]

In the mid-twentieth century, women like Parks who held their purses primly at the edge of their tightly closed knees could quietly demonstrate their virtue and poise. These qualities became the most celebrated part of the persistent folklore that describes Parks as simply a tired, tidy old lady on a bus. In describing why Parks was the perfect woman to launch the boycott, E. D. Nixon, former head of the Montgomery NAACP, even told a reporter, "She was clean," a comment that he likely meant in both a literal and figurative sense.[52] Nixon's language draws attention to the fact that male boycott organizers were concerned with the politics of respectability. Yet, this description of Parks also elides the facts that she had decades of experience as a civil rights activist by 1955 and was neither as traditionally feminine nor devoutly committed to nonviolence as legend would suggest. In fact, for much of her life until that point, Parks had practiced self-defense.

In her memoir, Parks recalled that she and her grandfather, who had been born enslaved and later became a follower of Marcus Garvey, would often stay up late guarding their porch with a double-barreled shotgun. At the age of 6, "I wanted to see him kill a Ku Kluxer."[53] When Parks was 10 years old, a white boy named Franklin insulted her and balled up his fist to hit her; she responded in this way: "I picked up a brick and dared him to hit me. He thought better of the idea and went away."[54] Parks's grandmother warned her that "if I wasn't careful, I would probably be lynched before I was twenty years old."[55]

Parks's grandmother's warnings did little to discourage her involvement in anti-racist political organizing. When she and her husband Raymond hosted political meetings, the Parks's kitchen table was "covered with guns."[56] She described herself as an "assistant tailor," a more masculine term than seamstress, and said she was not particularly tired.[57] In an interview she gave in 1978, Parks insisted that she "didn't tell anyone my feet were hurting . . . they wanted to give some excuse other than the fact that I didn't want to be pushed around."[58] Indeed, Parks spent much of the rest of her life resisting a narrative that defanged her political agency.

Contemporary memorials of Parks take her defiant action and turn it into something passive. These memorials are not alone in attempting to revise history by freezing her in a moment of quiet feminine dignity. Shortly after her arrest, the Black press worked hard to extol Parks's feminine, respectable virtues, perhaps in order to compensate for the fact that she was both a woman and a self-conscious, highly experienced political agent.[59] Ten years before refusing to give up her seat on a Montgomery bus, in 1945 she had become the third woman to join Montgomery's NAACP branch. She later became branch secretary and head of the local youth chapter.[60] And just four months before her arrest, she completed leadership training for civil rights activists at the Highlander Folk School in Monteagle, Tennessee. Yet, Montgomery activists reminded others that Parks was a pretty, Christian "lady" who was above all polite.[61]

Despite her family history and the fact that her husband owned a gun, there is no evidence that Parks carried a gun on December 1, 1955. As someone who had been active in protesting the humiliating treatment Black citizens routinely received on the city buses, Parks knew that city bus drivers had been endowed with police powers while on duty and drove armed. Parks, who preferred to walk so as not to have to suffer the indignity of having to change seats, also knew that she would likely be out-maneuvered if she tried to physically resist being moved by either the armed bus driver or police officers. Had she any doubts about how she might be treated in such a situation, the case of 15-year-old Claudette Colvin nine months earlier would have put them to rest. Because Colvin did not willfully give up her seat, allegedly kicking and scratching one of the police officers as they attempted to remove her, she was arrested and charged with assault.[62] Upon closer examination, then, it is perhaps fitting that Parks's purse has been used in an effort to secure her legendary status as an icon of the Civil Rights Movement because, by 1955, she had already strategically used her purse in order to resist Jim Crow bus policies.

Figure 5.3. After her arrest, Rosa Parks walked to court with her attorney Charles Langford on February 22, 1956. She carried a stylish black hexagonal-shaped purse and a pair of short white gloves. (Bettmann/Getty Images.)

Since men had stopped carrying pocketbooks, purses, and other movable containers with shoulder straps that might sway against their hips, in the 1950s the closest corollary to a purse in men's apparel was the briefcase. Rather than function as symbols of men's consumption, vanity, or body parts, men's briefcases elicited associations with white-collar work, contributing to the image of white businessmen of the gray flannel persuasion. Most photographs of Martin Luther King Jr. show him impeccably dressed in a suit while carrying his monogrammed briefcase. Rare images taken at the scene of his assassination at the Lorraine Hotel show his opened briefcase, revealing his shaving cream and a book he was reading.[63]

Had Parks carried a briefcase like King, she would have raised eyebrows. In a decade defined by conformity, anti-communism, and heightened homophobia, women and men active in the Civil Rights Movement needed to wear what was considered gender-appropriate clothing.[64] The purses that women like Rosa Parks, Daisy Bates, and others carried allowed them to blend in. Like Parks and Bates, Ella Baker also defied traditional gender roles. By the time of the Montgomery Bus Boycott in 1955, Baker already had amassed years of experience in civil rights leadership roles. Born in Virginia and raised in North Carolina, this "mother of the movement" first cut her political teeth challenging her high school's dress code. Though she did not own a pair herself, Baker's classmates asked her to challenge the school's policy forbidding students from wearing silk stockings. Baker surmised that the girls came to her because they "didn't have guts enough" to challenge the rule themselves.[65] She later worked as a field secretary and director of branches for the NAACP, cofounded the organization In Friendship, and organized a chapter of the Southern Christian Leadership Conference (SCLC) in Atlanta.

Before she moved to Atlanta, Bayard Rustin and Martin Luther King Jr. had to be convinced to hire Baker on a temporary basis. King preferred to work with another minister (and therefore man) rather than Baker.[66] When Baker arrived in Atlanta, however, she found that there was no designated office space and no supplies with which to work. She was the only staff member and recalled that "I had to function out of a telephone booth and my pocketbook."[67] Baker saw the versatile utilitarian powers of her pocketbook at a time when she was taking on enormous new responsibilities and was being surveilled by the FBI.[68] Though she did not discuss the appearance or construction of her pocketbook, or what she placed inside it, her statement makes clear that her purse served as a mobile office for the movement.

Three years later in the spring of 1960, Baker organized the conference at which SNCC was formed. She encouraged college students from across the country to gather on the campus of her alma mater, Shaw University. Baker had been inspired by four Black college students (later known as "The Greensboro Four") who successfully integrated a Woolworth's lunch counter a few months prior. She was also frustrated with the bureaucracy and patriarchal leadership of existing organizations. Like Parks, Baker was often surrounded by male figures of authority who doubted her leadership skills; she was also far more experienced than she was given credit for. Yet, she was impossible to ignore. Activist Bob Moses recalled that "she had this black woman's manner, and she carried that with her into the dangerous arena of radical politics."[69] Part of that manner was how Baker adorned her body and moved with self-assurance in the masculine sphere of politics. According to her biographer, "by the 1950s, she maneuvered within these spaces as a middle-aged Black woman with her purse tucked under her arm, her hat carefully placed, and her good southern manners."[70] The combination of Baker's pillbox hats and purses visually commanded respect, but only her purse offered her privacy in public and a mobile office that enabled her to launch into work at any time.

Baker inspired many young Black women active in the movement. One such woman was Roberta ("Bobbi") Yancy, a member of SNCC in the early 1960s.[71] As a young girl, Yancy had closely followed her Aunt Virginia's style. Growing up in Pennsylvania in a mostly white town, Yancy recalled that at the age of 4 or 5, she relentlessly begged her aunt to allow her to borrow and carry a long, thin red leather purse on a train trip to Pittsburgh. Though she had her own child-size "pocketbooks," Yancy insisted on carrying her aunt's red purse: "I have no idea why I was attached to it ... but I had to put up a fight to carry it."[72] Yancy was not aware that she was going to a funeral; perhaps her aunt thought the red bag was inappropriate for such a somber occasion. Yet, Yancy vividly remembers her unwillingness to back down about carrying that red purse. Her determination to fight for the right to carry a purse at a young age is particularly telling given the fact that Black women in the movement would be forcibly separated from their purses in jail.

After graduating with just two other Black students in her class at Barnard College, Yancy went to Atlanta to work closely with Ella Baker.[73] Yancy shared Baker's belief in the importance of being seen and listened to as a respectable middle-class Black woman. In her own words, she took care to play the part of "Miss Black Middle Class."[74] Yancy carefully planned out her part in demonstrations in advance. Before participating in a sit-in at a segregated diner in

Atlanta in December 1963, Yancy and two other Black women purchased stock in the company that owned it. When she arrived at the sit-in, Yancy presented herself as a part owner. Knowing she would likely be going to jail that day, she dressed with particular purpose.[75] By her own account, Yancy wore a "very, very nice" faux-mink coat.[76] She paired her coat with a gold-colored pleated skirt, striped sweater, black leather gloves, ankle boots with uncomfortable heels, and a leather "pocketbook," which had a zippered compartment in the front and multiple pockets inside. The outfit was part of her "college wardrobe."[77] In her pocketbook, Yancy packed a toothbrush, an item that she hoped would help sustain her throughout a potential stay in prison. Though Yancy felt it was important to dress in a way that would be perceived as respectable and feminine, she harbored a deep distaste for high heels. Knowing she would likely end up in jail for several days, she also placed a pair of flat shoes in her purse.[78]

Despite her protestations that she was a part-owner of the diner, the police entered and grabbed Yancy. She went limp and was dragged to a police car by white male police officers. At that moment, Mark Suckle snapped a photograph that appeared in the pages of *Jet* magazine on January 9, 1964.[79] Another SNCC activist, Judy Richardson, recalled that as the police dragged her away, Yancy "shouted 'Watch the fur, watch the fur.' She later told me the fur was fake, but the image endures."[80] The photograph in *Jet* shows Yancy being physically dragged from the scene. Yet, even in that moment, she insisted the two white policemen respect the integrity of her body and belongings.[81] In these images, Yancy can be seen donning her fur coat while holding her leather pocketbook out in the air, which kept it from being dragged and dirtied on the ground.[82] In fact, multiple family members had saved up to buy the purse and coat for Yancy, which they purchased for her to wear at the elite, nearly-all-white women's college she attended.[83] Once in jail, Yancy spent the next several days in solitary confinement, separated from her friends and possessions. As part of ongoing negotiations, her lawyer, Howard Moore, did manage to regain access to the fur coat, which Yancy used as a blanket to "make the concrete floor a bit softer" during her time in prison.[84] Yancy stayed in jail through the Christmas holiday, until the company that owned the diner finally agreed to desegregate its business, making the sit-in a success on multiple fronts.[85]

One year before Yancy's arrest, a sharecropper named Fannie Lou Hamer became active in the movement. Hamer had more humble beginnings than Yancy, growing up with nineteen siblings in Mississippi. She quit school after sixth grade to pick cotton. She eventually married, and, like countless poor women of color in the South, was sterilized without her knowledge or consent in 1961.[86] When civil rights workers descended on her hometown the next year, Hamer quickly became involved in the movement, and her charisma and courage attracted national attention. As one of the founders of the Mississippi Freedom Democratic Party (MFDP), Hamer testified on live television before the all-white Democratic Credentials Committee at the Democratic National Convention on August 22, 1964, in Atlantic City. By that time, the FBI had begun surveilling the activities of members of the MFDP under a counterintelligence program known as COINTELPRO.[87] Though she publicly endorsed nonviolent efforts, Charles Cobb, Jr. asserts that Hamer was also a gun-owner, as her mother had been. When asked how she survived terrorist threats, Hamer reportedly said, "I keep a shotgun in every corner of my bedroom and the first cracker even looks like he wants to throw some dynamite on my porch won't write his mama again."[88]

At the Democratic Convention, Hamer was summoned to the microphone to speak about how she had been arrested and assaulted after attempting to register to vote in 1962. On live television, she made her way through a crowd of mostly white male politicians. As she parted the crowd, she stepped forward, leading with her white purse in her left hand. At midcentury, American women often grabbed their purses, hats, and coats when they "went out," but Hamer grabbed only a trapezoid-shaped purse with a short strap as she approached the center of the room. Arriving at the table where she was to give her testimony, Hamer placed her purse standing up directly on the table next to her, partially blocking the camera's view of her and creating a physical barrier between her body, the Credentials Committee, the camera, and the viewing audience. Once at the table, Hamer bravely stated her personal address and shared the brutal details of her experience.[89] Throughout, her purse sat upright next to her as if her companion throughout the ordeal.

Although she never opened it while on camera, Hamer clearly wanted to keep her purse within inches of her body, reachable at a moment's notice. As was the case with the immigrant factory workers in the Triangle Shirtwaist Factory, Hamer's purse must have provided her with a measure of security, perhaps both psychological and physical. It also may have afforded her the reassurance that she looked "respectable" on live television. Though President Lyndon Johnson had not felt sufficiently threatened by Martin Luther King's testimony moments earlier, Hamer's live testimony was so gripping that Johnson convened an unplanned press conference in order to interrupt her televised speech.[90] The exact contents of Hamer's purse remain unknown, but knowing

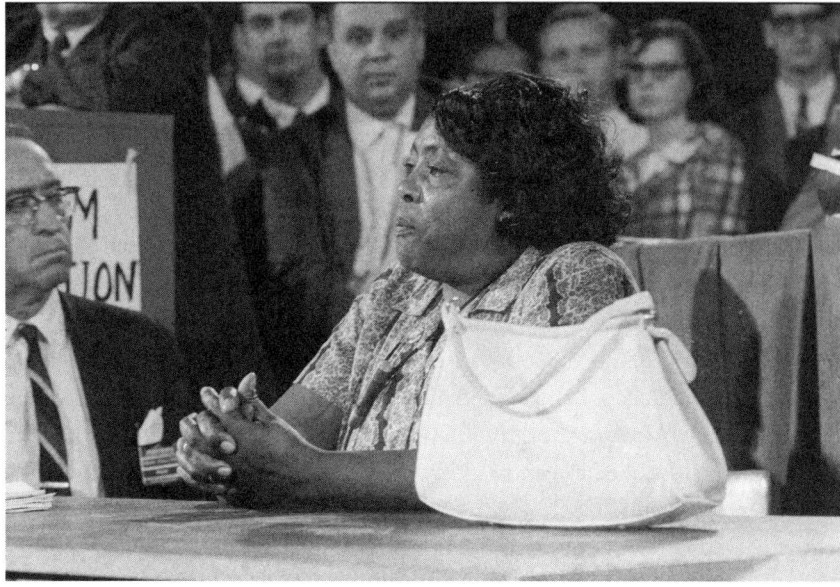

Figure 5.4. Fannie Lou Hamer testifying at the Democratic National Convention held in Atlantic City on August 22, 1964. Her closed white purse sits upright to her left. (August 22, 1964. Photograph and Prints Division, Library of Congress. LC-DIG-ds-07134.)

what she experienced and how she reportedly appointed her bedroom, one wonders what she decided to carry with her on a day she knew the world would be watching. Hamer's insistence on bringing her purse and placement of the purse in the direct view of cameras demonstrates that, like other activists, she saw her purse as a resource to sustain her through attempts to integrate space, vote, and even testify on live television.

Purses were not necessarily used in the same way by all activists who faced different stigmas and approached the movement with different sets of experiences. While Black women used purses to protect their bodies and desegregate Jim Crow spaces, white Southern women also used purses as toolkits. However, their whiteness often afforded them more direct access to these private spaces. As a white woman from Arlington, Virginia, Joan Trumpauer began joining sit-ins in the spring of 1960 and participated in the Freedom Rides that summer.[91] In June 1960, Trumpauer had recently returned from spending a year on the women's campus of Duke University where her participation in a sit-in with Black students from North Carolina College quickly got her in trouble: "The administration went ballistic," she recalled, and since she had never really wanted to attend a large, segregated university in the first place, she dropped out.[92]

The summer after her first year at Duke, Trumpauer returned to Arlington and began working with activists including Dion Diamond and Stokely

Carmichael. Both Diamond and Carmichael were attending Howard University and were members of the Non-Violent Action Group, cheekily referred to as NAG. The group hatched a plan to integrate the lunch counter of the Cherrydale Drug Fair in Arlington. As Trumpauer prepared for the sit-in, she considered what to wear and bring: "[Y]ou didn't want to have too much with you because you didn't know when you would get it back."[93] In June 1960, Trumpauer, Diamond, and others walked into the Cherrydale Drug Fair and faced a large group of white objectors. Photographs show Diamond facing a young white boy wagging a finger in his face, while Trumpauer appears to watch and listen from behind. What is easy to miss, however, is Trumpauer's purse on the far left of the image. On this important occasion, Trumpauer chose to bring a commodious wicker purse that can be seen standing upright on the counter next to her elbow.

In the early 1960s, famous white celebrities such as Audrey Hepburn, Grace Kelly, and Jane Birkin often carried trendy, expensive designer bags like the black quilted Chanel 2.55 or the tote-like Birkin bag. Many civil rights activists dressed

Figure 5.5. 19-year-old Joan Trumpauer and Dion Diamond stage a sit-in at the Cherrydale Drug Fair in Arlington, Virginia on June 9, 1960. A tall white man (center-right) wearing a plaid shirt glares at Trumpauer, while a white child (foreground) points his finger in Diamond's face. (Gene Abbott, courtesy of the DC Public Library, *Washington Star* Collection.)

up when they participated in protests, but iconic status-marking bags were not part of their uniform. More than fifty years after staging the sit-in, Trumpauer recalled that the wicker purse she carried that day "was less than a foot long and sort of oval-shaped."[94] Like many other non-designer purses made of wicker at that time, Trumpauer's purse was reminiscent of a modest basket. She would continue to participate in sit-ins for the next four years, and she brought this purse with her to many pickets and protests. In it, she often carried a pocket-sized copy of the Bible, which in the photograph sat just outside the purse on the counter near her elbow: "I had a small New Testament that I carried . . . it was less than six inches long."[95] Such a compact book left plenty of space for Trumpauer to store other items in her purse, and she often used that space to carry multiple items to read to keep her occupied during the sit-in. If she was arrested and allowed to take her purse to her cell, she would pass the time in jail reading. She recalled that, as a college student, she sometimes simply packed her homework.

Participating in a sit-in required short- and long-term logistical planning because participants often knew "it was jail without bail."[96] Years later, Trumpauer recalled that she often carried "the bigger [wicker] purse with the change purse in it . . . you always wanted to have some money with you to buy something if you were going to demonstrate in a store to show that you were welcome as a customer." Indeed, at the age of 78, Trumpauer still possessed the receipts of purchases she made at several sit-ins. The more seasoned she became as an activist, the more Trumpauer realized, "[Y]ou needed dimes to call your lawyer. But you didn't want to carry much, cause, it might get stolen."[97] Women like Trumpauer had to consider the safety, security, and practicality of what they packed when planning their participation.

In addition to the dimes and the Bible, women in Trumpauer's position knew they needed to bring other essential items: "If you were going to demonstrate and you thought you were gonna be arrested, and you might be in jail a couple days, you might . . . have a need for feminine products." Just as American women had been carrying tampons in their purses since the late 1930s, Trumpauer explained that she would "bring those 'cause you weren't gonna count on getting supplied them in jail."[98] Indeed, in preparation for her first Freedom Ride in June 1961, Trumpauer brought a purse and one small overnight bag packed with a few spare clothes, a book about Gandhi, toiletries, and a small mirror. She flew with Stokely Carmichael from Washington, DC, to New Orleans to join the second leg of the trip. After being arrested, charged, and convicted of "breach of the peace," she and fellow white rider Carol Ruth Silver were escorted from the city jail to the Hinds County Jail in Mississippi.

Upon their arrival, they were forced to leave their suitcases in a jail office. However, after "some verbal pleasantry," Silver noted in her diary, they "convinced the jailer to allow us our purses."[99] Separating a white woman from her purse seemed improper, even in these unusual circumstances. The two women were able to lean on gendered and racial modes of decorum to ensure they would have the necessary tools at hand.

For her part, Silver managed to smuggle cash, a book, and papers inside her purse. She also managed to sneak a "watch, which had been in my purse" and was "definitely contraband" but provided a "comforting reminder of the outside world, where minutes do count and time makes a difference."[100] The cash that white women had access to inside their purses enabled them to buy "cigarettes, candy, writing papers, and pencils. We rushed to buy cigarettes and to supplement the sweet, salty, nourishment-free prison diet with chocolate and peanuts."[101] Trumpauer, too, was allowed to bring a purse containing a toothbrush, among other items. The next day, the jailer also allowed the white women to make phone calls and get clothes and plastic bottles with toiletries from their suitcases. Silver noted that this was a privilege not afforded to "our Negro friends next door."[102] Given that they were not allowed to retrieve their suitcases, the contents of the Black women's purses could have proven even more vital. Unfortunately, existing sources do not confirm if the Black women jailed alongside them ever managed to gain access to their purses while in their cells, but Silver's observation confirms they were not afforded the same privileges as the white women.

Trumpauer kept a diary while in jail by writing on crumpled cloth paper she smuggled in. She stashed the paper in the crocheted and ruffled hem of her checkered skirt so it would not be confiscated.[103] In it, she noted that "we aren't supposed to have anything to read or anything glass." On Saturday June 11, she wrote, "I dressed up: flowered outfit, curly hair, polished shoes, lip stick."[104] Trumpauer also noted what she ate, read, and sang. She documented planning and then canceling a hunger strike, and noted how she exercised, when she menstruated, and what she wore each day.

Silver, who was imprisoned alongside Trumpauer, noted in her diary that "Trumpauer, who is a really devout Christian, insisted on dressing up this Sunday morning—she polished her white shoes (shoe polish was the furthest thing from my mind when I packed to come to jail) and put on her last vestige of clean clothing."[105] For Trumpauer, dressing up and looking tidy was important, even inside jail. But Silver also noted how the contents of Trumpauer's purse facilitated communication among inmates who could not see outside their cells: "Joan has a three-inch round mirror (although mirrors are strictly forbidden), and today we made the discovery that by holding the mirror through the bars out in the hall, we can actually see the Negro girls in the next cell with whom we have been singing and conversing."[106] The contraband mirror that Trumpauer smuggled in allowed the prisoners to establish a visual layout of the building in which they were held, which helped them to feel less disoriented. As Silver noted in her diary, "With our mirror we can also tell that ours is not a dead-end hall—a passageway to somewhere bends off the end of our corridor, and the cell on the other side is about ten feet away."[107]

Their purses functioned as toolkits, helping Trumpauer, Silver, and others survive those two weeks in jail. Though some prisoners opted to be bailed out of prison, Trumpauer was committed to SNCC's strategy of filling up the jails, and she insisted that her parents not post money on her behalf. Stokely Carmichael, who had been arrested with her, was sent to the men's section on a different floor of the Hinds County Jail. As in the women's jail, the men sang freedom songs to keep their spirits up. But their jailers soon ordered them to stop singing and threatened that the mess cart would no longer be accessible to them if they kept violating the rules. Carmichael recalled that many Freedom Riders were smokers and were deeply concerned about not being able to access cigarettes from the mess cart. The men's concerns about withdrawal from nicotine were alleviated, however, when the male prisoners stationed above them fashioned something like a make-shift reticule—a bag hanging from a string—and hung it within reach of the Freedom Riders. "We put in our orders and the money," Carmichael recalled. "The bag came back and the smoking and singing continued."[108] Just as bags had helped American women hide contraband for decades, so, too, did desperate men find ways to fashion bags in order to move illicit goods and maintain comfort.

After spending two weeks in the Hinds County Jail, both Carmichael and Trumpauer were transferred to Parchman, a maximum-security prison where they faced much harsher conditions. Not only did Trumpauer lose access to her purse when she was stripped of her belongings, but she was subjected to a vaginal cavity search before being placed in a cell normally reserved for death row inmates. She remained there for nearly two months.[109] Such a harrowing experience proved formative in solidifying her commitment to the movement but also must have reminded her that her whiteness would not save her from such violations.

After being released from prison that summer, Trumpauer went home to Virginia, taking a one-year hiatus from college. But in August 1961, she made a critical decision, deciding to become the first full-time white student to enroll at Tougaloo College, a "colored college" near Jackson, Mississippi. There she worked with SNCC, the Congress of Racial Equality (CORE), and the local office of the

NAACP, which was directed by Medgar Evers. Jackson was a far more dangerous environment than Arlington. On May 28, 1963, students and professors at Tougaloo College drove 10 miles to downtown Jackson to stage a sit-in at the segregated lunch counter at Woolworth's. Trumpauer had been recruited at the last minute and planned to work behind the scenes that day: "I was supposed to be a spotter at the picket line down the street, me and Lois Chaffee," Trumpauer recalled.[110] "Spotters" were generally white activists who could create diversions from sit-ins or watch (undetected) sit-ins unfold from the sidelines. The presence of spotters ensured that someone would be able to call with updates to organizational headquarters without getting arrested. Because she was prepared only to act as a spotter that day, Trumpauer did not expect to go to jail and therefore did not bring her larger wicker purse. Instead, she carried only a small coin purse.

When the picketers creating a diversion down the street from Woolworth's were quickly arrested, Joan Trumpauer and Lois Chaffee stood at a payphone and dug out a dime from Trumpauer's small coin purse to make their report.[111] Yet, the sit-in at Woolworth's took an unexpected turn. Instead of arresting those participating in the sit-in, more than ninety police officers stayed out of the store as violence erupted. The activists had not counted on the fact that local white students from Central High School would be on their lunch break at the time of the sit-in. When a mob of students quickly became aggressive, three Black students, Anne Moody, Pearlena Lewis, and Memphis Norman, bowed their heads to pray. Their prayers were met with kicks and punches; Norman was thrown to the ground and mercilessly kicked in the head.[112]

Because she had planned to serve only as a spotter, Trumpauer had no Bible or reading material to keep her occupied, or any supplies she would need if she was jailed. The coin purse she carried was a small souvenir from a trip she took to Denmark at the age of 15.[113] She kept the purse for more than four decades and, as she recalled more than fifty years after buying it, the purse was red to reflect the flag of Denmark, which features a white cross superimposed on a red background.

That day, the change purse contained only a phone number and some dimes that she had used to call Medgar Evers's office and make a purchase at Woolworth's.[114] After receiving the spotter's report, Evers wanted to head to Woolworth's to join the sit-in. Trumpauer, Chaffee, and John Salter convinced him that he would be murdered on the spot and therefore Salter should go instead.[115] Their prediction was unfortunately prescient; just over two weeks after that phone call, Evers would be shot dead in his own driveway in Jackson.[116]

Hoping to keep the sit-in going, Trumpauer and Salter emerged from the crowd and jumped on the stools alongside Anne Moody, who had made her way back to the counter after being pulled 30 feet by her hair.[117] Moody, who had worked for white families in Mississippi since the age of 9, knew from personal experience how white women could use allegations of purse theft to harm Black reputations and livelihoods.[118] While still in high school, Moody and her brother Junior had been falsely accused of stealing her white employer's change purse.[119]

Once Moody was joined at the Woolworth's counter by Trumpauer and Salter, there were now one Black and two white activists seated together. The boys in the white mob began to shout racial epithets and dump mustard and ketchup on the three, even putting out lit cigarettes on Salter's neck. Fred Blackwell, a 22-year-old photojournalist working for the *Jackson Daily News*, was inside of Woolworth's and seized the opportunity to jump on the lunch counter and start snapping pictures.[120] Blackwell captured several local white male high school students weaponizing condiments to use against the three protesters in what would become one of the most iconic images of the movement.

One of Blackwell's photographs caught a young white man pouring sugar down Trumpauer's back, while she faced Moody and clutched her red change

Figure 5.6. Joan Trumpauer is seated at the counter between Professor John Salter and fellow Tougaloo student Anne Moody. With her left hand, she clutches a small red change purse. (Photograph by Fred Blackwell, May 28, 1963, Woolworth's, Jackson, Mississippi, courtesy of Fred and Phyllis Blackwell.)

purse with her left hand. Another photograph taken just outside Woolworth's after the three-hour sit-in ended shows Moody holding onto a purse as well. Though she lost a shoe in the fracas, Moody somehow maintained control of her purse throughout the sit-in.[121] Because no one asked her during her lifetime, however, the contents of Moody's purse remain unknown.

During the era of Jim Crow, white women were often more able to maintain sole possession of their purses. For this reason, purses helped sustain their activism through sit-ins and jail terms. For Black women in particular, however, purses offered a "respectable" feminine way to arm themselves. Purses allowed them to access forbidden space and shield their bodies while appearing unthreatening to others. In the turmoil of the Civil Rights Movement, both Black and white women used purses to do far more than accessorize. Indeed, purses were the weapon of choice for women working to resist racist discrimination.

6

"Keith Carried a Clutch"

Queer Communities and Purses in the Late Twentieth Century

"Gay Bob" lives inside a discreet-looking archival box on the sixth floor of the San Francisco Public Library.¹ Quietly hidden away from the sights and sounds of the Tenderloin District, he lies still, approximately 13 inches tall and made of plastic. Perhaps the first explicitly gay doll, Gay Bob looks like a Ken doll and a cross between Paul Newman and Robert Redford.² In 1977, Harvey Rosenberg, a New York advertising executive who came up with the concept for Gay Bob, used $10,000 (approximately $54,500 in 2025) of his own money and the resources of his toy company, Gizmo Development, to manufacture the doll.³ As the *San Francisco Chronicle* explained in 1979, Bob "came packaged in a closet, fabulously attired in a cowboy flannel shirt and denim jeans and [unlike Ken] was 'anatomically correct.'"⁴

Gay Bob also carried a brown leather purse. Not only that, but he had hinge-able wrists that could be made limp, enabling him to carry his brown leather handbag at a dramatic angle. Cheeky advertisements for the toy suggested that Bob's hinge-able wrists allowed him to "play with himself without going blind."⁵ Obviously aimed at adults, Gay Bob was available for purchase through mail-order catalogues and specialty stores. A reported 10,000 units of the doll were sold, and he was prevalent enough that advice columnist Ann Landers claimed to have received 112 letters about him.⁶ If stories from the Natural History Museum, *Atlas Obscura*, *The Advocate*, and a 2022 podcast are any indication, his legacy endures.⁷

In 1977, however, most people were trying hard to avoid associations with anything explicitly gay. For example, after the release of Gay Bob, a conservative Toronto politician named Robert "Bob" Yuill announced that he would file a lawsuit against the toymaker. Yuill explained, the "reason I am irritated by this

Figure 6.1. Gay Bob, whose wrists are hinge-able, holds a brown purse with a long strap while standing inside his closet. Note the brown cowboy boots, plaid shirt, gold necklace, and stud in his left ear. (Author's photograph, July 2022, "Gay Bob," LGBTQIA Realia Collection. Collection No. GLC 119, James C. Hormel LGBTQIA Center, San Francisco Public Library.)

disgusting toy is that my son read about it in the paper and fell off his chair laughing." He continued, "[S]ince that time, I and I expect many other Bobs, have been the butt of many homosexual jibes."[8] In a culture dominated by a brand of homophobia that was deeply enmeshed with sexism, having one's masculinity ridiculed by other men was intolerable.

Long before Gay Bob's arrival, in the early twentieth century most gay men in America sought to pass as heterosexual, at least when in the company of heterosexuals.⁹ Beyond the stigmatized stereotype of the effeminate "fairy" who plucked his eyebrows and wore makeup, middle-class gay men were comfortable making only subtle sartorial statements, such as wearing red neckties or pale blue socks that only insiders could recognize as meaningful indicators of their sexuality.¹⁰ But in the early twentieth century, queer Americans were neither as isolated nor invisible as one would believe. In both rural and urban America, American men and women overcame tremendous obstacles, found each other, and nourished queer connections.¹¹

In the 1950s, however, the Cold War in general and the Lavender Scare in particular created an especially oppressive environment for queer people. During the Lavender Scare, thousands of federal employees were purged from government positions under the theory that they posed a risk to national security.¹² Even before the Lavender Scare, though, many people who knew they were lesbian or gay, especially those who were white and middle-class, spent years taking care not to dress in gender-subversive ways in public.¹³ In this context, early gay activist groups such as the Mattachine Society and Daughters of Bilitis self-consciously dressed in ways they hoped would undo stereotypes that lesbians and gay men were "abnormal" or "deviant."¹⁴ This strategy was also important when it came to staying out of jail. For decades, lesbians and gay men had to be careful not to fall afoul of municipal laws against cross-dressing, impersonation, or masquerading.¹⁵ Beginning in the late 1840s through World War I and beyond, more than sixty American cities passed such laws in every region of the nation.¹⁶ These laws sought to enforce the fiction that gender was an unchanging fact rather than a performance and process.¹⁷ In such cities, those who dressed in ways identifiable as "abnormal" were constantly at risk of harassment, arrest, and assault.¹⁸ And anti-cross-dressing laws were still at least selectively enforced in the 1950s, 1960s, and 1970s.

Though the American Psychiatric Association voted to remove "homosexuality" as a mental illness from the *Diagnostic and Statistical Manual of Mental Disorders* (DSM) in 1973, gays and lesbians were still frequently fired from their jobs, blackmailed, kicked out of their families and churches, harassed by the police, arrested, and publicly shamed.¹⁹ The same year that Gay Bob was released, former beauty queen and Christian fundamentalist Anita Bryant launched a campaign called "Save Our Children," which was designed to repeal a Miami-Dade County gay rights ordinance that banned discrimination based on sexual orientation. Her campaign was swift and devastating for gay Floridians. The Miami-Dade law was repealed by a 70 percent vote, which inspired other cities and states to pass anti-gay ordinances, especially those that banned so-called homosexuals from becoming teachers.[20] Trading on the belief that gay men were prone to pedophilia and sought to recruit young people to replenish their ranks, figures like Anita Bryant and evangelical pastor Jerry Falwell portrayed gay men and lesbians as sinister threats to humanity.[21]

Despite these insidious stereotypes and anti-gay laws, in the 1960s and 1970s, increasing (if still relatively small) numbers of gay men and lesbians felt more comfortable visually signifying their queerness in public spaces. And as multiple lesbian and gay activist organizations focused less on assimilation, more were willing to test gendered customs surrounding dress outside of their own homes. By the 1960s, purses had been deeply feminized as objects associated with women's bodies for many decades. This context made carrying a purse an efficient and nearly universal way in which gay men who dared to do so could announce their sexuality. For the same reasons, out purse-averse lesbians were often wary of carrying such feminized objects.

Purses played distinct roles in the lives of queer people in the second half of the twentieth century. Despite ongoing systemic oppression, in the 1960s, 1970s, and 1980s, cisgender gay men, cisgender lesbians, drag queens, and trans people consciously used purses to create privacy in public.[22] In uncertain places and times of danger, gay men and trans women used purses to guard their bodies while asserting and defending their queerness. These objects helped queer purse carriers enhance their agency and autonomy, enabling gender and sexual minorities to navigate public spaces more safely. In particular, purses played critical roles at the uprisings at Compton's Cafeteria in 1966 and the Stonewall Inn in 1969. Perhaps more than any other accessory in our sartorial system, purses functioned as an unusually potent symbol of sexuality.

Much like Black Americans fled the rural South hoping to escape the wrath of Jim Crow between World War I and World War II, LGBTQ+ people have often had to flee from their homes, families, churches, and workplaces. Those who had the means to do so traveled across cities, states, and even countries to cultivate community, create and sustain kin networks, and simply stay alive.[23] In the process, they searched for spaces like gay bars, lesbian bookstores, street corners, all-night diners, and private apartments where they could safely congregate. Purses, which ultimately facilitate their owner's ability to leave the home and navigate public space, have been particularly meaningful, if surprising, anchors for queer people in an often hostile landscape. In fact, queer people self-consciously carried purses (or stridently avoided carrying them, in some cases) to signal their sexual and gender identity, a move that sometimes subjected them to scrutiny and violence.

In the 1960s, trans women, drag queens, LGBTQ+ people, and sex workers (categories that sometimes overlapped) frequently met at Gene Compton's Cafeteria, a twenty-four-hour eatery located at the corner of Turk and Taylor Streets in San Francisco. The cafeteria was a favored haunt because it was open all night, offered cheap food, and provided a clean, centralized meeting space.[24] Though San Francisco had a long history of outlawing "cross-dressing" dating back to 1863, drag queens and trans women often gathered there in the wee hours of the morning to check in with each other to make sure each had made it safely through the night.[25]

In 1966, Compton's had also begun to serve as the meeting space for Vanguard, a new political organization led by (mostly white) drag queens and young gay men.[26] The group formed to organize resistance against harassment. Although Compton's was a relatively safe location, the "queens" were not out of harm's way. On July 18, members of Vanguard picketed Compton's to insist on equal treatment by the staff, a move that irritated the management.[27] Roughly one month later, the manager at Compton's called the police on the patrons.[28] When the police arrived, tensions quickly escalated, and soon the harassed customers turned tables and threw condiments as the conflict spilled out into the streets.[29]

Figure 6.2. This photograph showcases an exterior view of Gene Compton's Cafeteria in 1970. The 24-hour cafeteria was located on the first floor of the four-story Hyland Hotel on the corner of Turk and Taylor Streets. (Clay Geerdes, courtesy of the Tenderloin Museum.)

Figure 6.3. A rare interior view of Gene Compton's Cafeteria, circa 1966. Four bejeweled queens sit and chat while drinking coffee. (Photograph by Henri Leleu, Henri Leleu Papers [1997–13], GLBT Historical Society, San Francisco.)

Most Americans assume New York's Stonewall Riot of 1969 was the first mass expression of queer resistance. But the Compton incident three years earlier is a less well-known moment that illuminates how queer people attempted to carve out space in straight and cisgendered commercial areas.[30] It also highlights the persistent brutality that owners, fellow patrons, and the police visited on queer bodies in these spaces and how queer people resisted that brutality.

On the night of the Compton's uprising, a reported sixty drag queens were present, and many of them used their heavy purses to hit police officers in the face and below the belt.[31] What happened at Compton's is part of a much longer, nuanced set of stories that reveal how multiply marginalized Americans used bags, pocketbooks, and purses to insist on their safety and autonomy. Compared with queer dress practices before World War II, this use of the purse demonstrates a far more explicit sartorial survival strategy. In the upheaval of multiple liberation movements unfurling in the 1960s, purses played important political roles in liberating their holders.

As the rebellion at Compton's Cafeteria demonstrates, patrons used purses as defensive weapons. Just as importantly, however, purses have pocketed interiors that could carry and conceal other weapons. Felicia Elizondo, a transgender sex worker who frequented Compton's, attested to the necessity of carrying a purse filled with tools of survival: "We always had to load our handbags up . . . a half pint of Southern Comfort and [I] put the empty bottle in my bag. When people got out of line we'd crack it over their head. . . . Because if they were gonna mess with us, we weren't gonna let people hurt us."[32] As Elizondo's testimony shows, trans women who worked on the streets could not rely on help from the police. In such a context, purses helped them anticipate and prepare for harm. In fact, purses helped protect them in a transphobic, homophobic, and sexist climate that turned their bodies into sites of crime and fundamentally denied them their value and dignity.

Purses also played a key role as instruments of resistance in the more famous uprising at the Stonewall Inn in New York three years later. Though there are conflicting accounts of who did what on which night of the rebellion, it is clear that the police raided the bar, the patrons fought back, and trans women of color including Marsha P. ("Pay it no mind") Johnson helped lead the resistance. In one telling, on the second night of the riots, Johnson placed a brick in her bag and climbed up a lamppost. Once she reached the top, she threw her leaden bag directly on a police car and smashed the windshield.[33] For decades, newspapers had been breathlessly recounting tales of vulnerable white women who were victims of purse-snatchers. But for Johnson as well as other trans women, drag queens, and sex workers, purses were weapons, quietly keeping their owners armed and ready.

Bags and purses served important roles throughout Johnson's life. Because she spent much of her adult life on the streets or in transient housing, Johnson had to carry many of her possessions with her wherever she went. After graduating from high school in 1963, she left home with nothing more than 15 dollars and a bag of clothes to keep her company as she searched for a new home and community.[34] Similarly, "freedom bags" had helped Black women migrants start anew as they boarded northbound trains during the Great Migration.[35] When Johnson fled her home after being kicked out, her bag of clothes allowed her to pack up a mobile version of her former life and venture into a new one. Johnson and fellow trans activist Sylvia Rivera carried purses as emblems of their femininity, but they also visibly clung to them in street rallies, protests, and other politically charged spaces.

Johnson was not the only patron to carry a purse during the Stonewall riots. Unlike the uprising at Compton's Cafeteria, though, the rebellion at the Stonewall Inn was well documented. Fred McDarrah, a staff photographer for *The Village Voice*, took nineteen photographs capturing images of gay men, drag queens, and trans women outside Stonewall during and right after the hot,

Figure 6.4. In 1973, Marsha P. Johnson clutches a white purse and dark umbrella while smiling in the rain at a gay rights protest outside City Hall in New York City. Kady Vandeurs holds a "Gay Rights" poster behind her. (Photograph by Diana Davies, Manuscripts and Archives Division, Image ID 1582302, New York Public Library Digital Collections.)

historic nights of the riots.[36] When McDarrah approached one jubilant group for a picture in front of the Stonewall Inn, one participant recalled, "Half the kids—the ones who passed as straight anyway—ran away."[37] Those who stayed to have their photograph taken insisted on being seen and, in doing so, gambled with their futures.

Visibility through this kind of documentation was particularly frightening for trans women, lesbians, and gay men who were not yet out, and could be

Figure 6.5. "Drag Queen Chris" is featured second from the left, wearing cut-off jean shorts and carrying a leather bag with his right hand. Thomas Lanigan-Schmidt appears to the right of Chris in a striped t-shirt and dark pants. (Photograph by Fred McDarrah, circa June 29, 1969, Getty Images.)

arrested simply for "having buttons on the wrong side" of their shirt.[38] (As of this writing, men's shirts are still manufactured with buttons on the right, while on women's shirts buttons appear on the left.)[39] Many states also passed laws making it illegal to serve alcohol to gay people. Virginia passed such a law in the 1930s and was the last state in the nation to overturn its ban—in 1991.[40] Though gay bars still existed during these decades, they often did so undercover and with the constant threat of being raided. In addition, many gay bars were owned by the Mafia in the 1960s.[41] In such cases, owners often paid off the police to keep them at bay. Still, patrons always ran the risk of being arrested at a gay bar. Although many understandably did not want their presence at a gay rebellion documented, "Drag Queen Chris" stayed and stood in the front of the crowd, holding a leather purse high for the camera to capture. Though Chris does not otherwise appear to be in drag in this image, this single item signifies Chris's refusal to adhere to traditional gender expectations (and the laws that often backed them up).

Thomas (Tommy) Lanigan-Schmidt was also at Stonewall that night.[42] On the fiftieth anniversary of the riot, Lanigan-Schmidt commented on the significance of Chris's purse. He noted, "[T]here is one queen standing on the other side from me holding her purse. . . . [I]f you look at the purse's shape, you can see the outline of a brick. They didn't go around starting trouble, but they were always ready to defend themselves, and that brick in the purse came in handy."[43] Lanigan-Schmidt's insight confirms that Drag Queen Chris simultaneously held a defiant symbol of femininity and a potential weapon.

Beyond their potential as weapons, purses played symbolic and ritualistic roles in the lives of many young queer people. Just as many women recall acquiring their first purse as a rite of passage from girlhood, gay men have also highlighted formative interactions with purses as boys. Bradley Picklesimer, a drag artist who was born and raised in Lexington, Kentucky, in 1958, recalled dressing up for church as a child. Picklesimer and his younger sister, Elizabeth, would walk to Trinity Baptist Church on Sundays. He remembered that he had a "little camel suit on and my little shoes and everything. My little sister had her full dress, patent leather purse, patent leather shoes." He recalled that his sister, who would later come out as gay, wanted nothing to do with this patent leather purse, but he loved it. "She didn't want the purse and I wanted the purse and I would just carry it to church every Sunday." On such days, his father would inevitably receive a phone call from the church, complaining that "he has Elizabeth's purse again and he won't let go of it."[44] Despite repeated scoldings, Picklesimer clung to the purse, recalling the significance of this ritual many decades later.

Like Picklesimer's sister, many lesbians developed negative feelings about purses. Despite the personal preferences of individual members, early lesbian and gay activist groups thought carefully about how they dressed. The Daughters of Bilitis (DOB), the first lesbian rights organization in the nation, was founded in 1955. Created by four lesbian couples initially seeking opportunities to socialize with other lesbians, the Daughters of Bilitis attracted women with a higher-than-average level of education. Members typically met in private, wary of losing the class privilege they enjoyed by venturing out in public as a group.[45]

Phyllis Lyon and Del Martin, who met in Seattle around 1950 and later purchased a home and car together in San Francisco, emerged as early leaders of the group. As a couple, Lyon and Martin embodied the butch femme dynamic. Lyon, who often wore necklaces and earrings and carried a purse, described first meeting Martin by noting that "she was the first woman I'd ever seen wearing a briefcase!"[46] At midcentury, the briefcase was a potent symbol associated almost exclusively with middle-class businessmen and suburbia.[47] In this context, the sight of Martin in a green gabardine suit, carrying a briefcase instead of a purse, made a strong impression on Lyon. Indeed, Martin took on considerable risk in adopting this accessory.[48]

Despite Martin's own stylistic preferences, the DOB discussed and prescribed traditionally feminine dress in its early meetings. The minutes from a special meeting, held on November 9, 1955, indicate that the group even decided to host "a charm school to aid those who have difficulty walking in high heels."[49] In the first item listed on its Statement of Purpose in its monthly newsletter, *The Ladder*, the DOB also outlined a policy that required members to adopt "a mode of dress and behavior that was acceptable to society."[50] Despite this official rule, members recalled wearing men's jeans at private gatherings.[51]

It was difficult for members of the DOB to escape the feeling that they were being watched. In 1995, Phyllis Lyon recalled that, at the DOB's first national convention, all members wore skirts. The convention "drew a visit from the Homosexual Detail of the San Francisco Police Department." According to Lyon, the men were looking for evidence that the organization advocated dressing in men's clothing.[52] In fact, the FBI began spying on the DOB as early as March 1956.[53] Besides government agents, others outside the lesbian community were deeply interested in how lesbians were part of a "vast, sprawling grapevine, with a secret code of their own," as reporter Jess Stearn put it in 1964.[54] Without attributing his sources, Stearn claimed that, on Thursdays, lesbians in New York, Los Angeles, and San Francisco adorned themselves in green, while in Chicago they wore yellow, and in Connecticut they wore pink.[55]

Whether or not these observations were accurate, one item many lesbians did not adopt, regardless of color, was a purse. In the 1950s, white working-class butch lesbians rarely carried purses.[56] Those who wore men's pants had less reason to since men's pants came with integrated full-sized pockets that could provide privacy in public by holding several small objects. However, there was more to the decision not to carry a purse. One lesbian definitively stated, "[P]urses were not part of the butch ensemble . . . you know the butch doesn't carry a purse."[57] In one study, historians rightly concluded that butches' lack of familiarity with a purse was an assumed part of the culture—so much so that simply carrying a purse could discredit a woman's claim to a butch identity.[58]

Working-class women who did not have the privilege of private space in which to host their own social gatherings away from the public eye faced higher risks of arrest. The experiences of Matty, a lesbian bartender in Buffalo, New York, attest to the role that purses played in both spotting and fighting against accusations of cross-dressing. Matty was arrested in the mid-1960s for allegedly serving a drink to a minor. "The guy that was bartending [with me]," Matty recalled, "he was a gay guy, he was cracking up when" the police arrested Matty and dragged her out of the bar. "Because when they were taking me out, the girl I was seeing at the time" was worried because "I had nothing of a girl on" besides underwear.[59] In fact, butch lesbians—who the police targeted first— often strategically wore women's underwear beneath men's clothing in the hopes that it would help them evade laws forbidding cross-dressing. Yet, underwear was hidden and could not be readily seen by police as they quickly scanned a room during a raid.

Thinking quickly, Matty's date then ran "up to me and handed me her purse, she said, 'Here Matty, you forgot your purse.' And she handed me this huge purse, and I didn't even know how to carry the damn thing. There I stood looking at this purse wondering what the hell to do with it."[60] The impromptu strategy of Matty's date highlights the difference between purses and most other items of apparel. Although clothing can be layered and therefore easily hidden, purses are worn externally and are visible from most angles.[61] Matty's emphasis on the size of the purse suggests that she felt the size of the purse signaled the degree of femininity and heterosexuality of its carrier. Matty apparently accepted the purse from her date but remained worried that the police might look inside it and realize "this isn't even my purse."[62]

Clearly, Matty and her date were aware of laws against so-called cross-dressing. Both must have known that at any moment, Matty could be arrested for impersonating a man. Just as men did not want to be seen purchasing sanitary pads for their wives and equated the act to carrying a purse in public, as a butch lesbian, Matty wanted to communicate her distaste and unfamiliarity with purses. In fact, the way Matty told this story is as revealing as the story itself. She took pains to stress the hesitation with which she reluctantly touched the purse, even if it could have helped keep her out of jail. To further emphasize her lack of familiarity with purses, Matty also recalled that the gay man who laughed at her arrest noted that Matty "held it like you would a football." It is not without significance that Matty's friend chose to equate the foreign way Matty held the purse with the ball of one of the most violent and hyper-masculine American sports.

For women who identified with masculinity in the 1960s and 1970s, this aversion to purses was common and not new. The English lesbian writer Radclyffe Hall sometimes went by the name "John" and spent considerable time in men's clothing.[63] Hall did not carry a handbag and had extra pockets made for her skirt.[64] Decades later in 1975, lesbian writer Sasha Gregory-Lewis explained why purses were important for "dykes" to reject.[65] In an article published in *The Advocate*, she described discarding feminine clothing at the age of 13. Gregory-Lewis was keenly aware of how much purses had become deeply feminized and felt they represented a woman's heterosexuality and objectification. After all, for many decades men had been calling women they perceived as past their sexual prime "old bags." "Although I didn't have a word for it then," she explained, "I didn't want to be an object to men. I wanted people to relate to me as a human being." Later, she described discovering "the comfort and practicality" of boots and Levi's jeans "with all their pockets."[66]

Indeed, pockets offered more than carrying capacity. They have long given men opportunities for bodily arrangement and display that women have been denied. Etiquette guides dating back to the eighteenth century noted that thrusting one's hand inside a pocket was a masculine gesture that was considered vulgar and rude because it gave men the opportunity to hide their hands and keep them close to their genitals. Victorian mothers even went as far as stitching the pockets on their sons' clothing shut in order to prevent them from rudely putting their hands inside their pockets.[67]

After extolling the advantages of integrated pockets, Gregory-Lewis declared that "purses were an image of the sexual sell which I rejected."[68] Though she did not elaborate on exactly why she saw purses as part of "the sexual sell," or what she meant by this phrase, it seems clear that she linked purses to the objectification of women, heterosexuality, and the male gaze. Perhaps like Sigmund Freud, Gregory-Lewis even saw purses as material representations of women's genitals. Lesbian feminists like Gregory-Lewis insisted on the right to dress themselves in ways they saw as explicitly anti-feminine and anti-heterosexual. They identified purses as powerful symbols of women's objectification, and for some, abandoning purses was part of a larger queer and feminist political project.

The idea that purses were not for butches, dykes, or some feminists continued to have salience in the 1980s. In *Amazon: A Feminist Journal,* one writer identifying themself only as "SmpD," declared, "I see myself as a radical lesbian feminist. I wear blue jeans and T-shirts much of the time, I don't own a skirt or a designer handbag." Designer handbags, the author noted, "are definitely PI [politically incorrect]." She elaborated, noting that "make up, fancy perfumes, charm bracelets, and drip-dry wigs are also out," whereas "flannel shirts and overalls, knapsacks and construction boots, old army fatigues and undershirts, all of these are PC."[69] Among an entire constellation of feminized items of apparel, however, SmpD implied that fancy designer purses were the most incompatible with lesbian feminism since they implied that women were willing to invest significant portions of their income in a deeply feminized, seemingly heterosexual object.

In the 1970s, some cities and states continued to crack down on gay civil rights by enforcing local laws against cross-dressing. As of 1971, eleven states still had laws prohibiting cross-dressing.[70] Indeed, men who donned purses and other articles of clothing considered to be the exclusive property of women continued to be accused of impersonation or fraud. However, consensus on what constituted cross-dressing was often elusive. Did this mean wearing only one item of apparel designated for the so-called opposite sex? What about two? Or three? Did it matter if a person also wore one or more items of apparel meant for their sex? And how could such laws be enforced?[71]

Court cases illustrate how anti-cross-dressing laws were vague, even if purses were intended to be carried only by American women by the 1970s. In the 1974 case of the *City of Cincinnati v. Adams* (a.k.a. Harris), the defendant was accused of violating municipal ordinance Section 909-5, which forbade any person to "appear in a dress or costume not customarily worn by his or her sex, or in a disguise when such dress, apparel or disguise is worn with the intent of committing an immoral act." The defendant in this case was identified as a "male" who was wearing a "woman's wig, earrings and carrying a purse," among other items.[72] An undercover cop had spotted the defendant, arresting and charging him with a misdemeanor in the fourth degree.[73]

In its ruling, the court ultimately struck down the municipal ordinance, but not because the defendant's dress was found to be protected under the First Amendment's right to free expression. Indeed, the ruling explicitly stated, "Unlike pure speech, one's mode of dress is not an expression protected by the First Amendment unless such dress is specifically shown to be an expression of a philosophy, idealism or point of view." However, the court found the terms "not customarily worn" to be "unconstitutionally vague."[74] The case implied that other laws forbidding "transvestism" were also unconstitutional. Indeed, as expectations of respectable clothing for men and women evolved in the later part of the twentieth century, such laws were becoming unenforceable. What was "a costume not customarily worn by his or her sex," when women regularly wore pants and men had begun wearing their hair long?[75] Despite the fact that such municipal laws were being deemed unconstitutional, police continued to harass men and women they saw as violating gendered norms of dress.

Purses were not just of legal import at the city and state level. They were so powerful as symbols of lesbian and gay men's sexuality that they played a surprising role in international affairs. Since at least 1952, when the first edition of the DSM was published, the Immigration and Naturalization Service (INS) had been turning away gay and lesbian people from U.S. borders, barring the entrance of aliens with "psychopathic personality, or sexual deviation, or a mental defect."[76] The INS continued to explicitly prevent gay tourists and immigrants from entering U.S. borders through at least the 1970s, and people living with HIV were prevented from entering the country until 2010.[77] Legislators used the fact that psychiatrists had classified homosexuality as a mental illness in the DSM until 1973 as their rationale. But the government continued to deny entry to visitors on the basis of their supposed homosexuality until at least 1980.

For example, in August 1978, the city of San Francisco was still mourning the assassination of openly gay city supervisor Harvey Milk when two Mexican men who arrived at the San Francisco airport were at first denied entry. Edwardo Roman Martinez, 22, and Javier Cruz Garcia, 27, had traveled to San Francisco from Veracruz just one day after the Public Health Service announced it would no longer conduct examinations of so-called aliens to determine if they were gay. Yet, Martinez and Garcia were denied entry based on the "evidence" that one of them wore an earring and the other carried a "woman's handbag."[78]

These so-called exams were conducted visually and hastily. As an assistant INS commissioner explained, "When you only have fifty seconds to eyeball people, you just have to go on what you see. You look at the way they dress."[79] As in the case of Matty the bartender in Buffalo, looking for the presence or absence of a purse was thought to be an indisputable way to identify a gay interloper. Gay men, therefore, expressed a potent sign of their queerness when they attempted to carry a purse across national borders. But carrying a purse could mean more than being denied entry; it could result in the far more dangerous consequence of detainees having their passport stamped "sexual deviant."[80] Though the INS claimed it rarely turned away people for being gay, journalist Larry Bush reported in 1980 that a Washington INS official admitted privately "that the total number of exclusions on grounds of 'homosexuality' runs into the 'thousands' each year."[81]

Just two weeks after Martinez and Garcia were detained in California, border officials in Michigan denied approximately fifty women entry to the United States. Officials had learned that the Michigan Womyn's Music Festival drew many lesbians to the area. When Ariane Brunet and five other women tried to drive across the Canadian border to attend the festival, they were stopped at the border. After being flatly asked, "Are you a lesbian?" and a slew of other questions aimed at discerning their attitudes toward men, the women were asked, "Have you ever carried a purse?" Brunet lied and told border officials that she was heterosexual, knowing they would not allow her into the country otherwise.[82] Like Matty the bartender, border officials assumed lesbians never carried purses; thus, the follow-up question about a purse was apparently designed to catch Brunet in a lie, revealing that she was, in fact, a lesbian, even though she professed to be straight.

Laws against cross-dressing likely had a chilling effect on the number of gay men who were willing to wear purses in public. In the same year that Gay Bob premiered, researchers Karla Jay and Allen Young began distributing a survey in gay-owned periodicals around the nation. The questionnaire asked respondents several questions, but those relating to dress are of particular interest. Respondents were specifically asked "how often in connection with attracting sex partners" they wore a handbag or purse. They could choose from six answers, beginning with "always" and ending with "never." The survey also asked how respondents felt about the idea of purses.[83] In their book, *The Gay Report*, Jay and Young reported that, out of ninety-nine respondents, only one admitted to "very frequently" wearing a purse in connection with attracting sex partners. One answered, "somewhat frequently" and ninety-four said, "never." Only three respondents indicated that they had "very positive" feelings about purses, and fifty-one indicated they had "very negative" feelings.[84] Though still low, more respondents had positive feelings about jewelry and makeup than purses.

The respondents seemed to believe that wearing a highly visible external item of apparel deeply associated with women made one a "transvestite." More than one gay respondent referred to "transvestism" as a "sickness," adding that it would "be helpful to the cause of gay liberation if they could restrict extreme appearance and behavior to private gatherings, gay bars, drag balls, gay enclaves. . . ."[85] Jay and Young concluded that "the issue is not strictly one of garments, however, as the issue of cross-dressing by men has been made political."[86] Indeed, gay men's attitudes about "transvestites" likely reflect broader attitudes among many gay middle-class men who felt that drag was hurting the homophile movement. Though some gay men in the 1970s believed that dressing in drag or in other ways traditionally associated with women was a "revolutionary act," others worried that such practices attracted negative attention and confirmed straight people's assumptions that queer people were "deviant."[87] As a result, gender policing among gay people was not uncommon in the 1970s. One scholar argues that many gay men began to adopt a "macho" aesthetic as a reaction to widespread associations between gay men and effeminacy.[88] These survey results, which do not identify the race, age, or class of the respondents, likely obscure differences among groups. Nonetheless, they ultimately illustrate that most gay men were still reluctant to carry a purse in public when attempting to attract a partner in the 1970s.

Even if a man's comportment and dress otherwise strictly adhered to middle-class gender codes, the deployment of just a single item—the purse—continued to signal that he was gay in the 1980s. However, some men were unfazed by the potential implications of carrying a purse. In his collection of oral histories of Southern gay Black men, E. Patrick Johnson asked an interviewee named Jaime, who was enlisted in the military, how he could tell who else was gay in 1982. "Were there any codes or signals that people used to indicate that they were gay?," Johnson inquired. "Or, you know, clothing, wearing it a certain way. I mean anything that clued people?" Jaime responded, "Well, now there was a guy on my base. And I'll never forget his name was Keith. You know how the Europeans like to carry the man purses? Keith carried a clutch. And I mean in full uniform there's a man bag up under his arm."[89] Jaime identified this as a distinctly American phenomenon, noting that European men were able to carry purses without raising suspicions about their sexuality.

At that moment in the interview, Jaime stood up and physically demonstrated how Keith walked while holding his clutch. Keith knew that moving in a particular way with a purse held significant meaning.[90] Jaime added that Keith "walked across the base so everybody, you know, pretty much knew, you know, in that regard . . . honestly, everybody knew he was [gay]. It was just no question. But, he did his job, nobody said anything."[91] As he moved across the base, Keith navigated deeply entangled ideas about gender, race, and sexuality. He brazenly rejected the politics of gay respectability in 1982, one year into the

HIV/AIDS crisis, which was then referred to as GRID (Gay-Related Immune Deficiency). At the time, many straight people understood this disease as a "gay cancer."[92]

In 1994, Bill Clinton established the policy of "Don't Ask, Don't Tell" (DADT), which allowed gay service members to stay in the military as long as they remained in the closet.[93] When Keith was serving in 1982, however, the American military was still actively spending time and money spying on its recruits, dishonorably discharging gays and lesbians with no veterans' benefits.[94] Jaime reported, "I even had friends that had gotten found out or told on by a partner. Because that's all it takes in the military, somebody call your commander and say that person's gay. And they'll start investigating you."[95] Yet so long as Keith was otherwise silent about being gay, he was permitted to carry one deeply feminine signifier around the base. In this context, Keith's purse must have been important enough to him that he was willing to risk his livelihood and safety.

Although the presence or absence of a purse created potential challenges for Martinez, Garcia, Brunet, and Keith, for trans women, adding a purse to their ensemble when leaving the house also had consequences. Carrying a purse in a "natural" feminine manner (rather than like a football, as Matty did) was particularly critical. The significance of this fact was repeatedly discussed in the columns of queer periodicals. Published in the 1960s by Virginia Prince, who did not identify as a woman but adopted a woman's name, *Transvestia* was an independent magazine designed to serve "the needs of those heterosexual persons who have become aware of their 'other side' and seek to express it."[96] Prince was interested in normalizing "cross-dressing," and the magazine sought to distinguish itself from gay men's periodicals. Inside its pages, readers sometimes referred to themselves as "TVs." In the parlance of the time, this phrase was a more abbreviated, discrete version of the term "transvestites."[97]

In 1965, *Transvestia* published a long article titled "What Shall I Wear? The Right Clothes for You." The article suggested a detailed but affordable clothing budget. The author, who went by the name Beatrice, recommended that readers buy a new "evening clutch," which cost $2.95 once every three years, and a "leather handbag" which costs $10.95 every two years.[98] Echoing language from the 1920s and 1930s, readers were encouraged to keep their bags immaculately clean: "[R]emember, daintiness should be one of women's natural qualities." However, what is most striking about Beatrice's article is her strategic recommendation that readers "get a purse organizer at a boutique or notion counter." Not only would a purse organizer help those who lived at least part-time as women "find things more quickly," Beatrice claimed such efficiency would "prevent those longer awkward poses which might allow deliberate examination by those nearby." Indeed, many "TVs" and trans women attempted to keep their interactions with strangers brief, or they went out only at night when visibility would be limited. Further research might reveal they used purses to hide the size of their hands just as Grace Kelly, the princess of Monaco, famously used a Hermès bag to hide her pregnancy in 1956.[99]

Beatrice also endorsed a checklist of necessities to carry inside one's purse: "compact, lipstick, tissue, hankie, hairnet, keys, money, glasses, cigarettes and matches (if you smoke), photos—especially those of children (even if they are the neighbor's kids)." Beatrice also recommended carrying a form of identification (depending on your personal views of fact or fiction). Finally, she recommended a quick audit: "Before you go out, make sure everything is there."[100] This list suggests that purses played a role in helping "TVs" and trans women pass as cisgender women when they "went out." Beatrice found a purse so helpful in maintaining her safety that she was moved to recommend it to others. Filled with forms of identification and photographs of a fictional family that helped position purse carriers as mothers and wives, purses were especially helpful when "TVs" interacted with strangers.[101]

Later in 1965, *Transvestia* published another essay written by a person who was performing as a showgirl and, later, as part of a "sister act" on vaudeville. The author, identified as Jessica, described how a woman named Connie taught her how to move with a purse. After Connie buffed Jessica's nails, curled her hair, and laced her in a corset, she noted, "I was as ready as I'd ever be." Next, Connie handed Jessica a purse and said, "[N]ow we will just stroll down the street . . . away from the lot while I coach you on how to act like a girl does in public."[102] Following orders, Jessica took to the streets with Connie for a training session. "Now, said Connie, let's make with the purse! Don't carry it like a bag of sand, it is a pretty thing, a part of your wardrobe, handle it this way." Connie then demonstrated the correct way, "carrying it lightly with the arm slightly bent, sometimes by the strap, often held in the arm." Jessica "caught the idea, but the purse was the hardest thing to get accustomed to! I missed my pockets!" Jessica was further instructed to throw back her shoulders: "[L]et your body curve. . . . Don't just walk, strut!"[103] Walking "correctly" with a purse was key to passing as a cisgender woman in public.[104]

For people assigned male at birth who lived as women, purses offered the possibility of living and being seen as a cisgender woman. Victoria Schneider, who was born intersex but assigned male in 1951, was earning a living as a sex worker in San Francisco in 1996 when Vice Squad Officer Robert Porter arrested her for prostitution.[105] After he brought her to Central Station, Schneider said, "I told them I was female. . . . I grabbed my purse to present the identification, because I have several pieces of identification, including birth certificate, passport, driver's license, every kind of identification that could identify my gender as being female."[106] But the cop cuffed her and refused to let her reach her purse, which would have provided the indisputable evidence that she hoped would prevent her from being imprisoned with men.

When Officer Porter filled out his incident report, he noted what Schneider was wearing ("white tennis shoes, blue jeans, purple halter top, gray jacket") but did not mention a purse.[107] This description suggests the officer viewed Schneider's purse as merely ancillary to the rest of her outfit. And yet, later in the narrative Porter wrote describing the incident, Schneider's purse plays an important role. Porter exclusively used male pronouns to describe Schneider, even when referring to "his breasts," until he described Schneider reaching for "her purse."[108] It was as if the purse was the only conduit through which he could see Schneider as a woman; the purse functioned as her passport to femaleness and femininity. After the cops dumped out the contents of

Figure 6.6. Victoria Schneider, marching in the streets for the rights of sex workers with her black shoulder bag, circa 1990s. (Victoria Schneider Papers, GLBT Historical Society, San Francisco.)

Schneider's purse but refused to look at her identification to verify her claim, they illegally forced her to submit to a strip search to confirm that she was a woman. Schneider would later sue the police department of San Francisco, eventually winning 750,000 dollars from the city.

The presence of purses for trans women who used them as lifesaving, identity-affirming tools, and the potency of the purse as symbol of queerness for men continued to the end of the twentieth century and beyond. In 1999, Jerry Falwell, founder of Liberty University and *National Liberty Journal*, which circulated among 300,000 pastors, published a warning about a character from the children's television show, *Teletubbies* (1998–2001). In an article titled "Parents Alert: Tinky Winky Comes Out of the Closet," Falwell claimed that the character Tinky Winky was modeling the "homosexual lifestyle" for children. "The character," he alleged, "whose voice is obviously that of a boy, has been found carrying a red purse."[109] Falwell, who was 66 at the time he made this observation, had never seen the show, but was alarmed that Tinky Winky was "purple—the gay-pride color; and his antenna (growing from the top of his head) is shaped like a triangle—the gay-pride symbol."[110] (Keep in mind, the Teletubbies spoke in baby talk, as they were designed to appeal largely to a preverbal audience of babies and toddlers.)

In response to Falwell's claims, a representative for the company that licensed the program in the United States said, "The fact that he carries a magic bag doesn't make him gay. It's a children's show, folks."[111] Although Falwell claimed it was the combination of the purple color, triangle, and purse that concerned him, it seems that the purse most alarmed him. The year 1999 was also the heyday of Barney, another nonhuman purple-ish children's character, yet Falwell never issued a warning that Barney was modeling a gay "lifestyle."[112]

Progressive media outlets responded to Falwell's claim with derision. One week after he made his declaration, *Mother Jones* responded by publishing a cheeky article titled, "Parents Alert: Is Jerry Falwell Gay?"[113] Many members of the gay community responded with jeers as well. For example, in June 1999, GayCo Productions staged a sketch comedy show in Chicago called "Don't Ask, Don't Teletubby."[114]

Over the first half of the twentieth century, effeminacy had come to be seen as incontrovertible proof that a man was gay. By 1999, the notion of carrying a purse had become so deeply entangled with effeminacy, that it triggered the hyper-vigilant homophobia of men like Jerry Falwell. Though many treated Falwell's claim as an absurd joke, his brand of homophobia had serious consequences and the feelings behind his rhetoric were no laughing matter. In real

Figure 6.7. Appearing under the headline "Tinky Winky Kinky?," the Teletubbies character appears to taunt Jerry Falwell in this illustration by Eleanor Mill. Tinky Winky carries a purse in his right hand and offers Falwell a limp left wrist. (*Sojourner* 24, no. 8, April 1999, courtesy of Barrie Maguire, Newsart.com.)

life, men faced imminent harm if they carried a purse. This included straight men like Willie Houston, a Nashville bus driver.[115] Houston was enjoying a late summer night in July 2001 when he was out with his fiancée, Nedra Jones, and mutual friends Valerie and Melvin Holt, a married couple. Around 2:45 A.M., the group wrapped up a midnight river cruise on the *General Jackson Showboat*. Because Melvin Holt was blind, the group waited for most of the other passengers to disembark before attempting to leave. During that time, Houston's fiancée said she needed to use the restroom and asked him to hold her purse.

Whether or not he held misgivings, Houston agreed to hold Jones's purse, and he slung it over his shoulder as he waited for her to return. While she was still gone, however, Houston's blind friend, Melvin Holt, asked Houston to escort him to the bathroom. Still carrying Jones's purse, Houston took his friend's arm and guided him into the men's restroom. Unlike purse-averse lesbians, Houston simply placed it over his shoulder and walked to his destination.[116]

Witnesses said that inside the restroom Houston and Holt were confronted by 25-year-old Lewis Davidson III. Davidson had also been on the cruise and assumed that Houston and Holt were a gay couple when he began harassing them. Holt later testified that Davidson asked Houston if he was gay, to which he responded that his "'honey' was in the restroom, and he was merely holding her purse." Houston and Holt quickly exited the restroom to avoid any further conflict, but Davidson followed them out and continued harassing them. Then Houston and Holt found their dates and headed for their car, while Davidson headed to his. However, when Davidson got to his car, he grabbed a gun and approached Houston again, pointing the gun at him as Houston tried to unlock his car. Davidson shot a single fatal bullet into Houston's chest.[117] Davidson fled from the scene and was not arrested until nearly three months later. He was subsequently convicted of first-degree murder and sentenced to life in prison but was never charged with a hate crime.[118]

This case demonstrates that at least one American resorted to deathly violence to defend a perceived threat to his masculinity. This threat came in the form of a purse, which—by 2001—was an irredeemably gendered and sexualized object exclusively acceptable for women. In this case, Davidson must have believed that both men were gay, yet he only shot the man holding the purse. In short, his masculinity was so threatened by the entrance of a man with a purse into a space as intimate as a restroom that Houston's explanation made no difference to him.

Houston's tragic fate puts in sharp relief the courage gay men had to muster and the perils they faced for daring to carry a purse. Indeed, lesbians like Matty the bartender also faced harassment for refusing to carry a purse decades earlier. But Houston's violent story illustrates the power of this one object, which over the course of the twentieth century, Americans had decided revealed an inner and undeniable truth about its carrier's gender and sexuality. Many Americans believed this so deeply that carrying a purse could bring consequences as serious as imprisonment, deportation, and even death. Across the twentieth century, men's purses disappeared from advertisements and took on radically different meanings. Purses had the potential to ensure the safety of the queer patrons of Compton's cafeteria and the customers-turned-protesters at the Stonewall Inn, such as Marsha P. Johnson and Drag Queen Chris. Yet, women like Victoria Schneider still suffered when they could not control their purses. Purses could simultaneously protect some, while rendering others extremely vulnerable. Taken together, these experiences reveal the power of purses to reveal how queer people conceptualized, carried, and relied on these sartorial symbols to negotiate and communicate their sexuality.

Epilogue

When I became an aunt in 2013, I reveled in watching my niece learn new phrases and grapple with strange concepts and objects for the first time. I admit, though, that as someone who thinks carefully and constantly about gender, I struggled with what compliments to pay her and what gifts to buy her. I wanted to be an affirming presence, but I was afraid of reinforcing the gender stereotype that little girls exist to delight others in their pretty little cuteness, rather than their brains, bravery, and physical feats.

When she turned 2, I distinctly remember her being the recipient of not one, but two pink "Pretty Learning Purses," now sold as "My Smart Purse" by Fisher-Price. These gifts came from two different people who had no idea they had separately selected the same gift. This toy asserts that it contains "all baby's handbag essentials": a mirror, bracelet, credit card, cell phone, and keys. It is marketed to parents of babies aged 6 to 36 months old and claims to "encourage imaginative role play."[1] One of the automated recorded phrases it emits is the command "Let's go shopping!" I thought about the limiting gendered messages this item seemed to be teaching little girls who would become women in a couple of decades. And then I thought about the places that purses have taken the women in this book and the things their purses allowed them to carry along the way. Rather than rolling my eyes at this toy, I wanted to share these other stories with my niece.

Today, I think about all the women whose stories did not make it into this book. I have primarily and intentionally focused on women who were not famous or powerful, and it has been harder to access their purses for this reason. But there are also many compelling stories about famous women and their purses. For example, when Aretha Franklin died in 2018, I learned that she refused to sing on stage before being paid in full in cash, which she then stashed in her purse. Throughout her career, she kept her cash-filled purse close on stage within her sight during her performances, including her last live performance at a benefit for Elton John's AIDS Foundation in 2017, at a time when

Figure E.1. This pink "Pretty Learning Purse" (now marketed as "My Smart Purse") was still available for purchase at the time of this writing. Intended for use by baby girls between the ages of 6 and 36 months, the purse speaks and tells players, "Let's go shopping!" (Photograph courtesy of Sarah Cochran, August 2024.)

her net worth was a reported 80 million dollars.[2] Throughout her career, she used her purses—once modest and later designer and often made by Chanel—to demand R-E-S-P-E-C-T. She used her purse to make sure she did not get stiffed as so many other Black performers in the mid-twentieth century did.

This book is largely about ordinary women, but I'm also reminded of another extraordinary woman whose story never found a home in the preceding chapters. After the death of Supreme Court Justice Ruth Bader Ginsburg in September 2020, I watched a documentary called *Making the Case*.[3] In this short film, Ginsburg showed off some of her favorite purses and shared the story behind how she acquired each one. She identified a large grayish, lavender bag that had, in her words, "a zillion pockets." Echoing the thoughts of suffragists more than a century earlier, she elaborated, "I love pockets." Ginsburg

EPILOGUE

Figure E.2. Taken during a performance at the BET Honors Awards on February 8, 2014, a few years before her death, Aretha Franklin touches her bejeweled clutch, which she often rested on a piano where it remained reachable and within sight. (Larry French, Getty Images.)

explained that everywhere she traveled across the world, she took this bag with her, and in it she carried a copy of the Constitution. Then, with her hands inside purple netted gloves, Ginsburg reached into one of those pockets and pulled out a physical copy of the Constitution. To Ginsburg, it was important to have both her bag and the document she so cherished within arms' length everywhere she went. I immediately remembered how, inside her red alligator bag, Susan B. Anthony carried the transcript of her trial after her arrest for illegally voting. And I thought of Nellie Bly with her passport in her gripsack flying around the world. I wondered if Ginsburg knew these stories.

No matter how famous and powerful or meager and modest their owner, purses have mattered. Today, I wonder how many women and men—who no one ever thought to interview about their purse—share similarly strong feelings about their bags. What privileges and burdens do their bags provide them? If you've made it this far in this book, you, too, likely have a relationship with a bag, or perhaps many bags. You might hate purses or you might love them. The chances are good that you have received a purse as a gift, bought one on a whim, or held onto a bag you used to carry but can't quite bring yourself to throw out.

As several news columns, fashion magazines, websites, and social media accounts dedicated to purses attest, in the twenty-first century purses are likely more deeply embedded in American life than ever. In 2004, *The Wall Street Journal* spoke with Janet Northen, a 48-year-old advertising executive who carried a Coach tote bag that measured 13 by 12 by 8 inches. She told the *Journal* that she carried far more than she needed at any given time, but "the minute I take something out is when I need it. So I carry the world." Most of the time, the paper reported, Ms. Northen's bag "is so crowded and her life so busy, she's not even sure what she is carrying."[4] And while most of us are not carrying around Coach bags or the Constitution, we are all still here reading, writing, thinking about, and, of course, carrying purses.

Many of us complain about how heavy our bags are and the shoulder pain they sometimes cause. We bemoan the fact that we cannot find things when we most need them, even as our bags remain our companions and we insist that no one else touch them without our explicit permission. Indeed, some purse owners have come to see their bags as a burden, perhaps not knowing how this item of apparel gave their mothers, grandmothers, gay great-uncles, great-grandmothers, and great-great-grandmothers privacy in public and ready access to the things that helped them feel safe, dignified, and authentic. Purses have proven to be critical tools at many important moments, and they have simultaneously felt burdensome. Ultimately, they have provided adaptable means and materials for women's activism, expanding their agency, providing privacy, and helping them cross boundaries at so many unexpected corners.

For their part, many lesbians still convey a strong distaste for purses. A host of online articles and websites dedicated to "burses" (butch purses) suggest that purses still feel too feminine to those who do not identify as straight women.[5] And the emergence of the "murse" (a.k.a. man purse) reinforces the fact that purses are still feminized enough that Americans need a cheeky portmanteau when they are in the possession of men.[6] Though homophobia and transphobia are in some ways as virulent and insidious as ever, I hope that American men who carry purses face less danger of being assaulted than they did when Willie Houston was murdered in 2001.

In her eighties at the time of this writing, the civil rights activist Roberta ("Bobbi") Yancy—who held her leather purse up in the air and told the police to "watch the fur!" as they dragged her from a sit-in in 1964—now carries one of three purses. Each is made of fabric instead of leather because they are lighter and easier on her back and shoulders. She has had to adjust the way she carries a cross-body purse since she had a mastectomy, and she now uses it to carry tissues, lozenges, and a folding cane that helps her stay balanced as she navigates the streets and subterranean passageways of New York City.[7] She still hates heels and doesn't bother with them these days. Though Yancy appears infrequently in the historical literature on the Civil Rights Movement, her experiences provide just one example of the burdens—both material and psychological—that Black women carried throughout the twentieth century.

Today, purses continue to live rich lives as emotional agents as well. A 2014 study demonstrates that purses act as transitional and memory objects for aging women, especially those grappling with dementia.[8] For women who are unable to physically leave memory units in nursing homes, purses are a place to keep their most meaningful objects together and close by. In fact, they are the best approximation of home for a displaced person who feels both physically and cognitively lost without their purse on their lap or at their feet to anchor them in a strange place. After all, most purses contain literal proof of our identity, and their familiar heft, feel, and sight help us feel safe. When women with dementia keep them close, purses often remain one of the last vestiges of their privacy and dignity. Any good bag prevents the material mundanities of our lives—our pills, tissues, glasses, vitamins, half-melted snacks, beauty products, pepper spray, first-aid, and family photos—from spilling out our secrets. Being able to both see and hold their bags helps assure geriatric patients that, though they may have been stripped of their surroundings and even their memories, no one else is in possession of their identity.[9]

Starting in 2020, some pundits predicted that the global COVID-19 pandemic would kill the purse. Who needs a purse when so many people shifted to working from home in their pajamas? But the pandemic caused only a brief dip in sales in 2020, more than recovering to pre-pandemic sales by 2023. By one estimate, the handbag market in the United States is projected to reach over 13 billion dollars in 2025.[10] Perhaps now we appreciate leaving the house more than ever and plan for these occasions at least as much as we did before. Every morning millions—perhaps billions—of women engage in the ritual of packing their bags as they imagine their day and prepare to meet the world.

Today, purses continue to be one of the most important objects in American women's lives. Though historians are often hesitant to make predictions, even in a future shaped by contactless payment and keyless entry, the purse will remain a partner to the body. When our bodies bleed, ache, hunger, thirst, and seek comfort, purses will be there, ready to meet their material needs. In the digital age, when so much information about what we read, think, write, desire, and consume is readily available online, the small measure of privacy that a purse affords us will be even more sacred. We will still have a place for purses; they will persist as our companions wherever we find ourselves, reassuring and reminding us of who we are. And if we want to take the histories of women and of gender and sexual minorities seriously, it is time we open up purses, look inside, and listen to their stories.

Notes

INTRODUCTION

1. For further discussion and eighteenth-century artistic representations of this association, see Barbara Burman and Ariane Fennetaux, *The Pocket: A Hidden History of Women's Lives, 1660–1900* (New Haven, CT: Yale University Press, 2019), 46–47.
2. Burman and Fennetaux argue that this process was neither smooth nor linear. *The Pocket*, 13, 19. See also Caroline Cox, *The Handbag: An Illustrated History* (New York: HarperCollins, 2007), 23, and Hannah Carlson, *Pockets: An Intimate History of How We Keep Things Close* (Chapel Hill, NC: Algonquin Books, 2023).
3. Carlson, *Pockets*, 113. See also Burman and Fennetaux, *The Pocket*, 36; Ann D. Gordon, ed., *The Selected Papers of Elizabeth Cady Stanton and Susan B. Anthony* (New Brunswick, NJ: Rutgers University Press), June 24, 1899, Vol. 6, 301.
4. Burman and Fennetaux, *The Pocket*, 19.
5. Burman and Fennetaux, *The Pocket*, 37.
6. Carlson, *Pockets*, 111.
7. Cox, *The Handbag*, 23.
8. Lauren Camerlengo, "The Ubiquitous Miser's Purse," master's thesis, Cooper-Hewitt, Parsons, 2010.
9. Cox, *The Handbag*, 29–30.
10. *Mary Poppins*, directed by Robert Stevenson (Burbank, CA: Walt Disney Studios, 1964).
11. Elizabeth Cady Stanton, "The Pocket Problem," *Utica Sunday Journal*, May 26, 1895. Cited by Carlson, *Pockets*, 120–121, note 259; Elizabeth Cady Stanton, "A trailing dress and no pocket," in *Selected Papers of Elizabeth Cady Stanton and Susan B. Anthony*, Vol. 6, 1895–1906, June 24, 1899, 301. In this entry, Stanton describes one of her "unhappy acquaintances" who was severely injured while holding too many items and tripping over her trailing dress as she attempted to catch a car. See also "Fashions Against Suffrage," *New York Tribune*, June 14, 1899, 7.
12. Gilman, "Male Attire," *New York Times*, March 5, 1905.
13. "The Fashion Now," *Boston Daily Globe*, May 22, 1887.
14. "Purse," noun, Old English, *Oxford English Dictionary*, accessed December 19, 2023.
15. Luanne von Schneidemesser, "Miscellany, Purse and Its Synonyms," *American Speech* 55, no. 1 (Spring 1980): 74–76.
16. von Schneidemesser, "Purse and Its Synonyms," 74.
17. Cox, *The Handbag*, 18.
18. "Bag," slang, *Oxford English Dictionary*, III.17, https://www.oed.com/dictionary/bag_n?tab=meaning_and_use#29734700, last revised July 2023, accessed December 21, 2023.
19. The *Oxford English Dictionary* notes that in the United States, the term "bag" was used as "a disparaging term for a woman; (originally) a sexually promiscuous woman; (later) an unattractive or elderly woman." "Old bag," colloquial (orig. U.S.), derogatory and offensive, *Oxford English Dictionary*, https://www.oed.com/dictionary/old-bag_n?tl=true, accessed December 18, 2023. The *OED* cites the following example from 1947: "Around comes this old bag again . . . and he . . . quavers . . . 'I've seen that old broad somewhere before.'"

N. Johnson, *Letters* (1981), 35. A second example from the 1940s includes the following quote from the University of Virginia's student newspaper: "They got a campaign goin' around here to try to stick us students six rocks just to go . . . and listen to some old bag yell her fool head off." *Cavalier Daily* (University of Virginia), October 22, 1949, 4, no. 1.

20. It is notable that these meanings have specific resonance in America, where they were used in these ways before other English-speaking countries. For more information, see Kelsie B. Harder and W. L. McAtee, "'Handbag' or 'Purse'?," *American Speech* 36, no. 2 (1961): 154–156; Schneidemesser, "Purse and Its Synonyms," 74–76.
21. "Handbag," noun, https://www.oed.com/dictionary/handbag_n?tab=meaning_and_use#12052691, accessed December 21, 2023.
22. Schneidemesser, "Purse and Its Synonyms," 75.
23. For example, see Burman and Fennetaux, *The Pocket*; Carlson, *Pockets*; Laura F. Edwards, *Only the Clothes on Her Back: Clothing and the Hidden History of Power in the 19th-Century United States* (New York: Oxford University Press, 2022); Tiya Miles, *All That She Carried: The Journey of Ashley's Sack, A Black Family Keepsake* (New York: Random House, 2021).
24. For example, see Claire Wilcox, ed., *Handbags: The Making of a Museum* (New Haven, CT: Yale University Press, 2012); Sigrid Ivo, *Bags: A Selection of Bags and Purses, Amsterdam* (Amsterdam: Pepin, 2011); Claire Wilcox, *A Century of Handbags: Icons of Style in the 20th Century* (New York: Chartwell Books, 1997); Farid Chenoune, ed., *Carried Away: All About Bags* (New York: Vendome Press, 2005); Vanda Foster, *Bags and Purses: The Costume Accessories Series* (London: B.T. Batsford, 1982); Caroline Cox, *The Handbag: An Illustrated History* (New York: HarperCollins, 2007).
25. Other books that take a more journalistic or popular approach to bags include Winifred Gallagher, *It's in the Bag: What Purses Reveal and Conceal* (New York: HarperCollins, 2006); Carmel Allen, *The Handbag: To Have and to Hold* (London: Carlton Books, 1999); Sophie Gachet, *The Handbag Book: 400 Designer Bags That Changed Fashion* (New York: Harry N. Abrams, 2024); and Julia Werner and Dennis Braatz, *For the Love of Bags* (Augsburg, Germany: TeNeues, 2015).
26. Mesh bags, which required a great deal of labor through at least the 1910s, were not only popular; trade magazines considered them a kind of jewelry. By one estimate, two-thirds of middle-class women had at some point been involved in making them. Winfield Dunham, "Making the Mesh Ring Purse," *American Jeweler*, March 1, 1910, 30. For more information on the kinds of souvenirs—including baskets, boxes, and purses—that indigenous people made and sold to Victorian Americans, see Ruth B. Phillips, *Trading Identities: The Souvenir in North American Native Art from the Northeast, 1700-1900* (Hong Kong: University of Washington Press, 1998).
27. This book builds on decades of foundational scholarship in gender history and feminist theory. Collectively, these works have shaped my understanding of gender as a historically contingent performance and process. My thinking has been particularly influenced by the work of Joan Scott, Gail Bederman, Susan Stryker, Judith Butler, Jack Halberstam, and Sara Ahmed, to name a few. Black feminist thought on intersectionality has also guided much of my thinking, especially the work of Kimberlé Crenshaw and Evelyn Brooks Higginbotham. Finally, I also benefit from scholarship on the role of clothing and material culture in women's lives. Gail Bederman, *Manliness and Civilization: A Cultural History of Gender and Race in the United States, 1880-1917* (Chicago: Chicago University Press, 1995); Joan Wallach Scott, "Gender: A Useful Category of Historical Analysis," *American Historical Review* 1, no. 5 (1986): 1053–1075; Susan Stryker, *Transgender History*, 2nd ed. (Berkeley, CA: Seal Press, 2017); Sara Ahmed, *Living a Feminist Life* (Durham, NC: Duke University Press, 2017); Judith

Butler, *Gender Trouble: Feminism and the Subversion of Identity* (New York: Routledge, 2006); Jack Halberstam, *Female Masculinity* (Durham, NC: Duke University Press, 1998); Kimberlé Crenshaw, "Mapping the Margins: Intersectionality, Identity Politics, and Violence Against Women of Color," *Stanford Law Review* 43, no. 6 (1991): 1241–1299, and "Demarginalizing the Intersection of Race and Sex: A Black Feminist Critique of Antidiscrimination Doctrine, Feminist Theory and Antiracist Politics," University of Chicago Legal Forum, 1989, 139–167; Evelyn Brooks Higginbotham, "African American Women's History and the Metalanguage of Race," *Signs* 17, no. 2 (1992): 251–274; Miles, *All That She Carried*; Edwards, *Only the Clothes on Her Back*; Burman and Fennetaux, *The Pocket*; and Carlson, *Pockets*.

28. Carey Goldberg, "Oldest Mummy 'Found' on Museum Shelf, *The New York Times*, April 27, 1996; David Brown, "Nevada Mummy Caught in Debate over Tribal Remains," *The Washington Post*, May 5, 1996.
29. Catherine Gouédo, "Bags: The Archeological Evidence," in *Carried Away*, 179–181.
30. Julia Laite, "The Emmet's Inch: Small History in a Digital Age," *Journal of Social History* 53, no. 4 (Summer 2020): 963–989, https://academic.oup.com/jsh/article/53/4/963/5315914, accessed December 21, 2023. Cited in Miles, *All That She Carried*, 311, note 8.
31. Darby Penney and Peter Stastny tell this story more fully in *The Lives They Left Behind: Suitcases from a State Hospital Attic* (New York: Bellevue Literary Press, 2008).
32. "Willard Asylum for the Chronically Insane," *Atlas Obscura*, accessed April 13, 2021, https://www.atlasobscura.com/places/willard-asylum-for-the-chronic-insane; Penney and Stastny, *The Lives They Left Behind*, Prologue.
33. Penny and Stastny, *The Lives They Left Behind*, x–xi.
34. Jon Crispin, photographer, telephone conversation with author, December 9, 2024.
35. This patient's full name has been obscured to protect her privacy.
36. Jon Crispin, "Willard Suitcases," Anna B. H., Images 7–12, https://willardsuitcases.photoshelter.com/gallery-image/Anna-B-H/G0000tJ2IKQBLbg4/I0000ZbF88gUzsmA, accessed August 28, 2021.
37. This phrase and the title of the book are inspired by Tim O'Brien's collection of short stories on Vietnam. Published in 1990, O'Brien's book begins by discussing the literal materials soldiers carried in their rucksacks (i.e., ponchos, photographs, machetes, and grenades) as they "humped" along while fighting in Vietnam. However, the book also explores the psychological weight of the burdens they carried (i.e., shame, panic, horror). While not about war, this book simultaneously considers the barriers faced and burdens carried by historically marginalized people, including but not exclusively women. But it also explores the surprising ways in which people used purses to create more space, privacy, and privileges for themselves. O'Brien, *The Things They Carried* (Boston: Mariner Books, 1990).
38. Lou Taylor, "Fashion and Dress History: Theoretical and Methodological Approaches," *The Handbook of Fashion Studies,* ed. Sandy Black et al. (London: Bloomsbury Academic, 2013), 23–43.
39. Elizabeth Lapovsky Kennedy and Madeline Davis, *Boots of Leather, Slippers of Gold: The History of a Lesbian Community* (New York: Routledge, 1993), 160.
40. See William Eskridge Jr., *GayLaw: Challenging the Apartheid of the Closet* (Cambridge, MA: Harvard University Press, 1999), 27, Appendix A2, 338–341. See also Chapter 2 of Stryker, *Transgender History*.

CHAPTER 1

1. Aunt Charlotte Raines, "Georgia Narratives," FWP, Vol. 4, Part 3, 190–191.
2. For these reasons, transcripts of the interviews reflect the subjective memories of interviewees, as well as the biases of white interviewers, transcribers, and editors. Despite these limitations,

they remain immensely valuable to historians. Indeed, patterns emerge in these interviews that mere coincidence or bias cannot explain away. For further discussion of these sources and the challenges inherent in working with them, see Charles L. Perdue Jr., Thomas E. Barden, and Robert K. Phillips (eds.), *Weevils in the Wheat: Interviews with Virginia Ex-Slaves* (Charlottesville: University Press of Virginia, 1976), xi–xlv. Stephanie M. H. Camp, "The Pleasures of Resistance: Enslaved Women and Body Politics in the Plantation South, 1830–1861," *Journal of Southern History* 68, no. 3 (August 2002): 536–537, note 6; Helen Bradley Foster, *New Raiments of Self: African American Clothing in the Antebellum South* (New York: Berg, 1997), 8–11. See also George P. Rawick, *From Sundown to Sunup: The Making of a Black Community* (Westport, CT: Greenwood, 1972), 174–175; Edward Baptist, *The Half Has Never Been Told: Slavery and the Making of American Capitalism* (New York: Basic Books, 2016); Catherine Stewart, *Long Past Slavery: Representing Race in the Federal Writer's Project* (Chapel Hill: University of North Carolina Press, 2016).

3. Foster, *New Raiments of Self*, 7.

4. For example, when William Henry Towns was interviewed by Levi Shelby, Jr., he was asked to recall rhymes and riddles from his childhood in Alabama. Towns had been born in 1854, seven years before the Civil War began and, though he was in his eighties at the time of the interview, he recalled that "us young'uns" had "a song or two an' a few riddles." Then, perhaps at Shelby's request, he sang:

> Hawk an' de buzzard went down to de lawl,
> When de hawk got back he had a broken jaw.
> Lady's pocketbook on de Judge's banch
> Haden' had no use for a pocketbook sence.

5. Hundreds of photographs document what FWP interviewees looked like at the time of their interview, and these images reveal details about the clothing they were wearing at the time. All of the images were taken outside and many of the women were sitting in chairs, standing still in front of their homes, or actively engaged in washing clothing. Of over 90 images of formerly enslaved women, many are wearing aprons tied at the waist, only one dons a coat, and none of the images feature a woman holding a purse. Because they had been visited at their homes by government employees, most of which were apparently not expecting such visitors, it stands to reason that they would not be wearing coats or carrying purses. Many of them may have still associated purses with white "ladies" or were unable to purchase purses for themselves due to financial constraints.

6. A few scholars have highlighted the historical significance of clothing to enslaved people, concluding that clothing helped them develop and sustain their own communities: Stephanie M. H. Camp, "The Pleasures of Resistance: Enslaved Women and Body Politics in the Plantation South, 1830–1861," *Journal of Southern History* 68, no. 3 (August 2002): 533–572; Foster, *New Raiments of Self*. See also Shane and Graham White, *Stylin': African American Expressive Culture from Its Beginnings to the Zoot Suit* (Ithaca, NY: Cornell University Press, 1999). More recent scholarship illustrates how creative readings of textiles can reveal "hidden histories," and these works can dramatically expand our understanding of the many meanings of historical textiles for women and enslaved people. See Barbara Burman and Ariane Fennetaux, *The Pocket: A Hidden History of Women's Lives: 1660–1900* (New Haven, CT: Yale University Press, 2020); Tiya Miles, *All That She Carried: The Journey of Ashley's Sack, A Black Family Keepsake* (New York: Random House: 2021); Laura F. Edwards, *Only the Clothes on Her Back: Clothing and the Hidden History of Power in the 19th-Century United States* (New York: Oxford University Press, 2022).

7. For example, see South Carolina's "Negro Act of 1735."
8. Michael Zakim, "A Ready-Made Business: The Birth of the Clothing Industry in America," *The Business History Review* 73, no. 1 (Spring 1999): 62–63. See also "Sartorial Ideologies: From Homespun to Ready-Made," *American Historical Review* 106, no. 5 (December 2001): 1553–1586.
9. Linda Baumgarten, "'Clothes for the People': Slave Clothing in Early Virginia," *Journal of Early Southern Decorative Arts*, 14, no. 2 (1988): 40.
10. Foster, *New Raiments of Self*, 79, 135.
11. "The style and quality of clothing," Baumgarten notes, "depended upon their occupation, as well as their perceived visibility to the white community." "'Clothes for the People,'" 38.
12. Baumgarten, "'Clothes for the People,'" 38, 40–41.
13. Stephanie Camp, *Closer to Freedom: Enslaved Women and Everyday Resistance in the Plantation South* (Chapel Hill: University of North Carolina Press, 2004), 60, 79, 80, 82.
14. Wooden shoes were typically provided only in winter or not at all, and interviewees rarely mentioned coats. Children typically received even less clothing than adults. In his narrative, Frederick Douglass (1851) notes that, as an enslaved child, he was "kept almost naked—no shoes, no stockings, no jacket, no trowsers, nothing on but a coarse tow linen shirt reaching only to my knees." *Narrative of the Life of Frederick Douglass, An American Slave* (London: H.G. Collins, 1851), 30.
15. Adeline Marshall, "Texas Narratives," Part 3, 46.
16. Marshall, "Texas Narratives," 106.
17. Marshall, "Texas Narratives," 211.
18. According to Miles, "The badges, meant to be worn visibly on the body, displayed an enslaved person's occupation and announced the master's permission for that person to be mobile for the named work." *All That She Carried*, 83.
19. Isaiah Butler, "South Carolina Narratives," Vol. 14, Part 1, 159.
20. In many states throughout the country, free people of color also had to carry freedom papers to prove that they were not enslaved. In England and America, some of the wealthiest enslavers who sought to prominently display their wealth and power even forced slaves to wear silver collars engraved with their owner's name and address. Baumgarten has documented this phenomenon through her analysis of eighteenth-century portraits and estate inventories. "'Clothes for the People,'" 33.
21. For an example of a slave collar with bells, courtesy of the Holden Family Collection, see "'Purchased Lives': The American Slave Trade from 1808 to 1865," Bullock Museum, Texas, https://www.thestoryoftexas.com/discover/artifacts/slave-collar-with-bells, accessed April 26, 2022.
22. Miles notes that the sack she studied in *All That She Carried* was most likely made in a cotton factory in South Carolina in the 1850s. Miles, 32.
23. Historians of gender have long recognized the importance of objects in general and textiles in particular to women's history. "Because far more women were accustomed to using needles than pens," Laurel Thatcher Ulrich has argued, "textiles may offer the richest unexplored body of information in early American women's history." Ulrich, "Of Pens and Needles: Sources in Early American Women's History," *Journal of American History* 77, no. 1 (June 1990): 205.
24. Solomon Northup, *Twelve Years a Slave: Narrative of Solomon Northup, a Citizen of New-York, Kidnapped in Washington City in 1841, and Rescued in 1853*, 167. Documenting the American South, https://docsouth.unc.edu/fpn/northup/northup.html, accessed December 12, 2024.

25. Northup, *Twelve Years a Slave*, 167.
26. Northup, *Twelve Years a Slave*, 167.
27. Northup, *Twelve Years a Slave*, 178.
28. Northup, *Twelve Years a Slave*, 178.
29. Northup, *Twelve Years a Slave*, 166.
30. Richard Orford, "Georgia Narratives," Vol. 4, Part 3, 150.
31. Sarah Ashley, "Texas Narratives," Vol. 16, Part 1, 34–35.
32. Irella Battle Walker, "Texas Narratives," Vol. 16, Part 4, 122.
33. Jennifer Morgan, *Laboring Women: Reproduction and Gender in New World Slavery* (Philadelphia: University of Pennsylvania Press, 2004), 36.
34. Morgan, *Laboring Women*, 146.
35. Joe Clinton, "Arkansas Narratives," Vol. 2, Part 2, 32.
36. As Joe Clinton recalled, Brown even ordered "Uncle Nat" to "go git some boards en make er coffin for dis n***er what I done kilt." Clinton, "Arkansas Narratives," Vol. 2, Part 2, 32.
37. "Rube Witt (Marshall)," Portraits of African American ex-slaves from the U.S. WPA, September 7, 1937, Library of Congress, Prints and Photographs Division, Washington, DC.
38. Rube Witt, "Texas Narratives," Vol. 16, Part 4, 209.
39. Hannah Carlson, *Pockets: An Intimate History of How We Keep Things Close* (Chapel Hill, NC: Algonquin Books, 2023), 7.
40. There is some disagreement among historians as to whether Walker was born enslaved or free. For example, Leslie Harris claims he was born enslaved, while Edward Baptist argues that he was born free in North Carolina and briefly lived in Charleston. Baptist claims that Walker personally witnessed the torture and execution of thirty enslaved men whose plans to stage a rebellion had been discovered. Leslie Harris, *In the Shadow of Slavery: African Americans in New York City, 1626–1863* (Chicago: University of Chicago Press, 2003), 174; Baptist, *The Half Has Never Been Told*, 195.
41. Walker knew what he was doing when he signed his name and said so in the pamphlet: "What is the use of living," he said, "when I am in fact dead." Baptist, *The Half Has Never Been Told*, 197.
42. Baptist, *The Half Has Never Been Told*, 196.
43. Baptist, *The Half Has Never Been Told*, 197.
44. Northup, *Twelve Years a Slave*, 303.
45. Elizabeth Hyde Botume, *First Days Amongst the Contrabands* (Boston: Lee and Shepard, 1892), 67.
46. Miles, *All That She Carried*, 4.
47. "Ashley's Sack. How much can one bag carry?," Middleton Place, 2021, https://www.middletonplace.org/news-and-events/ashleys-sack-how-much-can-one-bag-carry/, accessed December 11, 2024.
48. Miles, *All That She Carried*, 31.
49. Miles, *All That She Carried*, 93. At least one popular example of an artist's rendering of a slave coffle suggests the possibility that sack carrying was either a gendered part of these forced marches or perhaps perceived as a gendered act. "Edward Stone's Coffle Gang" (1940) features enslaved women carrying sacks behind shoeless enslaved men who have their hands tied behind their backs and are chained together. This illustration appears to have been based on a description written by Reverend James H. Dickey, who claimed to have encountered a coffle of slaves in Bourbon County, Kentucky in 1822. J. Winston Coleman, Jr., *Kentucky in Slavery Times* (Chapel Hill: University of North Carolina Press, 1940), 145–146.
50. Baptist, *The Half Has Never Been Told*, xxiii.

51. Miles, *All That She Carried*, 103.
52. "U.S. Journal: Gee's Bend, Ala." *New Yorker*, March 22, 1969, 102–108.
53. For more information, see Terri Klassen, "Representations of African American Quiltmaking: From Omission to High Art," *Journal of American Folklore*, Vol. 122, No. 485 (Summer, 2009): 297–334; Maris Curran, "The Master Quilters of Gee's Bend Alabama," November 13, 2018, https://www.nytimes.com/2018/11/13/opinion/quilts-while-i-yet-live.html, accessed February 8, 2025.
54. Fannie Tatum, "Arkansas Narratives," Vol. 2, Part 6, 257. Likewise, at the age of 81, Annie Bridges of Missouri recalled, "We all wore 'jeans' an' wrap'd an' ole' sack 'round our legs." Bridges, "Missouri Narratives," Vol. 10, 44.
55. Tatum, "Arkansas Narratives," 257.
56. Fannie Wheeler, "Arkansas Narratives," Vol. 2, Part 7, 115.
57. Rosa Simmons, "Arkansas Narratives," Vol. 2, Part 6, 157.
58. Laura Bell, "North Carolina Narratives," Vol. 11, Part 1, 100.
59. Walter Johnson, *Soul by Soul: Life Inside the Antebellum Slave Market* (Cambridge, MA: Harvard University Press, 1999), 137–145.
60. Tom Hawkins, "Georgia Narratives," Vol. 4, Part 2, 132.
61. Ida Henry, "Oklahoma Narratives," Vol. 13, 136.
62. Waters McIntosh, "Arkansas Narratives," Vol. 2, Part 5, 18–19.
63. McIntosh, "Arkansas Narratives," 18–19.
64. Lina Hunter, "Georgia Narratives," Vol. 4, Part 2, 257.
65. Hunter, "Georgia Narratives," 257.
66. Walter Johnson, *Soul by Soul*, 189.
67. Analyses of the texts of runaway advertisements published in the late eighteenth century show that both men and women brought clothing with them when they ran away, though ads spilled more ink enumerating what men had taken with them. Jonathan Prude, "To Look upon the 'Lower Sort': Runaway Ads and the Appearance of Unfree Laborers in America, 1750-1800," *Journal of American History* 78, no. 1 (June 1991). 124–159, especially 144.
68. According to Prude, "it is impossible to overstate the role of dress in these advertisements…the intensity with which clothing was noticed is astonishing." In a large study of runaway advertisements involving over 1,700 people published between 1750 and 1800, Prude found that the average ad mentioned 9.6 articles of clothing. The number of clothes most Americans owned only increased in the nineteenth century. Prude, "To Look upon the 'Lower Sort,'" 143.
69. Simon B. Abbott, "30 DOLLARS REWARD," *Charleston Mercury*, June 30, 1836, Freedom on the Move, https://app.freedomonthemove.org/advertisements/6a07f229-d929-41c6-af88-911d297df24b?limit=12&page=1, accessed September 18, 2021.
70. Josephine Brown, *Biography of an American Bondman*, as described by C. Riley Snorton, *Black on Both Sides: A Racial History of Trans Identity* (Minneapolis: University of Minnesota Press, 2017), 77. In 1860, William Craft detailed this escape in *Running a Thousand Miles for Freedom*. Craft, *Running a Thousand Miles for Freedom; Or, the Escape of William and Ellen Craft* (London: William Tweedie, 1860).
71. Laura Edwards, *Only the Clothes on Her Back: Clothing and the Hidden History of Power in the 19th-century United States* (New York: Oxford University Press, 2022). See also Chapter 2 of Tamika Y. Nunley, *At the Threshold of Liberty: Women, Slavery, and Shifting Identities in Washington D.C.* (Chapel Hill: University of North Carolina Press, 2021).
72. "Brought to Jail," runaway slave advertisement, *Milledgeville Federal Union*, September 1845.

73. "$50 reward," *Wilmington Chronicle,* August 4, 1847; "$100 reward," *Wilmington Chronicle,* September 8, 1847; "$50 reward," *Raleigh Register,* July 31, 1847; "$100 reward!" *Raleigh Register,* September 4, 1847.
74. Laura Edwards uncovers several such legal cases in *Only the Clothes on Her Back* and "James and His Striped, Velvet Pantaloons: Textiles, Commerce, and the Law in the New Republic," *Journal of American History,* (September 2020): 336–61.
75. Jacobs, *Incidents in the Life of a Slave Girl* (New York: Cosimo Books, 1861), 312–313.
76. Caroline Cox, *The Handbag: An Illustrated History* (New York: HarperCollins), 8–9.
77. William Wells Brown in *The Rising Son; or. The Antecedents and Advancement of the Colored Race* (Boston: A.G. Brown and Co, 1874), 536. Cited in Catherine Clinton's *Harriet Tubman: The Road to Freedom* (New York: Little, Brown and Co., 2004), 131.
78. Clinton, *Harriet Tubman,* 131.
79. Clinton, *Harriet Tubman,* see Chapter 6, "The Moses of Her People."
80. One surviving example created by the Female Society of Birmingham (England) includes an image of a lone, distressed enslaved mother holding a baby. Made in 1827, it can now be found at the Victoria and Albert Museum. Reticule, Victoria and Albert Museum, https://collections.vam.ac.uk/item/O68954/reticule-lines-samuel/, accessed February 8, 2025.
81. The U.S. government did not pay Tubman her pension until 1899, when she was 77 years old. She would live another 14 years. Janelle Hobson, "Between History and Fantasy: Harriet Tubman in the Artistic and Popular Imaginary," *Meridians* 12, no. 2 (2014): 52, 58.
82. Hobson, 54.
83. Earl Conrad, *Harriet Tubman* (Washington, DC: Associated Publishers, 1943), 71.
84. On October 6, 1873, the *Auburn Daily Bulletin* published a story about the incident. Clinton, *Harriet Tubman,* 201.
85. Camp, *Closer to Freedom,* 2004, 6.
86. See Morgan, *Laboring Women.*
87. Jacobs, *Incidents in the Life of a Slave Girl,* 66.
88. Elizabeth Clark-Lewis, *Living In, Living Out: African American Domestics in Washington, D.C. 1910–1940* (Washington, DC: Smithsonian Books, 1994), 94.

CHAPTER 2

1. Nellie Bly, *Around the World* (New York: Pictorial Weeklies, 1890); electronic edition, https://digital.library.upenn.edu/women/bly/world/world.html, accessed December 13, 2024.
2. Bly, *Around the World.*
3. Bly, *Around the World.*
4. Brooke Kroeger, *Nellie Bly: Daredevil, Reporter, Feminist* (New York: Times Books, 1994), 141. Until its closure in 2019, Bly's satchel could be seen on display at the Newseum in Washington, DC.
5. Bly claimed to have packed "two traveling caps, three veils, a pair of slippers, a complete outfit of toilet articles, ink-stand pens, pencils, and copy-paper, pins, needles and thread, a dressing gown, a tennis blazer, a small flask and a drinking cup, several complete changes of underwear, a liberal supply of handkerchiefs and fresh ruchings [*sic*], and most bulky and compromising of all, a jar of cold cream to keep my face from chapping in the varied climates I should encounter." Bly, *Around the World.*
6. Bly, *Around the World.*
7. Bly, *Around the World.*
8. For more information on the legal, political, and cultural evolution of marriage in America, see Hendrik Hartog, *Man and Wife in America: A History* (Cambridge, MA: Harvard

University Press, 2002); Nancy Cott, *Public Vows: A History of Marriage and the Nation* (Cambridge, MA: Harvard University Press, 2000); Priscilla Yamin, *American Marriage: A Political History* (Philadelphia: University of Pennsylvania Press, 2012); Clare Virginia Eby, *Until Choice Do Us Part: Marriage Reform in the Progressive Era* (Chicago: University of Chicago Press, 2014).

9. See Jessica Ellen Sewell, *Women and the Everyday City: Public Space in San Francisco, 1890–1915* (Minneapolis: University of Minnesota Press, 2011).

10. See Sarah Deutsch, *Women and the City: Gender, Space, and Power in Boston, 1870–1940* (New York: Oxford University Press, 2000); Sewell, *Women and the Everyday City*. More recently, see Georgina Hickey's work on urban gender segregation. *Breaking the Gender Code: Women and Urban Public Space in the Twentieth-Century United States* (Austin: University of Texas Press, 2023).

11. For more information on how turn-of-the-century built environments shaped gender ideologies and vice versa, see Sewell, *Women and the Everyday City*. For an intriguing discussion on the controversy of women taking up space by wearing large hoop-skirts and tall theater hats, see Emily Remus, *A Shopper's Paradise: How the Ladies of Chicago Claimed Power and Pleasure in the New Downtown* (Cambridge, MA: Harvard University Press, 2019), Chapters 2 and 3.

12. For more information on window shopping, see Sewell, *Women and the Everyday City*, 26–27, and Emily Remus, *A Shopper's Paradise*.

13. Sewell, *Women and the Everyday City*, 2.

14. Sandweiss, "Image and Artifact: The Photograph as Evidence in the Digital Age," *Journal of American History* 94, no. 1 (2007): 194.

15. This was true even in the 1860s, when long exposure times necessitated that photographers use immobilizing posing stands. Andrea Volpe, "Cartes de Visite Portrait Photographs and the Culture of Class Formation," *Looking for America: The Visual Production of Nation and People*, ed. Ardis Cameron (Malden, MA: Blackwell Publishing, 2005), 45–48.

16. Michael Lesy, "Visual Literacy." *Journal of American History* 94, no. 1 (January 2007): 153.

17. Shawn Michelle Smith, *American Archives: Gender, Race, and Class in Visual Culture* (Princeton, NJ: Princeton University Press, 1999), 95.

18. I borrow this concept from Marilyn F. Motz's work on women's assemblage of photograph albums. "Visual Autobiography: Photograph Albums of Turn-of-the-Century Midwestern Women," *American Quarterly* 41, no. 1 (March 1989), 63. As Shawn Michelle Smith argues, "[W]e might find a disruptive potential in the conjunction of commodification, mechanical reproduction, and feminized consumption. In circulation and display we might see women claiming self-authorship and self-ownership." *American Archives*, 97.

19. Rachel Teukolsky, "Cartomania: Sensation, Celebrity, and the Democratized Portrait," *Victorian Studies* 57, no. 3 (Spring 2015), 468.

20. Here, I do not mean to suggest that all women would have faced the same choices or consequences. For example, African American women may have used their portraits to combat racist assumptions that they were overly sexual; immigrant women likely used American styles as a meaningful way in which to assert their "American-ness"; working-class women would likely have to choose their Sunday clothes (distinguished from their "work clothes"), whereas middle-class women's wardrobes may have enabled them to buy a new dress for the occasion. Kathy Peiss, *Cheap Amusements: Working Women and Leisure in Turn-of-the-Century New York* (Philadelphia: Temple University Press, 1986), 44.

21. Volpe, "Cartes de Visite Portrait Photographs," 43.

22. Allison K. Lange, *Picturing Political Power: Images in the Women's Suffrage Movement* (Chicago: University of Chicago Press, 2020), 27.

23. Teukolsky, "Cartomania," 462. Lange argues that *cartes de visite* cost 2 to 3 dollars per dozen. *Picturing Political Power*, 60.
24. Teukolsky, "Cartomania," 464.
25. Volpe, "Cartes de Visite Portrait Photographs," 51.
26. Liam Buckley, "Self and Accessory in Gambian Studio Photography," *Visual Anthropology Review* 16, no. 2 (Fall/Winter 2000–2001), 76.
27. Liam Buckley argues that "while the photograph was used to monitor and to control identity, it was also used to create new images and to posit new identities, proliferating the possibilities for representing and circulating the self." Props played a critical role in this representation. "Self and Accessory in Gambian Studio Photography," 71.
28. Smith, *American Archives*, 93.
29. Teukolsky, "Cartomania," 463.
30. For example, see "The modern Cornelia, a veritable rum 'un,'" *Frank Leslie's Illustrated Newspaper*, July 31, 1869, Prints and Photographs Division, Library of Congress.
31. Lange, *Picturing Political Power*, 27.
32. Sojourner Truth, *Narrative of Sojourner Truth, a northern slave, emancipated from bodily servitude by the state of New York, in 1828* (Boston: 1850), 13, https://digital.library.upenn.edu/women/truth/1850/1850.html#1, accessed July 24, 2024. See also Nell Irvin Painter, *Sojourner Truth: A Life, a Symbol* (New York: W.W. Norton, 1997), 4.
33. Lange, *Picturing Political Power*, 67.
34. Painter, *Sojourner Truth*, 3.
35. Darcy Grimaldo Grigsby, *Enduring Truths: Sojourner's Shadows and Substance* (Chicago: University of Chicago Press, 2015), 155.
36. "Shadow" was a nineteenth-century reference to a photograph, which had to be developed in darkness. Lange, *Picturing Political Power*, 69.
37. "Sojourner Truth," *Revolution*, 44. Cited in Lange, *Picturing Political Power*, 70, note 70.
38. The Library of Congress citation notes that Cunningham's portrait is part of the visual materials from the National Urban League records.
39. It is also imperative to note that a large majority of Black women had worked for wages outside the home long before most white women did. The image of the cover for "Hannah! (I Want My Hannah)" sheet music highlights this fact by showing a Black woman leaving the home with a purse, in which she would have kept her wages.
40. Lange, *Picturing Political Power*, 70.
41. "Alligator purse," National Susan B. Anthony Museum and House, https://susanb.org/alligator-purse/, accessed February 8, 2024.
42. "Limited edition 'Ms. Anthony' Alligator Bag Available for Pre-order," National Susan B. Anthony Museum and House, https://susanbanthonyhouse.org/blog/limited-edition-ms-anthony-alligator-bag-available-for-pre-order/, accessed February 8, 2025.
43. "Suffragists Seek Votes by Distribution of Literature," *San Francisco Chronicle*, September 30, 1911, 7. Cited in Sewell, *Women and the Everyday City*, 149.
44. For more information, see Lange, *Picturing Political Power*.
45. Stanley (illegible) to Eva Tanguay, December 14, 1910; J. Hilton Thomas to Eva Tanguay, December 15, 1910, Professional, Fan Letters, 1910–1938, Eva Tanguay Papers, Benson Ford Research Center, Henry Ford Museum of American Innovation. For an extensive analysis of Tanguay's career, see Kathleen Casey, *The Prettiest Girl on Stage Is a Man: Race and Gender Benders in American Vaudeville* (Knoxville: University of Tennessee Press, 2015), Chapter 1.
46. Douglas Gilbert, *American Vaudeville: Its Life and Times* (New York: MacGraw-Hill and Company, 1940), 329; Jane Westerfield, "An Investigation of the Lifestyles and Performance

of Three Singer-Comediennes in American Vaudeville," PhD diss. (Ball State University, Muncie, IN, 1987), 46.
47. See Steve Massa, *Rediscovering Roscoe: The Films of "Fatty" Arbuckle* (Orlando, FL: Bear Manor Media, 2020), Chapter 4.
48. Roscoe Arbuckle himself knew the power of a good purse. Although he told one reporter in January 1922 that he was broke, one month earlier he reportedly bought his estranged wife, Minta Durfee, a "$1,000 jeweled purse for Christmas." Greg Merritt, *Room 1219: The Life of Fatty Arbuckle, the Mysterious Death of Virginia Rappe, and the Scandal That Changed Hollywood* (Chicago: Chicago Review Press, 2013), Chapter 16, 241.
49. Kemp R. Niver, "Early Motion Pictures: The Paper Print Collection in the Library of Congress," Motion Picture, Broadcasting, and Recorded Sound Division, Washington, DC, 1985, 100.
50. Georgina Hickey, *Breaking the Gender Code*, 4. For more on the creation of "comfort stations" built for women after 1900, see pp. 49–56.
51. As Elizabeth Alice Clement has shown, indeed, many working-class women at this time occasionally performed sex work to help keep the family afloat during difficult times. Clement, *Love for Sale: Courting, Treating and Prostitution in New York City, 1900–1945* (Chapel Hill: University of North Carolina Press, 2006), xxxv, xcii.
52. For more on "white slavery," see Clement, *Love for Sale*, and Gail Bederman, *Manliness and Civilization: A Cultural History of Gender and Race in the United States, 1880–1917* (Chicago: University of Chicago Press, 1995).
53. Hickey, *Breaking the Gender Code*, 26.
54. Deutsch, *Women and the City*, 11.
55. "A Simple Purse," *Los Angeles Times*, August 6, 1916.
56. Hickey, *Breaking the Gender Code*, 5.
57. Sewell, *Women and the Everyday City*, 5.
58. Wendy L. Rouse, *Her Own Hero: The Origins of the Women's Self-Defense Movement* (New York: New York University Press, 2017).
59. Cited in Deutsch, *Women and the City*, 73.
60. See Elizabeth Clark-Lewis, *Living In, Living Out: African American Domestics in Washington D.C., 1910–1940* (Washington, DC: Smithsonian Books, 1994). For an illuminating case study, see Elsa Barkley Brown and Gregg Kimball's analysis of the "moral geography" of Richmond, Virginia. "Mapping the Terrain of Black Richmond," *Journal of Urban History* 21, no. 3 (March 1995): 296–346.
61. Hickey, *Breaking the Gender Code*, 56–57.
62. At a time when bloomers were ridiculed and women were still wearing corsets, women who rode bicycles were considered scandalous. Yet, Davidson became a cycling enthusiast, founding the Lady Cyclists' Association in 1892 and penning a *Handbook for Lady Cyclists* four years later. Davidson never married and spent much of her life living with two other women. Perhaps it is not surprising that she also encouraged women to embrace new opportunities through travel without male escorts as well. Amanda Hess, "Overlooked No More: Lillias Campbell Davidson, an Early Advocate for Women's Cycling," *New York Times*, August 3, 2018.
63. Lillias Campbell Davidson, *Hints to Lady Travelers: At Home and Abroad* (London: Elliott and Thompson Limited, 2011; originally published by Iliffe and Son, 1889), 7. For more on women's etiquette books from this time period, see Hickey, *Breaking the Gender Code*, 15–20.
64. Davidson, *Hints to Lady Travelers*, 7.
65. Davidson, *Hints to Lady Travelers*, 82.

66. Davidson, *Hints to Lady Travelers*, 83.
67. Davidson, *Hints to Lady Travelers*, 83.
68. "Greatest Novelty in Years!," *Harper's Weekly*, August 25, 1894.
69. Thin "envelope purses" were popular in the 1910s, and the rectangular-shaped "clutch" was perhaps the most popular style in the 1930s.
70. Advertisement 17, "Purse with Vanity Box," *The Youth's Companion*, October 19, 1916, 90, 42, 610.
71. Salvatore Picciotto, Vanity case, Google Patent, US 1518103 A, March 27, 1924.
72. In the Great Depression, when more Americans were desperate for money, concerns about the security of purses would only continue to grow.
73. "A Serious Defect," *New York Observer and Chronicle,* December 27, 1894, 72, 52.
74. "Plenty of Pockets in Suffragette Suit," *New York Times*, October 10, 1910.
75. Charlotte Perkins Gilman, "Male Attire," *New York Times*, March 5, 1905.
76. Gilman's character "never had dreamed of how it felt to have pockets. Behind her newspaper she let her consciousness… rove from pocket to pocket, realizing the armored assurance of having all those things at hand, instantly get-at-able, ready to meet emergencies. The cigar case gave her a warm feeling of comfort—it was full; the firmly held fountain pen, safe unless she stood on her head; the keys, pencils, letters, documents, notebook, checkbook, bill folder—all at once, with a deep rushing sense of power and pride, she felt what she had never felt before in all her life—the possession of money, of her own earned money—hers to give or to withhold, not to beg for, tease for, wheedle for—hers."
77. Charlotte Perkins Gilman, *Herland*, see Chapter 7, Project Gutenberg, https://www.gutenberg.org/files/32/32-h/32-h.htm, accessed February 9, 2025.
78. "A Serious Defect," 72, 52.
79. "A Serious Defect," 52. Italics mine.
80. "Women trust their memory," *Chicago Defender,* June 28, 1913, 8.
81. "Ground for much speculation," *Chicago Daily Tribune*, June 27, 1897, 26.
82. "Ground for much speculation," *Chicago Daily Tribune*, June 27, 1897, 26.
83. "Ground for much speculation," *Chicago Daily Tribune*, June 27, 1897, 26.
84. I have consulted several hundred articles in the archives of periodicals such as *Women's Wear Daily*, *Vogue*, but especially urban periodicals like *Harper's Weekly*, *The New York Times*, *The New York Tribune*, *The Los Angeles Times*, as well as Black-owned papers like *The New Amsterdam News*, *The Chicago Defender*, and many smaller newspapers available through the Chronicling America database.
85. "Honesty Brings Life Position," *The Chicago Defender*, July 31, 1909, 2.
86. Guilfoyle, "Street-Rats and Gutter-Snipes: Child Pickpockets and Street Culture in New York City, 1850–1900," *Journal of Social History* 37, no. 4 (Summer 2004), 859.
87. Guilfoyle, "Street-Rats and Gutter-Snipes," 859. According to the *Oxford English Dictionary*, the phrase "moll-buzzer" is a compound noun that dates to the 1850s. The term refers to a thief who targets women's handbags and pockets. https://www.oed.com/dictionary/moll-buzzer_n?tab=factsheet#36188918, accessed December 28, 2023.
88. Guilfoyle, "Street-Rats and Gutter-Snipes," 876.
89. "Went for Her Purse," *The Atlanta Constitution*, December 6, 1894, 5.
90. W. E. B. Du Bois, "The Negro Criminal" and "The Philadelphia Negro" (Philadelphia: University of Pennsylvania Press, 1899), 263.
91. "Attacks on White Women," *The Chicago Defender*, September 29, 1919, 18.
92. "White Man, Blackened Face, Snatches Purse," *The Chicago Defender*, October 3, 1914, 6.
93. "Umbrella Routs a Footpad," *The Chicago Defender*, January 27, 1912, 6.

94. Henry Angelino, "Shoplifting: A Critical Review," *The Midwest Sociologist* 15, no. 2 (Spring 1953): 18.
95. "St. Louis Pickpockets Steal Purses from Stores' Customers," *Women's Wear Daily* 27, no. 93, October 22, 1923, 25. For more on women and shopping in the nineteenth and early twentieth centuries, see Remus, *A Shopper's Paradise*. On shoplifting, see Elaine S. Abelson, *When Ladies Go A-Thieving: Middle Class Shoplifters in the Victorian Department Store* (New York: Oxford University Press, 1989).

CHAPTER 3

1. Leon Stein, *The Triangle Fire* (New York: A. Carroll and Graf/Quicksilver Books, 1962), 201.
2. Letter to Michael and Hugh Owens from Pauline Newman, May 1951, International Ladies' Garment Workers' Union Archives, Cornell University, Kheel Center for Labor-Management Documentation and Archives, Ithaca, NY, https://trianglefire.ilr.cornell.edu/primary/letters/PaulineNewman.html, accessed December 5, 2024.
3. Miriam Finn Scott, "The Factory Girl's Danger," *The Outlook: An Illustrated Weekly Journal of Current Life*, April 15, 1911, 817.
4. "List of Victims," https://trianglefire.ilr.cornell.edu/victimsWitnesses/victimsList.html, accessed June 28, 2020.
5. Claire Wilcox, *A Century of Bags: Icons of Style in the Twentieth Century* (New York: Chartwell Books, 1997), 16–18.
6. "Continues with Female Workers' Testimony," December 11–12, 1911, Vol. 1, Sec. 6, 552. Decades later, Mary Domsky-Abrams told Leon Stein that in the trial, "The bosses lawyers made all sorts of excuses, attempting to defend the employers for keeping the door locked, in the face of another girl's testimony that even when the fire already had broken out, and she was among the first to reach the elevator, she had to show the watchman the contents of her pocketbook...." Mary Domsky-Abrams, "My Reminiscences of the Fire," Leon Stein interviews, date unknown. *Remembering the 1911 Triangle Shirtwaist Fire*, Cornell University, https://trianglefire.ilr.cornell.edu.
7. Miriam Finn Scott's article stated Becky's age as 18. However, victim lists published elsewhere note that she was just 16 at the time of her death. Scott, "The Factory Girl's Danger," 817.
8. For examples of previous scholarship on working women in turn-of-the-century America, see Alice Kessler-Harris, *Out to Work: A History of Wage-Earning Women in the United States* (New York: Oxford University Press, 1982); Kathy Peiss, *Working Women and Leisure in Turn-of-the-Century New York* (Philadelphia: Temple University Press, 1986); Joanne Meyerowitz, *Women Adrift: Independent Wage Earners in Chicago, 1880–1930* (Chicago: University of Chicago, 1988); Annalise Orleck, *Women and Working-Class Politics in the United States, 1900–1965* (Chapel Hill: University of North Carolina Press, 1995); Nan Enstad, *Ladies of Labor, Girls of Adventure* (New York: Columbia University Press, 1999). For information on working women as labor activists during this time, see Lara Vapnek, *Breadwinners: Working Women and Economic Independence, 1865–1920* (Urbana: University of Illinois Press, 2009), and Heather Mayer, *Beyond the Rebel Girl: Women and the Industrial Workers of the World in the Pacific Northwest, 1905–1924* (Corvallis: Oregon State University Press, 2018). For information about urban women in mid- to late-nineteenth-century New York City, see Mona Domosh, "'The New York Woman': A Fashionable Moral Geography," *Environment and Planning D: Society and Space*, 19 (2001), 573–592.
9. Here I take inspiration from Robin D. G. Kelley's study of the importance of dressing up for Black working class laborers in the 1930s and 1940s. "'We Are Not What We Seem:'

Rethinking Black Working Class Opposition in the Jim Crow South," *Journal of American History* 80, no. 1 (June 1993): 75–112.
10. Georgina Hickey, *Breaking the Gender Code: Women and Urban Public Space in the Twentieth-Century United States* (Austin: University of Texas Press, 2023), 15.
11. Orleck, *Common Sense and a Little Fire*, 218.
12. Lauren C. Santangelo, *Suffrage and the City: New York Women Battle for the Ballot* (New York: Oxford University Press, 2019), 3, 14.
13. U.S. Department of Labor, Bureau of Labor Statistics, *Regularity of Employment in the Women's Ready-to-Wear Garment Industries*, Bulletin 183 (Washington, DC: Government Printing Office, 1915), 22.
14. *Regularity of Employment in the Women's Ready-to-Wear Garment Industries*, 26.
15. In 1924, the Johnson-Reed Immigration Act slowed the tide of these unwanted immigrants, excluding Asian immigrants altogether.
16. For a nuanced discussion of treating in turn-of-the-century New York City, see Kathy Peiss's *Cheap Amusements* and Elizabeth Alice Clement, *Love for Sale: Courting, Treating, and Prostitution in New York City, 1900–1945* (Chapel Hill: University of North Carolina Press, 2006).
17. Enstad, *Ladies of Labor, Girls of Adventure*, 9.
18. Letter from Pauline M. Newman to Michael and Hugh Owens, May 1951, International Ladies' Garment Workers' Union Archives, Cornell University, Kheel Center for Labor-Management Documentation and Archives, Ithaca, NY, https://trianglefire.ilr.cornell.edu/primary/letters/PaulineNewman.html, accessed December 5, 2024; Clare Lemlich, "Life in the Shop," cited by Leon Stein, ed., *Out of the Sweatshop: The Struggle for Industrial Democracy* (New York: Quadrangle/New Times Book Company, 1977).
19. Garment worker and labor activist Clara Lemlich noted that the workers were unlikely to be able to spend more than 50 cents on a hat. Lemlich, "Why the Waistmakers Strike," *New York Evening Journal*, November 28, 1909.
20. Perry Mason also sought to appeal to new customers by advertising separate compartments for coins and bills and free monogramming. The monogramming would personalize a pocketbook and make it easier to recover lost or stolen bags. "Pocketbooks and Bags," *The Youth's Companion*, January 20, 1910, 84, 3.
21. Nan Enstad, *Ladies of Labor, Girls of Adventure* (New York: Columbia University Press, 1999). These findings confirm Kathy Peiss's earlier study that argued that, for working-class women, "dress became a cultural terrain of pleasure, expressiveness, romance and autonomy." Peiss, *Cheap Amusements*, 64.
22. Enstad, *Ladies of Labor, Girls of Adventure*, 6.
23. Enstad, *Ladies of Labor, Girls of Adventure*, 3–4.
24. Lillian D. Wald, *The House on Henry Street* (New York: Henry, Holt, and Co., 1915), 190.
25. Jane Addams, *The Spirit of the Youth and the City Streets* (New York: Macmillan and Co., 1909).
26. Jane Addams, *Twenty Years at Hull House* (New York: Macmillan and Co., 1911), 267–268.
27. For context, 12 dollars in 1911 was roughly equivalent to 390 dollars in 2025. "Survivor Oral Histories," interview with Pauline Pepe, unidentified interviewer, March 19, 1986, International Ladies' Garment Workers' Union, Cornell University, Archives at the Kheel Center for Labor-Management Documentation and Archives, Ithaca, NY.
28. "Survivor Oral Histories," Pepe, 1986.
29. As historian Rob Schorman has argued, "[C]lothing provided a means of exerting control over personal space in a time of flux and turmoil, of expressing one's attitude toward others

and asserting one's place within society, of establishing both physical and metaphorical boundaries against perceived threats." *Selling Style: Clothing and Social Change at the Turn of the Century* (Philadelphia: University of Pennsylvania Press, 2003), 124.
30. Leon Stein, "Complete Transcript of Triangle Fire," library notes, 65. http://digitalcommons.ilr.cornell.edu/triangletrans/18, accessed June 28, 2020.
31. Stein, *The Triangle Fire*, 193–194.
32. Stein, *The Triangle Fire*, 109.
33. For a nuanced discussion of the significance of several widely published photographs taken at the scene of the fire, see Ellen Wiley Todd, "Photojournalism, Visual Culture, and the Triangle Shirtwaist Fire," *Labor: Studies in Working Class History of the Americas* 2, no. 2 (Summer 2005), 9–27.
34. Stein, *The Triangle Fire*, 86.
35. Stein, *The Triangle Fire*, 86–87.
36. "Razor strap" may have referred to a razor strop, a strip of leather used to polish straight razors. Stein, *The Triangle Fire*, 87.
37. Stein, *The Triangle Fire*, 87.
38. Stein, *The Triangle Fire*, 92.
39. Stein, *The Triangle Fire*, 88. Presumably, the reporter is referring to seeing a skull and cross bones.
40. The remaining part of the transcript was preserved and transcribed through a cooperative effort between the New York County Lawyer's Association and the Kheel Center at Cornell University.
41. Testimony of Mary Bucelli (A. Mary Cisco), "Testimony by Factory Workers," adjourned to December 11, 1911, Vol. 1, Sec. 4, 331, https://ecommons.cornell.edu/items/1bda7972-3186-47 5b-9b4e-4edbf3cf30b5.
42. Domsky-Abrams, "My Reminiscences of the Fire."
43. Bucelli, "Testimony by Factory Workers," Vol. 1, Sec. 4, 337; also in that same testimony of female workers, statements of machine operator and witness Anna Gullo, Vol. 1, Sec. 5, 364–365, and "Opening Statement by Mr. Bostwick for the People," Vol. 1, Sec. 1, 12. Refer additionally to Letter from Pauline M. Newman to Michael and Hugh Owens, May 1951, 6036/008, 17. See also David von Drehle, *Triangle: The Fire That Changed America* (New York: Grove Street Press, 2003), 144.
44. von Drehle, *Triangle*, 140. See also Domsky-Abrams, "My Reminiscences of the Fire."
45. Bucelli, "Testimony by Factory Workers," Vol. 1, Sec. 4, 336.
46. "Testimony by Factory Workers," and sworn testimony by Max Harris, co-defendant/owner, Vol. 3, Sec. 7, 1853; Stein, *The Triangle Fire*, 23–24.
47. Untitled [Notice of fire], *Ladies' Garment Worker,* April 1911. *Remembering the 1911 Triangle Factory Fire*, Cornell University, https://trianglefire.ilr.cornell.edu/primary/index.html.
48. Clara Lemlich, "Why the Waistmakers Strike," *New York Evening Journal,* November 28, 1909.
49. "Transcripts of Criminal Trial against Factory Owners" and "Testimony by Female Workers" (see sworn statement of Yetta Lubitz), December 11, 1911, Vol. 1, Sec. 5, 431–445, https://ecommons.cornell.edu/items/6513709e-bd6e-43dd-9bb4-b477767c020b.
50. Orleck, *Common Sense and a Little Fire*, 32.
51. Orleck, *Common Sense and a Little Fire*, 66.
52. Orleck, *Common Sense and a Little Fire*, 310; Letter from Pauline M. Newman to Michael and Hugh Owens, May 1951, 6036/008.
53. Quoted in David Huyssen, *Progressive Inequality: Rich and Poor in New York, 1890–1920* (Cambridge, MA: Harvard University Press, 2014), 162.

54. Orleck, *Common Sense and a Little Fire*, 32–33.
55. Letter from Pauline M. Newman to Michael and Hugh Owens, May 1951, 6036/008.
56. It should be noted that Newman made these statements in a letter written in 1951, more than four decades later. Nonetheless, she was a staunch union activist who spent the rest of her life working for the International Ladies' Garment Workers' Union; these figures would have been part of her formative experiences as a worker and organizer. For more information on Newman, see Orleck's excellent book *Common Sense and a Little Fire*.
57. See "Testimony by Female Workers," Vol. 1, Sec. 5, 532. Years after the fire, Mary Domsky-Abrams told Leon Stein that on the day of the fire, she and her coworker Minnie Bornstein went "to the dressing room. Suddenly, she recalled she had left her purse on her machine and she wanted to go back and get it. I told her that we should get dressed over first, and she could pick up her purse on the way back." Domsky-Abrams, "My Reminiscences of the Fire."
58. "Complete Transcript of Triangle Fire," 1516, 1528, https://ecommons.cornell.edu/collections/8136d906-eb78-4ec3-a806-fb745b453f26. Italics mine.
59. "Continues with Female Workers' Testimony," December 11–12, 1911, Vol. 1, Sec. 6, 663; Stein, "Complete Transcript of Triangle Fire," library notes, 24 (reference from missing transcript p. 718).
60. In her prize-winning book *Domestic Work*, poet Natasha Trethewey imagines just such a moment for Black women in the South. In "Drapery Factory," set in 1956 Mississippi, the narrator explains, "She does remember the men / she worked for . . . Her lips tighten speaking / of quitting time when / the colored women filed out slowly / to have their purses checked, / the insides laid open and exposed / by the boss's hand. / But then she laughs / when she recalls the soiled Kotex / she saved, stuffed into a bag / in her purse" (St. Paul, MN: Graywolf Press, 2000).
61. "Testimony by Female Workers," and sworn testimony by Isaac Harris, co-defendant/owner, Vol. 3, Sec. 7, 1868.
62. "Testimony by Female Workers," and sworn testimony by Isaac Harris, co-defendant/owner, Vol. 3, Sec. 7, 1865.
63. "Human Hair Wigs, Waterfalls, Rats, Mice, Curls, Fronts & c. – How they are Made and all About Them," *The New York Times*, August 3, 1866, 8.
64. "Continues with Female Workers' Testimony," December 11–12, 1911, Vol. 1, Sec. 6, 553.
65. "Continues with Female Workers' Testimony," December 11–12, 1911, Vol. 1, Sec. 6, 550.
66. "Continues with Female Workers' Testimony," December 11–12, 1911, Vol. 1, Sec. 6, 551.
67. "Continues with Female Workers' Testimony," December 11–12, 1911, Vol. 1, Sec. 6, 663.
68. Stein, *The Triangle Fire*, 202. The transcript for this portion of the trial is unfortunately missing; thus, I have had to rely on Stein's description and quotations. He consulted the full transcript in the early 1960s.
69. Domsky-Abrams, "My Reminiscences of the Fire."
70. Domsky-Abrams, "My Reminiscences of the Fire."
71. Stein, *The Triangle Fire*, 199.
72. According to Sarah Deutsch, "[M]en and women shared few spaces on equal terms." *Women and the City: Gender, Space, and Power in Boston, 1879–1940* (New York: Oxford University Press, 2000), 24.
73. Deutsch, *Women and the City*, 12; Santangelo, *Suffrage and the City*, 8–10. For more information on how women shaped and negotiated city spaces at this time, see Daphne Spain, *How Women Saved the City* (Minneapolis: University of Minnesota Press, 2001); Jessica

Ellen Sewell, *Women and the Everyday City: Public Space in San Francisco, 1890–1915* (Minneapolis: University of Minnesota Press, 2011); and Hickey, *Breaking the Gender Code*.
74. See Clement, *Love for Sale*.
75. For more information, see Joanne Meyerowitz, *Women Adrift*.
76. Emma supposedly closed her letters to Dreiser by signing, "I remain your / Sister Emma." Dreiser himself had left his family to work in Chicago at the age of 15. By contrast, Emma left her lover in Chicago for a married man named L. A. Hopkins, with whom she ran away to Canada before eloping. Hopkins, as it turns out, brought shame on the couple by stealing thousands from his employer. Theodore Dreiser, *Sister Carrie* (Mineola, NY: Dover Publications, 2004), iv, 1–2; first published New York: Doubleday, 1900.
77. Dreiser, *Sister Carrie*, 3.
78. Dreiser, *Sister Carrie*, 2.
79. Barbara Y. Welke, "When All the Women Were White, and All the Blacks Were Men: Gender, Class, Race, and the Road to *Plessy*, 1855–1914," *Law and History Review* 13, no. 2 (Autumn 1995), 269–271.
80. See Hickey, *Breaking the Gender Code*, 35–37.
81. Dreiser, *Sister Carrie*, 4.
82. Dreiser, *Sister Carrie*, 5.
83. Dreiser, *Sister Carrie*, 7.
84. As described by Joanne Meyerowitz, Carrie's story parallels that of a real woman traveling to Chicago from Emporia, Kansas, who recalled clutching her purse "tightly in one hand, and my bag in the other, shaking my head at redcaps." Meyerowitz, *Women Adrift*, 22.
85. Dreiser, *Sister Carrie*, 7.
86. Dreiser, *Sister Carrie*, 51.
87. According to historian Ann Douglass, in 1920, there were close to 20,000 working actresses; in 1870, there had been only 780. Ann Douglass, *Terrible Honesty: Mongrel Manhattan in the 1920s* (Farrar, Straus, and Giroux, 1996), 380.
88. Rennold Wolf, "The Highest Salaried Actress in America," *Green Book Magazine*, July 1912, 8, 782.
89. Dreiser, *Sister Carrie*, 319.

CHAPTER 4

1. In the 15 years between 1912 and 1927, the number of Americans who had electricity in their homes increased by nearly 50 percent. Vinikas, *Soft Soap, Hard Sell: American Hygiene in an Age of Advertisement* (Ames: Iowa State University Press, 1992), 23.
2. For example, *Ladies Home Journal*, founded in 1883, became the first magazine to have 1 million subscribers in 1903. https://www.desmoinesregister.com/story/money/business/2014/04/24/meredith-earnings-fall-37-percent/8089633/, accessed November 1, 2023.
3. Theodore Peterson, *Magazines for the Twentieth Century*, 2nd ed. (Urbana: University of Illinois Press, 1964), 58–59; cited by Vinikas, *Soft Soap, Hard Sell*, 9.
4. Vinikas, *Soft Soap, Hard Sell*, 55.
5. Vinikas, *Soft Soap, Hard Sell*, xi.
6. Vinikas, *Soft Soap, Hard Sell*, xii.
7. William Leach, *Land of Desire: Merchants, Power, and the Rise of a New American Culture* (New York: Vintage Books, 1993), 112. In *Selling Mrs. Consumer*, published in 1929, Christine Frederick argued that American women held 80 to 90 percent of the purchasing power in American households. Frederick, *Selling Mrs. Consumer* (New York: The Business Bourse, 1929), 12–13. Cited by Emily Remus, *A Shoppers' Paradise: How the Ladies of Chicago*

Claimed Power and Pleasure in the New Downtown (Cambridge, MA: Harvard University Press, 2019), 8. Though Frederick was likely focused on white women, according to Lizabeth Cohen, Black women also held a great deal of purchasing power. Cohen, *A Consumer's Republic: The Politics of Mass Consumption in Postwar America* (New York: Vintage Books, 2003), 50, 147.

8. Because these figures do not include fabric or metal (i.e., mesh) bags, they undercount the total number of purse factories and pursemakers. Julius Klein, Manufacturers, by Specified Industries, Statistical Abstract of the United States, Department of Commerce, 1925 edition (published 1926), Part 12, 760, no. 727, https://www.census.gov/library/publications/1926/compendia/statab/48ed.html, accessed July 28, 2024.

According to census.gov, the Statistical Abstract of the United States was published between 1878 and 2012 and was "the authoritative and comprehensive summary of statistics on the social, political, and economic organization of the United States." Yet, consistently tracking the growth of the purse industry across multiple decades is challenging. For some years, the data are missing altogether and in others the categories of data collected varied from year to year. For example, the Statistical Abstract of the United States published in 1910 tracked the sale of all pocketbooks in 1880, 1890, 1900, and 1905 but only leather pocketbooks in 1914, 1919, 1921, and 1923. Statistical Abstract of the United States, Department of Commerce, 1910 edition (published 1911), Part 3, 190, no. 110, https://www.census.gov/library/publications/1911/compendia/statab/33ed.html, accessed July 28, 2024.

9. Vinikas cites "The People as Consumers," a chapter in the 1933 work *Recent Social Trends in the United States*, which was commissioned by President Hoover in 1929 (New York: McGraw-Hill, 1933), 898, 900.

10. *Recent Social Trends in the United States*, 898.

11. Roseann Mandziuk, "'Ending Women's Greatest Hygienic Mistake': Modernity and the Mortification of Menstruation in Kotex Advertising, 1921–1926," *Women's Studies Quarterly* 38, no. 3 (Fall/Winter 2010), 45.

12. Vinikas, *Soft Soap, Hard Sell*, 56.

13. On the Tulsa Race Massacre of 1921, see Randy Krehbiel, *Tulsa, 1921: Reporting on a Massacre* (Norman: University of Oklahoma Press, 2019); James S. Hirsch, *Riot and Remembrance: The Tulsa Race War and Its Legacy* (New York: Houghton Mifflin, Co., 2001); and Tim Madigan, *The Burning: Massacre, Destruction, and the Tulsa Race Riot of 1921* (New York: St. Martin's Press, 2003). For a popular telling of the Great Migration, see Isabel Wilkerson, *The Warmth of Other Suns* (New York: Random House, 2010).

14. See Annie Menzel's illuminating discussion of how state public health boards used the Sheppard Towner Act to surveil and discipline Black midwives through mandatory bag inspections. Menzel, "The Midwife's Bag, or the Objects of Black Infant Mortality," *Signs: Journal of Women in Culture and Society* 46, no. 2 (2021): 283.

15. Andrea Tone, *Devices and Desires: A History of Contraceptives in America* (New York: Hill and Wang, 2001), 122. For more on the history of the Miss America Pageant, see Amy Argetsinger, *There She Was: The Secret History of Miss America* (New York: Simon and Schuster, 2021).

16. Lara Freidenfelds, *The Modern Period: Menstruation in Twentieth Century America* (Baltimore: Johns Hopkins University Press, 2009), 30.

17. See Chapter 1 of Courtney Q. Shah's *Sex Ed, Segregated* (Rochester, NY: University of Rochester Press, 2015).

18. These booklets were vague and primarily intended to promote their products to American, Canadian, and Australian households in the 1930s. Marie Pauline Callender, "Marjorie

May's Twelfth Birthday," Museum of Menstruation, http://www.mum.org/marma38.htm, accessed November 3, 2023.
19. Correspondence, Series II, Margaret Sanger Papers, Sophia Smith Collection and Smith College Archives. For an example, see April 1936, Folder 002681-011-0198.
20. "In its hiddenness, especially from men," Freidenfelds argues, "menstruation was treated as part of this women's domain of reproductive knowledge and labor." *The Modern Period*, 21.
21. Onnie Lee Logan as told to Katherine Clark, *Motherwit* (New York: E.P. Dutton, 1989), 51.
22. Logan, *Motherwit*, 51.
23. Logan, *Motherwit*, 51.
24. Freidenfelds, *Modern Period*, 30.
25. Freidenfelds, *Modern Period*, 23.
26. Freidenfelds, *Modern Period*, 23.
27. Sociologist Henry Angelino was skeptical of such claims and suggested this theory "warrant[s] more study." Angelino, "Shoplifting: A Critical Review," *The Midwest Sociologist* 15, no. 2 (Spring 1953): 18–19.
28. Freidenfelds, *Modern Period*, 30–31.
29. Freidenfelds, *Modern Period*, 35.
30. Freidenfelds, *Modern Period*, 31.
31. Advertisement, Cellucotton Products, Co., *Vogue* 60, no. 6, September 15, 1922, 111.
32. The first advertisement for Kotex appears to have been published in a January 1921 issue of *Good Housekeeping*. Purchasing these products through the mail was also an option.
33. "Kotex, How War Nurses Found a New Use for Cellucotton," *Cosmopolitan* 70, no. 2, February 1921, 117. For more information on the first five years of Kotex advertisements in *Good Housekeeping*, see Mandziuk, "Ending Women's Greatest Hygienic Mistake," 46.
34. An early advertisement from 1921 assured readers that they could "send us sixty-five cents and we will send you one box of a dozen Kotex in plain wrapper." Kotex pads could also be purchased from "Kotex cabinets," which effectively were vending machines installed in women's restrooms that ejected one pad for 10 cents. "Kotex, At stores and shops that cater to women," *Ladies Home Journal* 38, no. 1, January 1921, 77. "Kotex, How War Nurses Found a New Use for Cellucotton," *Cosmopolitan* 70, no. 2, February 1921, 117.
35. Three years later, Kotex began selling prewrapped boxes, eliminating the need for store employees to wrap the boxes in front of customers. Freidenfelds, *Modern Period*, 137.
36. Freidenfelds, *Modern Period*, 136–137.
37. Freidenfelds, *Modern Period*, 137.
38. "Kotex," *Vogue*, September 15, 1922, 111.
39. Mandziuk, "Ending Women's Greatest Hygienic Mistake," 47.
40. "Kotex," *Ladies Home Journal*, March 1923, 168.
41. See Advertisement, Cellucotton Products, Co., *Vogue* 60, no. 6, September 15, 1922, 111. For further discussion, see Mandziuk, "Ending Women's Greatest Hygienic Mistake," 42–62.
42. Kat Eschner, "The Surprising History of Kotex Pads," *Smithsonian Magazine*, August 11, 2017, https://www.smithsonianmag.com/innovation/surprising-origins-kotex-pads-180964466/#:~:text=For%20Kotex%2C%20the%20first%2Dever,way%20women%20dealt%20with%20menstruation, accessed August 6, 2024.
43. Freidenfelds, *The Modern Period*, 43; Rebecca Rego Barry, "Was Lydia E. Pinkham the Queen of Quackery?," *JSTOR Daily*, November 17, 2022, https://daily.jstor.org/was-lydia-e-pinkham-the-queen-of-quackery/, accessed November 3, 2023.
44. Advertisement, Lydia E. Pinkham Medicine Co., *Red Book Illustrated* 2, no. 5, March 1904, 622. Despite the fact that Lydia Pinkham had been dead since 1883, advertisements published

several times in 1904 and 1905 encouraged women to write directly to her, as a "woman whose experience with woman's diseases covers a great many years." Rather than relying on the endorsements of doctors, Pinkham's company relied on women to promote their product. In 1903, *Red Book Illustrated* printed an ad for Pinkham's compound, claiming it was endorsed by a female lecturer for the Women's Christian Temperance Union. Advertisement, "Rev. Maguerite St. Omer Briggs," *Red Book Illustrated* 2, no. 1, November 1903, 140. Advertisement, "Household Cares," *Red Book Illustrated* 3, no. 4, August 1904, 562. Advertisement, "STOP! WOMEN! And Consider the All-Important Fact," Lydia E. Pinkham Medicine Co., *Red Book Magazine* 6, no. 1, November 1905, 164. See also Advertisement, "STOP! WOMEN! And Consider the All-Important Fact," Lydia E. Pinkham Medicine Co., *Red Book Magazine* 5, no. 2, June 1905, 296.

45. Advertisement, "Tired Mothers," *Red Book* 3, no. 6, October 1904, 840.
46. "Are You Well and Strong?," Lydia Pinkham's Vegetable Compound, *Indianapolis Times*, November 14, 1930, 22.
47. "Carry Your Medicine in Your Handbag," *Maryland Independent*, November 28, 1930, 3; "Carry Your Medicine in Your Handbag," *Maryland Independent*, September 5, 1930, 7; and *The Washington Times*, February 20, 1931, 12. For identical or similar ads in other small newspapers published between 1930 and 1931, see also the *New Britain Herald*, *The Midland Journal*, *The Ronan Pioneer*, *The Frontier*, *The Coolidge Examiner*, *The Bismarck Tribune*, *The Waterbury Democrat*, *The Ely Miner*, *White Bluffs Spokesman*, and more.
48. "Cramps Almost Killed Me," *The Bismarck Tribune*, October 21, 1931, 8.
49. Interestingly, the previous illustration of floating hands dropping a box of tablets into an open purse was replaced by a far more personalized headshot of a woman in severe pain.
50. "How Do Sportswomen Manage?," *The Washington Times*, January 25, 1932.
51. "MUM," *Ladies Home Journal* 47, no. 9, September 1930, 115.
52. "A Minute Alone . . ." *Ladies Home Journal* 48, no. 9, September 1931, 76.
53. The line "Seal up your lips and give no words but mum" appears in Shakespeare's *King Henry VI, Part 2*, published in the sixteenth century.
54. Advertisement 33, "Trademarks Registered," *American Druggist and Pharmaceutical Record*, December 26, 1910, G26.
55. "Midol a New Analgesic Preparation," *American Druggist and Pharmaceutical Record*, December 1, 1911, 59, 9, C58.
56. Advertisement-30, no title, *American Druggist and Pharmaceutical Record*, April 1, 1922, 70, 4; Display Ad-20, "Again?" *Chicago Daily Tribune*, December 3, 1929, 22.
57. "Again?" *Chicago Daily Tribune*, December 3, 1929, 22.
58. Display Ad-20, "Again?" *Chicago Daily Tribune*, December 3, 1929, 22. Advertisements, Midol Tablets, Sears, Roebuck and Co. Catalogue, Fall 1935, 780; 1936, 716; Fall 1937, 826; Fall 1938, 764; Spring 1939, 676; Fall 1939, 902.
59. Advertisements, Kurb Tablets, *Hearst's International/Cosmopolitan*, September 1937, 130; October 1937, 136; November 1937, 86; May 1958, 151; June 1938, 145; August 1938, 123; September 1938, 129; October 1938, 129; November 1938.
60. "For Women's Trying Days," *Cosmopolitan*, June 1938, 145.
61. Advertisement, Per-stik, *Ladies Home Journal* 52, no. 6, June 1935, 118. See also Advertisement, Per-stik, *Ladies Home Journal* 51, no. 8, August 1934, 87.
62. "Discoveries in Beauty," *Vogue*, November 15, 1935, 88.
63. "A Minute Alone . . ." *Ladies Home Journal* 48, no. 9, September 1931, 76.
64. Vinikas, *Soft Soap, Hard Sell*, xvi; Peiss, *Hope in a Jar*, 7.
65. Advertisement, Hinze Ambrosia, Inc., *Good Housekeeping* 92, no. 4, April 1932, 125.

66. Advertisement, *Red Book Magazine* 16, no. 5, March 1911, 991.
67. "The use of cosmetics," Vincent Vinikas argues, "served to modify the recent changes in women's status in America; in applying them, women could both acknowledge recent alterations in gender identity and mute the more threatening ambiguities that accompanied the emergence of the New Woman." Vinikas, *Soft Soap, Hard Sell*, 46. In *Manliness and Civilization*, Gail Bederman makes a similar argument about growing fears that men were turning soft and becoming more womanlike.
68. Joanne Meyerowitz, *Women Adrift: Independent Wage Earners in Chicago, 1880–1930* (Chicago: University of Chicago, 1988), 5; Georgina Hickey, *Breaking the Gender Code: Women and Urban Public Space in the Twentieth-Century United States* (Austin: University of Texas Press, 2023), 15.
69. The census results from 1920 proved that, for the first time, the majority of Americans (54 percent) lived in urban (defined as having a population of 2,500 people or more) instead of rural areas. Women had uniformly been excluded from jury service in America until 1870, when Wyoming became the first territory to allow women to serve as jurors. In 1898, Utah became the first state to institute a law preserving a woman's right to serve on a jury. After the passage of the Nineteenth Amendment in 1920, many states began to seat women on juries. However, it was not until 1975 that the Supreme Court enshrined women's constitutional right to serve on juries. Though the majority of women who worked outside the home were unmarried in 1920, married women constituted 20 percent of the workforce. Important differences across race should be noted. Black women had always worked outside the home in larger numbers than white women. Women of all races contributed mightily to the family's overall income, even if they were not being paid a living wage. United States Census, History, https://www.census.gov/history/www/programs/geography/urban_and_rural_areas.html, accessed November 11, 2023; Joanna Grossman, "Women's Jury Service: Right of Citizenship or Privilege of Difference," *Stanford Law Review* 46, no. 5 (May 1994): 1132–1136. See also Sarah Deutsch, *Women and the City: Gender, Space, and Power in Boston, 1879–1940* (New York: Oxford University Press, 2000); Claudia Goldin, "The Work and Wages of Single Women, 1870–1920," *Journal of Economic History* 40, no. 1 (March 1980): 81–83.
70. Vinikas, *Soft Soap, Hard Sell*, 57.
71. Peiss, *Hope in a Jar*, 6–7.
72. Peiss, *Hope in a Jar*, 5.
73. Harry Burke, "Women Cigarette Fiends," *Ladies Home Journal* 39, no. 6, June 1922, 19.
74. In the early 1920s, a new smoking shop and lounge aimed exclusively at women opened on East Fifty-fourth Street in New York City. Claiming to the be the first of its kind in America, the shop sold "tobacco handbags, containing pipe, tobacco pouch, cigarette case, purse and, of course, mirror and powder." Burke, "Women Cigarette Fiends," 132.
75. "Smoke, do you?," *The Evening Star*, August 1, 1922, 11.
76. The fashion trade journal *Women's Wear Daily* began publication in 1910 and is still in publication at the time of this writing. Robert Friedel, *Zipper: An Exploration in Novelty* (New York: W.W. Norton and Co., 1994). See Chapter 1, "Witty Inventions and Thinking Men," 1–25. "Handbags," *Women's Wear Daily* 30, no. 96, April 24, 1925, 36; "Handbags," *Women's Wear Daily* 30, no. 120, May 22, 1925, 36; "Omaha Shops Stress Bags, Zipper Type Presented," *Women's Wear Daily*, September 18, 1925, 34.
77. Isabel Sheldon, "The Shopper's Notebook: Tricky Handbag with Dial Offers you Quick Smoke," *Los Angeles Times*, September 2, 1935, A6.
78. Isabel Sheldon, "The Shopper's Notebook," *Los Angeles Times*, August 2, 1937.

79. "Handbags: Bags Demand Elsewhere," *Women's Wear Daily* 31, no. 38, August 14, 1925, 36; "Handbags," *Women's Wear Daily* 30, no. 120, May 22, 1925, 36.
80. Advertisement, Sears, Roebuck and Co., *Good Housekeeping* 89, note 6, December 1929, 220.
81. Amos Parrish, "What's in Fashion Now," *Los Angeles Times*, March 7, 1934, 6.
82. Advertisement, Ronson, *Cosmopolitan* 87, no. 5, November 1929, 140.
83. *Essence* was not established until 1970. For more information, see Chapter 1, "Scattered Pages," of Noliwe M. Rooks, *Ladies Pages: African American Women's Magazines and the Culture That Made Them* (New Brunswick, NJ: Rutgers University Press, 2004), 4.
84. I was unable to locate any advertisements for Kotex products in *Half-Century Magazine*, though Kotex had only been advertising for the last four years of the magazine's circulation. Internet Archive, *Half-Century Magazine*, https://archive.org/details/pub_half-century-magazine?query=kotex&sin=TXT&sort=date, accessed November 11, 2023. *Jet Magazine*, aimed at both Black men and women, would not begin publication until 1951.
85. Display Ad, "Wood's Cut Rate," *The Philadelphia Tribune*, July 21, 1932, 3.
86. Display Ad, "Very Special! Kotex," *New Journal and Guide*, January 20, 1934, 10.
87. Display Ad, "The Standard Toilet Goods," *Atlanta World*, January 13, 1932, 3. A search for the term "Kotex" in the Proquest Black historical newspaper database, between the years 1920 and 1940, produced eighty-six advertisements. Almost all of them were small advertisements for local pharmacies, drug stores, or dry goods stores. Lara Freidenfelds has argued that many Black women relied on homemade menstruation rags into the 1940s, yet these ads suggest that some middle-class Black women likely knew about (if not purchased) Kotex products in the 1930s. One advertisement in the *Los Angeles Sentinel* featured Kotex, Modess, Midol, douching products, and products that purported to aid with "marital hygiene" like "Cerene," which called itself "Madam's Best Friend." Display Ad 19, *Los Angeles Sentinel*, June 21, 1934, 7.
88. See Display Ad 50, *New Journal and Guide*, January 14, 1933, A11.
89. "Perhaps Your Doctor Has Already Told You About Tampax," *Evening Star*, August 23, 1936, 11. Italics in original.
90. "Perhaps Your Doctor Has Already Told You About TAMPAX," *Evening Star*, September 13, 1936, 11; Advertisement, TAMPAX, "You Have Given Us Unbelievable Freedom," *Good Housekeeping* 104, no. 4, April 1937, 190; Advertisement, TAMPAX, *Good Housekeeping* 104, no. 5, May 1937, 209; Advertisement, TAMPAX Inc., *Cosmopolitan*, July 1938, 105; Advertisement, TAMPAX Inc., *Red Book Magazine* 71, no. 4, August 1938, 93. Even when advertisements for Tampax did not explicitly mention purses, they were at least occasionally still shown in illustrations. See Advertisement, TAMPAX Inc., *Ladies Home Journal*, 53, no. 10, October 1936, 111.
91. Advertisement, Kotex, *Ladies Home Journal* 39, no. 5, May 1922, 145.
92. According to Freidenfelds, "[W]omen also hid menstruation from their sons." Mike Ozols recalled how his Eastern European–born mother Mara "never kept stuff like that [pads or tampons] around." *The Modern Period*, 18.
93. This advertisement showed the product in an open box. Advertisement, TAMPAX Inc., *Good Housekeeping* 108, no. 2, February 1939, 216.
94. "There's One Less Disadvantage in Being a WOMAN," *Evening Star*, September 13, 1936, 15; Advertisement, TAMPAX, "You Have Given Us Unbelievable Freedom," *Good Housekeeping* 104, no. 4, April 1937, 190.
95. "There's One Less Disadvantage in Being a WOMAN," 15.
96. "Bag," slang, *Oxford English Dictionary*, III.17, https://www.oed.com/dictionary/bag_n?tab=meaning_and_use#29734700, last revised July 2023, accessed December 21, 2023.

97. "Old bag," slang, *Oxford English Dictionary*, https://www.oed.com/dictionary/old-bag_n?tl=true, accessed December 18, 2023.
98. Hurston, "Story in Harlem Slang," *Zora Neale Hurston: Novels and Stories* (Library of America, 1995), 1006, https://storyoftheweek.loa.org/2012/03/story-in-harlem-slang.html, accessed December 7, 2024. Though the *OED* cites Hurston's text as a distinct usage of the term "pocketbook" as slang, it is somewhat ambiguous whether or not the character is referring to her actual purse or her genitalia.
99. Maya Angelou, *I Know Why the Caged Bird Sings* (New York: Random House, 2009), 72. "Pocketbook," noun, U.S. slang [esp. regional (Southern)] (euphemism): "the female external genitals; the vagina." *Oxford English Dictionary*, 3rd ed. (December 2007).
100. Angelou, *I Know Why the Caged Bird Sings*, 271.
101. Fibs appears to have been the first Kotex tampon produced to compete with Tampax. See Museum of Menstruation, http://www.mum.org/fibs.htm, accessed October 21, 2023.
102. See Hannah Carlson, *Pockets: An Intimate History of How We Keep Things Close* (Chapel Hill, NC: Algonquin Books, 2023), Chapter 4, "Pocket Sexism."
103. Freidenfelds, *The Modern Period*, 31. "Look, we didn't have book bags then," recalled Ida Smithson. "We carried our books in our arms. And no specific place to put your books or anything; you put them under your desk. You know, you had a chair, and in the chair, underneath, it had a rack where you put your books. The only way you could carry one was to carry it in your lunch bag! [Hearty laughter.] And I don't think you want to be carrying something like that in your lunch bag! Unless you carried it in your bosom, now. You know, we could always find somewhere!"
104. Sharra Louise Vostra, *Under Wraps: A History of Menstrual Hygiene Technology* (Lanham, MD: Lexington Books, 2008), 75–76.
105. J. David Hacker and Evan Roberts, "Fertility Decline in the United States 1850–1930: New Evidence from Complete Count Datasets," *Annales de Demographie Historique* 138, no. 2 (June 2019): 1.
106. Tone notes that "measuring use of contraceptives is inherently difficult, especially for an age when birth control was criminal, few people recorded their experiences with contraceptives, and medical marketing and opinion surveys of national practices did not exist." *Devices and Desires*, 79.
107. "Highlights," May 23, 1935. Birth Control: History, 1931–1953, Box 78, Folder 5, Planned Parenthood Federation of America Records, 1918–1974, Sophia Smith Collection, Smith College Library.
108. "Feminine Hygiene," Preface, 1933. Conferences, American Conference on Birth Control and National Recovery, Data, 1934. Stella Hanau, October 27, 1933, Box 83, Folder 13, Sophia Smith Collection, Smith College Library.
109. "Feminine Hygiene," 10, 1933. Conferences, American Conference on Birth Control and National Recovery, Data, 1934. Planned Parenthood Federation of America Records, 1918–1974, Sophia Smith Collection, Smith College Library.
110. In the winter of 1947, the company advertised folding douchebags with syringes for traveling, including the Ayvette White Plastic Syringe, which was "sturdy, long-wearing" and had the extra benefit of folding "up into purse-size while not in use." Albert Lasker, Advertising, Commercial Contraceptives, 1934–1943, Box 76, Folder 3, 56, Planned Parenthood Federation of America Records, 1918–1974, Sophia Smith Collection, Smith College Library.
111. Tone, *Devices and Desires*, xv.
112. Tone, *Devices and Desires*, 184.

113. This organization was previously called the American Birth Control League. Margaret Sanger was its "Honorary Chairman."
114. Letter to 747 Public Health Officials, Birth Control Federation of America, Inc., September 6, 1939, Public Health Mailings, 1919–1941, Box 99, Folder 11, 3, Planned Parenthood Federation of America Records, 1918–1974, Sophia Smith Collection, Smith College Library.
115. Public Health Officials, Wisconsin, Public Health Mailings, 1939–1941, Box 99, Folder 11, 128, Planned Parenthood Federation of America Records, 1918–1974, Sophia Smith Collection, Smith College Library.
116. For more information on the history of pockets, see Barbara Burman and Ariane Fennetaux, *The Pocket: A Hidden History of Women's Lives, 1660–1900* (New Haven, CT: Yale University Press, 2020), and Carlson, *Pockets*.
117. Einav Rabinovitch-Fox, *Dressed for Freedom: The Fashionable Politics of American Feminism* (Urbana: University of Illinois Press, 2021), 118.
118. Rabinovitch-Fox, *Dressed for Freedom*, 144–147.
119. The "auxiliary" part of the title was dropped in July 1943. "Army and Navy—WAAC to WAC," *TIME Magazine*, July 12, 1943, https://time.com/archive/6766228/army-navy-waac-to-wac/, accessed August 4, 2024. See also D'ann Campbell, "Women in Combat: The World War II Experience in the United States, Great Britain, Germany, and the Soviet Union," *Journal of Military History* 57 (April 1993): 303. See also https://www.army.mil/women/history/wac.html, accessed August 4, 2024.
120. Martha Hall, Belinda T. Orzada, and Dilia Lopez-Gydosh, "American Women's Wartime Dress: Sociocultural Ambiguity Regarding Women's Roles During World War II," *Journal of American Culture* 38, no. 3 (September 2015): 239.
121. For more information, see Leisa D. Meyer, *Creating G.I. Jane: Sexuality and Power in the Women's Army Corps during World War II* (New York: Columbia University Press, 1998); M. Michaela Hampf, "'Dykes' or 'Whores': Sexuality and the Women's Army Corps in the United States during World War II," *Women's Studies International Forum* (January/February 2004): 13–30; and Marilyn Hegarty, *Victory Girls, Khaki-Wackies, and Patriotutes: The Regulation of Female Sexuality during World War II* (New York: New York University Press, 2008).
122. For more information on the long struggle to create satisfactory uniforms for women in the WAC and WAVES, see Hannah S. Friesen, "Skirted Soldiers: An Account of American Women's Military Service during World War II," master's thesis (San Diego State University, 2021).
123. Amanda Mae Willey, "Fashioning Femininity for War: Material Culture and Gender Performance in the WAC and WAVES during World War II," PhD diss. (Kansas State University, 2015), 142.
124. Meyer, *Creating G.I. Jane*, 154.
125. Women's Army Corps Handbook, Chapter IX, "This Business of Being Feminine," Fort Des Moines, Iowa, 1944, 11, https://gateway.uncg.edu/islandora/object/wvhp%3A17412#page/15/mode/1up, accessed August 4, 2024.
126. Women's Army Corps Handbook, Chapter X, "What to Wear," Fort Des Moines, Iowa, 1944, 12. It is also worth noting that Japanese American women forced to relocate to internment camps and women held in concentration camps during the Holocaust who were of reproductive age would have lacked privacy and may not have had access to menstrual products. Women held captive and starved during the Holocaust may have at least temporarily lost the ability to menstruate (amenorrhea). For a remarkable story about how

Holocaust survivor Camilla Gottlieb managed to keep her purse filled with important documents through the Holocaust and for decades thereafter, see "Camilla's Purse," National Museum of American History, https://americanhistory.si.edu/explore/exhibitions/camillas-purse, accessed February 10, 2025.
127. Carlson, *Pockets*, 125–127.
128. Campbell, "Women in Combat," 303–304.
129. Women's Army Corps Handbook, Fort Des Moines, Iowa, 1944, 12.
130. Katherine Keene Papers, 1941–1977, MC 817 8.3.1, Box 5, Schlesinger Library, Harvard University, Cambridge, MA.
131. "Army and Navy - WAAC to WAC," July 12, 1943.
132. See "Fit as a Fiddle . . ." and "Off to Work We Go!" Kotex advertisements, *McCall's*, 1942. Cited by Friesen, "Skirted Soldiers," 88.
133. *Woman's Home Companion*, July 1953, 80. Physicians: Fees, Folder 00539, New York Academy of Medicine, 1933–November 1, 1965.
134. Pursettes Tampons, Museum of New Zealand, https://collections.tepapa.govt.nz/object/702372, accessed July 30, 2023.
135. Freidenfelds, *Modern Period*, 149.
136. Freidenfelds, *Modern Period*, 141.

CHAPTER 5

1. Rosa Parks with Jim Haskins, *My Story* (New York: Puffin Books, 1992), 79. Parks's biographer similarly notes that Parks "purposely dropped her purse and sat down in a seat in the whites-only section to pick it up." Jeanne Theoharis, *The Rebellious Life of Mrs. Rosa Parks* (Boston: Beacon Press, 2013), 61.
2. Parks also knew that it was important to dress the part of a pure, virtuous, and polished woman when she wore a dress, white gloves, and a black purse to her court hearing four days after her arrest. Parks arrived at court accompanied by E. D. Nixon, who once told her, "Women don't need to be nowhere but in the kitchen." Parks with Haskins, *My Story*, 82; Theoharis, *The Rebellious Life of Mrs. Rosa Parks*, 88. For more on the critical role Black women played in the Montgomery Bus Boycott movement, see JoAnn Robinson's memoir *The Bus Boycott and the Women Who Started It: The Memoir of Jo Ann Gibson Robinson* (Knoxville: University of Tennessee Press, 1987).
3. Parks with Haskins, *My Story*, 78–79.
4. In recent decades, scholars have highlighted Black women's disproportionate involvement in the Civil Rights Movement, noting that Black women constituted the foundation of the movement by filling the pews of church meetings and walking to work during bus boycotts. For excellent recent examples of such work, see Tanisha Ford, *Liberated Threads: Black Women, Style, and the Global Politics of Soul* (Chapel Hill: University of North Carolina Press, 2015); Theoharis, *The Rebellious Life of Mrs. Rosa Parks*; and Danielle McGuire, *At the Dark End of the Street: Black Women, Rape, and Resistance, A New History of the Civil Rights Movement from Rosa Parks to the Rise of Black Power* (New York: Vintage Books, 2010). Slightly older works include Bettye Collier-Thomas and V. P. Franklin, *Sisters in the Struggle: African American Women in the Civil Rights-Black Power Movement* (New York: New York University Press, 2001); Vicki L. Crawford, Jacqueline Anne Rouse, and Barbara Woods, eds., *Women in the Civil Rights Movement: Trailblazers and Torchbearers, 1941–1965* (Bloomington: Indiana University Press, 1990); Peter Ling and Sharon Montieth, eds., *Gender and the Civil Rights Movement* (New Brunswick, NJ: Rutgers University Press, 2004). Though a few women loom large (Rosa Parks, Coretta Scott King, Ella Baker, and

Fannie Lou Hamer all have at least one biography), many other female activists have not received the fuller critical treatment they deserve. Dorothy Height, Daisy Bates, Septima Clark, Diane Nash, Jo Ann Robinson, and Joan Trumpauer are just a few women who need more scholarly attention, to say nothing of the thousands of unnamed women who were the foot soldiers of the movement.

5. Few historians have examined the role of clothing in the Civil Rights Movement. Though Tanisha Ford does not specifically examine purses in her illuminating work on Black women's "soul style," this chapter benefits from and builds on her excellent scholarship. Ford, *Liberated Threads*. See also Marisa Chappell, Jenny Hutchinson, and Brian Ward, "'Dress modestly, neatly, as if you were going to church': Respectability, Class, and Gender in the Montgomery Bus Boycott and the Early Civil Rights Movement," in Ling and Montieth, eds., *Gender and the Civil Rights Movement*, 69–100.

6. Indeed, Clark-Lewis has noted, "Just as each girl had carried a freedom bag when she was taken on the train, she was now given another freedom bag to carry to her first live-in job. Somehow, her identity was folded inside that bag. And because there was as yet no fit place for her in society, she carried her own identity with her from place to place." Elizabeth Clark-Lewis, *Living In, Living Out: African American Domestics in Washington, D.C. 1910–1940* (Washington, DC: Smithsonian Books, 1994), 94.

7. Ella Baker and Marvel Cooke, "The Bronx Slave Market," *The Crisis*, November 1935, 330, https://books.google.com/books?id=4lcEAAAAMBAJ&lpg=PA321&pg=PA321#v=onepage&q&f=false, accessed January 3, 2024.

8. Marvel Cooke, "Slavery . . . 1939 Style," *New York Amsterdam News*, May 27, 1939. See also "Women Make 'Slave' Sts. Immoral," *New York Amsterdam News*, December 2, 1950, 6. Images accompanying these articles show Black women carrying both paper bags and what appear to be leather purses.

9. Baker and Cooke, "The Bronx Slave Market," 330.

10. Clark-Lewis, *Living In, Living Out*, 94.

11. Sarah Deutsch, *Women and the City: Gender, Space, and Power in Boston, 1879–1940* (New York: Oxford University Press, 2000), 21.

12. Evelyn Brooks Higginbotham, *Righteous Discontent: The Women's Movement in the Black Baptist Church, 1880–1920* (Cambridge, MA: Harvard University Press, 1993), 187.

13. For example, see Chappell, Hutchinson, and Ward, "'Dress modestly, neatly, as if you were going to church,'" 69–100. Barbara Y. Welke has suggested that some wealthy Black women even used their dress and "conspicuous respectability" to evade Jim Crow segregation on public transportation. Welke, "When All the Women Were White, and All the Blacks Were Men: Gender, Class, Race, and the Road to *Plessy*, 1855–1914," *Law and History Review* 13, no. 2 (Autumn 1995): 261–316. For an explanation of why, by 1963, some young members of SNCC eschewed conventionally respectable middle-class attire for the denim overalls of sharecroppers; see Tanisha C. Ford, "SNCC Women, Denim, and the Politics of Dress," *Journal of Southern History* 79, no. 3 (August 2013): 625–658.

14. See Victoria Wolcott, *Remaking Respectability: African American Women in Interwar Detroit* (Chapel Hill: University of North Carolina Press, 2001).

15. For an interdisciplinary discussion about the surveillance of Black bodies in America, see Simone Browne, *Dark Matters: On the Surveillance of Blackness* (Durham, NC: Duke University Press, 2015).

16. Reginald Thomas (*The HistoryMakers* A2004.111), interviewed by Larry Crowe, July 27, 2004, HistoryMakers Digital Archive, Session 1, Tape 1, Stories 6 and 9. Up until the 1960s, when John F. Kennedy became the first U.S. president to abandon the habit of wearing a hat, many Americans wore hats whenever they stepped outside.

17. According to Alison Lurie, gloves were important whenever a woman might "be introduced to strangers. If she forgot or misplaced them and had to touch the hand of a strange man with her own bare hand, she was aware of having made—inadvertently or not—a sexual gesture." *The Language of Clothes* (New York: Random House, 1981), 242.
18. According to the third edition (December 2007) of the *Oxford English Dictionary*, "pocketbook" has been used in the American South as early as 1942 as a euphemism for a woman's vagina. In 1942 and in 1969, Zora Neal Hurston and Maya Angelou included dialogue in their texts that referred to not letting anyone "snatch" or "see" your pocketbook.
19. Tera W. Hunter, *To Joy My Freedom: Southern Black Women's Lives and Labor after the Civil War* (Cambridge, MA: Harvard University Press, 1997), 195.
20. Timothy Tyson, *Radio-Free Dixie: Robert F. Williams and the Roots of Black Power* (Chapel Hill: University of North Carolina Press, 2001), 56.
21. Roberta "Bobbi" J. Yancy, oral history interview by author, Zoom, June 28, 2021.
22. Daisy Bates, *The Long Shadow of Little Rock* (Fayetteville: University of Arkansas Press, 1986), 11–12.
23. Bates, *The Long Shadow of Little Rock*, 12.
24. After the Ku Klux Klan began burning crosses on her front lawn and firing shots into her home, even bombing it in 1959, Bates stayed up late and guarded the home with a .45-caliber automatic pistol, which she and her husband lovingly referred to as "Old Betsy." Tyson, *Radio-Free Dixie*, 153, 165.
25. Josephine Baker spoke before the official program began. Bennetta Jules-Rosette, *Josephine Baker in Art and Life: The Icon and the Image* (Urbana: University of Illinois Press, 2007), 235–237.
26. Charles E. Cobb Jr., *This Non-Violent Stuff'll Get You Killed: How Guns Made the Civil Rights Movement Possible* (New York: Basic Books, 2014), 8.
27. The Honorable Bobbie Steele (*The HistoryMakers* A2002.109), interviewed by Larry Crowe, July 1, 2002, HistoryMakers Digital Archive, Session 1, Tape 2, Story 16.
28. Stokely Carmichael with Ekwueme Michael Thelwell, *Ready for Revolution: The Life and Struggles of Stokely Carmichael* (New York: Scribner, 2003), 471.
29. Carmichael, *Ready for Revolution*, 471. Quoted in Cobb, *This Non-Violent Stuff'll Get You Killed*, 3.
30. Carmichael, *Ready for Revolution*, 366–367.
31. The two recruits were Carol Martin and Doris Wilkerson. Carmichael, *Ready for Revolution*, 366–367.
32. Doug McAdam, *Freedom Summer* (New York: Oxford University Press, 1988), 7.
33. Cynthia Washington, "We started from different ends of the spectrum," *Southern Exposure*, "Generations: Women in the South," 4, no. 4 (Winter 1976): 14.
34. Cobb, *This Non-Violent Stuff'll Get You Killed*, epigraph.
35. Washington, "We started from different ends of the spectrum," 14–15.
36. Washington, "We started from different ends of the spectrum," 14.
37. Ford, *Liberated Threads*, 75.
38. Ford, *Liberated Threads*, 77–78; Barbara Ransby, *Ella Baker and the Black Freedom Movement: A Radical Democratic Vision* (Chapel Hill: University of North Carolina Press, 2003), 259.
39. Ford, *Liberated Threads*, 75.
40. Yancy, oral history interview by author, Zoom, June 28, 2021.
41. William Waller Hening, "Act X: An Act for Preventing Negro Insurrections," in *The Statutes at Large: Being a Collection of All the Laws of Virginia, from First Session of the Legislature in the Year 1619* (New York: R. & W. &. G. Bartow, 1823), 481.

42. Howard Odum, *Race and Rumors of Race: The American South in the Early Forties* (Chapel Hill: University of North Carolina, 1943; repr. Baltimore: Johns Hopkins University Press, 1997), 100. Citations here refer to 1997 edition.
43. Cobb, *This Non-Violent Stuff'll Get You Killed*, 126.
44. Robyn Spencer addresses the significance of women's roles within the Black Panther Party (BPP), highlighting how women like Lewis challenged sexism within the group. "Engendering the Black Freedom Struggle: Revolutionary Black Womanhood and the Black Panther Party in the Bay Area, California," *Journal of Women's History* 20 (2008): 96. See also Spencer's book *The Revolution Has Come: Black Power, Gender, and the Black Panther Party in Oakland* (Durham, NC: Duke University Press, 2016). In addition, see Ashley Farmer, *Remaking Black Power: How Black Women Transformed an Era* (Chapel Hill: University of North Carolina Press, 2019).
45. Indeed, with a few important exceptions, much of the existing scholarship on self-defense and armed resistance focuses on men. This work examines men like Robert F. Williams, the gun clubs established by Southern Black veterans of World War II and the Korean War, as well as organizations like the Black Panther Party for Self-Defense (which initially had no female members). In *This Non-Violent Stuff'll Get You Killed*, Charles Cobb argues that "we do not know what many women who were active in the movement were thinking, or whether and how they organized for self-defense" (12). For other examples, see Timothy Tyson's *Radio-Free Dixie* and Lance Hill's *The Deacons for Defense: Armed Resistance and the Civil Rights Movement* (Chapel Hill: University of North Carolina Press, 2004).
46. Full-size bronze statues of Parks with a purse appear in Montgomery, Alabama; Greenville, South Carolina; Washington, DC; and Flint, Michigan, to name just a few cities.
47. Erected in 2013 and sculpted by Eugene Daub and codesigned by Rob Firmin, the statue of Parks in DC was the first to be commissioned by Congress since 1873. It was also the first full-length statue of an African American in the U.S. Capitol. See https://www.aoc.gov/art/other-statues/rosa-parks, accessed October 10, 2019.
48. These bags fastened at the top, as was typical of designs in that decade.
49. By contrast, the statue in Flint shows Parks in a more active position, standing upright with a purse draped over her left shoulder. The statue in Greenville, South Carolina, is similar, though it also portrays Parks holding a pigeon. The pose is a curious choice, given that its purpose is to memorialize a woman known for refusing to literally stand up.
50. Black Women Oral History Project, Interviews, 1976–1981. Rosa Parks, OH-31, 11. Schlesinger Library, Radcliffe Institute. Cited in Theoharis, *The Rebellious Life of Mrs. Rosa Parks*, 60. See also McGuire, *At the Dark End of the Street*, 120–121.
51. Though this aspect of her activism is often forgotten, Parks worked as an anti-rape activist early in her tenure as secretary of the Montgomery chapter of the NAACP. In 1944, Parks investigated the brutal rape of Recy Taylor and helped lead a campaign to pressure the governor to indict the perpetrators. Clearly, Parks was not afraid to work outside socially prescribed gender norms. For more information, see McGuire, *The Dark End of the Street*, 3–39; Theoharis, *The Rebellious Life of Mrs. Rosa Parks*, 17–45, 51.
52. Parks with Haskins, *My Story*, 125.
53. Theoharis, *The Rebellious Life of Mrs. Rosa Parks*, 3.
54. Parks with Haskins, *My Story*, 22.
55. On another occasion, when a white boy tried to push Parks off the sidewalk, she recalled that she "turned around and pushed him." Parks with Haskins, *My Story*, 23, 48.
56. Chappell, Hutchinson, and Ward, "'Dress modestly, neatly, as if you were going to church,'" 89; Theoharis, *The Rebellious Life of Mrs. Rosa Parks*, 14–15. See also McGuire, *At the Dark End of the Street*.

57. Theoharis, *The Rebellious Life of Mrs. Rosa Parks*, 84.
58. Theoharis, *The Rebellious Life of Mrs. Rosa Parks*, 70.
59. Chappell, Hutchinson, and Ward, "'Dress modestly, neatly, as if you were going to church,'" 83.
60. Chappell, Hutchinson, and Ward, "'Dress modestly, neatly, as if you were going to church,'" 86.
61. Jo Ann Robinson, who slept with a gun under her pillow, said that Parks was a "lady . . . [who] was too sweet to even say damn in anger." Chappell, Hutchinson, and Ward, "'Dress modestly, neatly, as if you were going to church,'" 89.
62. Chappell, Hutchinson, and Ward, "'Dress modestly, neatly, as if you were going to church,'" 85. See also "Arrested for refusing to give up bus seat in 1955, she's fighting to clear her record," NPR, October 26, 2021, https://www.npr.org/2021/10/26/1049240521/claudette-colvin-civil-rights-rosa-parks-bus-arrest, accessed December 10, 2024.
63. "Found: Photos of King's Assassination Scene," *American History* 44, no. 3 (August 2009): 8.
64. For more information on the pressures faced by civil rights activists during the Cold War, and how they leveraged that pressure against the American government, see Mary Dudziak, *Cold War Civil Rights: Race and the Image of American Democracy* (Princeton, NJ: Princeton University Press, 2000).
65. Ransby, *Ella Baker*, 59.
66. Ransby, *Ella Baker*, 180.
67. Ransby, *Ella Baker*, 181.
68. Ransby, *Ella Baker*, 129.
69. Ransby, *Ella Baker*, 257.
70. Ransby, *Ella Baker*, 257.
71. Ransby, *Ella Baker*, 258.
72. Yancy, oral history interview by author, Zoom, June 28, 2021.
73. Heather Loepere and Marianna Najman-Franks, "Jailed in a Fur Coat," *Columbia Spectator*, https://www.columbiaspectator.com/news/2019/02/26/jailed-in-a-fur-coat-bobbi-yancy-bc-62-reflects-on-decades-long-career-as-radical-civil-rights-activist/, accessed June 29, 2021.
74. Yancy, oral history interview by author, Zoom, June 28, 2021.
75. *Jet* magazine does not specify the date of the sit-in and Yancy was uncertain of the exact dates when I interviewed her nearly sixty years later. However, Courtney Pace asserts that the protest began on December 23, when seventeen protesters were arrested, a number that the *New York Times* confirms. Pace further contends that Yancy was arrested the next day, on Christmas Eve, and held on 100 dollars' bail. Yancy, Prathia Hall, and Lillian Gregory had all purchased stock in Dobbs International before staging their portion of the sit-in on the second day of the protest. As co-owners of the restaurant, they were still refused service. Courtney Pace, *Freedom Faith: The Womanist Vision of Prathia Hall* (Athens: University of Georgia Press, 2019), 90; "Head of Integration Group Is Arrested in Atlanta Sit-in," *New York Times*, December 23, 1963, 35.
76. Yancy, oral history interview by author, Zoom, June 28, 2021.
77. Yancy arrived at Barnard in 1959, graduating in 1962. For more information on Yancy, see Roberta Yancy, Civil Rights Collection, 1960-1977, New York Public Library, Schomburg Center for Research in Black Culture, Manuscripts, Archives and Rare Books Division. https://archives.nypl.org/scm/20838, accessed February 10, 2025. Deirdre Clemente argues that, a few years later, Black college students at places like Barnard turned away from wearing formal dress and went for a more casual look. She notes that, by 1967, Sherry Suttles "no longer wore ironed dresses but donned rolled-up jeans and beaded necklaces." Clemente,

Dress Casual: How College Students Redefined American Style (Chapel Hill: University of North Carolina Press, 2014), 6.
78. Yancy, oral history interview by author, Zoom, June 28, 2021.
79. Mark Suckle, "The Week's Best Photos," *Jet*, January 9, 1963, 31.
80. Judy Richardson, "SNCC: My Enduring 'Circle of Trust,'" in *Hands on the Freedom Plow: Personal Account by Women in SNCC* (Champaign: University of Illinois Press, 2010), 353.
81. John Britton, "Reliving the Xmas Pageant," *Jet*, January 9, 1964, 6, 31.
82. Yancy, oral history interview by author, Zoom, June 28, 2021.
83. Yancy, oral history interview by author, Zoom, June 28, 2021.
84. Loepere and Najman-Franks, "Jailed in a Fur Coat."
85. Yancy spent Christmas and several days thereafter in jail. Yancy, oral history interview by author, Zoom, June 28, 2021.
86. Kay Mills, *This Little Light of Mine: The Life of Fannie Lou Hamer* (Lexington: University Press of Kentucky, 2007), 21.
87. Mills, *This Little Light of Mine*, 113.
88. Cobb, *This Non-Violent Stuff'll Get You Killed*, 124; Nicholas J. Johnson, *Negroes and the Gun: The Black Tradition of Arms* (New York: Prometheus, 2014), 13.
89. For more biographical information on Hamer, see Chana Kai Lee's *For Freedom's Sake: The Life of Fannie Lou Hamer* (Urbana: University of Illinois, 2000); and, more recently, Keisha N. Blain, *Until I Am Free: Fannie Lou Hamer's Enduring Message to America* (Boston: Beacon Press, 2021).
90. By the time LBJ's superfluous announcement was over, Hamer had finished testifying. Yet, Johnson was ultimately unsuccessful in silencing Hamer because the evening news outlets replayed her speech that evening.
91. Around this time, Joan's married surname was Trumpower, but she spelled it incorrectly (Trumpauer) when speaking to the press in order to protect her in-laws. Today, she uses her maiden name (Mulholland), but because she is widely known as Trumpauer in most historical sources, I refer to her that way here. Joan Trumpauer Mulholland, oral history interview by author, January 22, 2020.
92. Trumpauer, oral history interview by author, January 22, 2020.
93. Trumpauer, oral history interview by author, January 22, 2020.
94. Trumpauer, oral history interview by author, January 22, 2020.
95. Trumpauer, oral history interview by author, January 22, 2020.
96. Trumpauer, oral history interview by author, January 22, 2020.
97. Trumpauer, oral history interview by author, January 22, 2020.
98. Trumpauer, oral history interview by author, January 22, 2020.
99. Carol Ruth Silver, *Freedom Rider Diary: Smuggled Notes from Parchman Prison* (Jackson: University Press of Mississippi, 2014), 31.
100. Silver, *Freedom Rider Diary*, 33.
101. Silver, *Freedom Rider Diary*, 33.
102. Silver, *Freedom Rider Diary*, 34.
103. Joan Trumpower and her Freedom Rider Diary. "About Me," Personal Archives.
104. Joan Trumpauer, Freedom Rider Diary, Jackson, Mississippi, June 8–23, 1961, Personal Archives, Transcribed by M. J. O'Brien. Published in Faith S. Holsaert, Martha Prescod Norman Noonan, et al., *Hands on the Freedom Plow: Personal Accounts by Women in SNCC* (Urbana: University of Illinois Press, 2010), 67–75. For more biographical information on Trumpauer, see M. J. O'Brien's *We Shall Not Be Moved: The Jackson Woolworth's Sit-In and the Movement It Inspired* (Jackson: University Press of Mississippi, 2013), 32–41; Loki Mulholland and Angela Farewell, *An Ordinary Hero: The True Story of Joan Trumpauer*, DVD (2013); Loki

Mulholland and Angela Fairwell, *She Stood for Freedom: The Untold Story of a Civil Rights Hero, Joan Trumpauer Mulholland* (Shenzhen, China: Shadow Mountain, 2016).
105. Silver, *Freedom Rider Diary*, 37.
106. Silver, *Freedom Rider Diary*, 37.
107. Silver, *Freedom Rider Diary*, 37.
108. Stokely Carmichael with Ekwueme Michael Thelwell, *The Life and Struggles of Stokely Carmichael (Kwame Ture)* (New York: Scribner, 2003), 198.
109. Joan Trumpauer Mulholland, oral history interview with John Dittmer, Library of Congress, 2013.
110. Lois Chaffee was a white faculty member at Tougaloo. The student and professor planned to work together, as faculty and students often did at Tougaloo. O'Brien, *We Shall Not Be Moved*, 41; Trumpauer, oral history interview by author, January 22, 2020.
111. Trumpauer, oral history interview with author, January 22, 2020; Emily Wagster Pettus, *Los Angeles Times*, February 10, 2015. It is possible that all three were spotters and made multiple calls independently or as a collective. For more information, see O'Brien, *We Shall Not Be Moved*.
112. Moody, *Coming of Age in Mississippi* (New York: Dell Publishing, 1968), 265–266.
113. Trumpauer, oral history interview by author, January 22, 2020.
114. O'Brien, *We Shall Not Be Moved*, 41.
115. O'Brien, *We Shall Not Be Moved*, 51.
116. O'Brien, *We Shall Not Be Moved*, 22.
117. Moody, *Coming of Age in Mississippi*, 266.
118. The most explicit example of the ways in which purse-snatchings drew attention to interactions between Black males and white females involved Bill "Bojangles" Robinson, a world-renowned tap dancer and one of the most famous Black performers of the early twentieth century. In 1930, newspapers reported that Robinson exited his hotel room in Pittsburgh just as a white woman's purse was snatched from her. Upon hearing the woman's screams, Robinson dropped his bags, pulled out his revolver, and pursued the suspect. However, a nearby Irish policeman saw a Black man running down the street, mistook Robinson for the thief, and shot him. Robinson dropped to the ground after catching a bullet near his elbow. Allegedly, the policeman later visited Robinson at the hospital, apologized, and said, "All black men look alike to me." "Bojangles Forgives Cop Who Shot Him for Bag Snatcher," *The Chicago Defender*, October 11, 1930, 5.
119. According to Moody, Junior "stood there trembling with fear, a horrified look on his face," as Moody's white boss, Mrs. Burke, "shook him down and turned his pockets inside out." Shortly after, Mrs. Burke found the purse herself in her own home. Although Moody had suffered countless indignities while working for Mrs. Burke, the humiliation of watching her little brother have his pockets emptied finally prompted her to quit. Moody, *Coming of Age in Mississippi*, 155–156.
120. O'Brien, *We Shall Not Be Moved*, 282.
121. The photograph in which Moody holds a purse while standing outside of Woolworth's was taken just after the sit-in by Fred Blackwell. Associated Press, May 28, 1963, Woolworth's, Jackson, Mississippi.

CHAPTER 6

1. "Gay Bob," LGBTQIA Realia Collection, Collection No. GLC 119, James C. Hormel LGBTQIA Center, San Francisco Public Library.
2. "Meet Gay Bob," https://www.kqed.org/arts/13880161/meet-gay-bob-the-1977-doll-that-urged-people-to-come-out-of-the-closet, accessed November 10, 2023.

3. Val Hatcher, "What About Gay Bob?," Natural History Museum, Los Angeles County, https://nhm.org/stories/what-about-gay-bob, accessed August 15, 2022.
4. *San Francisco Chronicle*, August 28, 1979, 20.
5. Hatcher, "What About Gay Bob?"
6. Hatcher, "What About Gay Bob?"; "Gas rationing, the Gay Bob doll and more," *St. Louis Post Dispatch*, August 3, 2023, originally published 1978; "Dear Ann Landers," *San Francisco Chronicle*, February 4, 1979, 94.
7. Michael Waters, "The Story Behind Gay Bob, the World's First Out and Proud Doll," *Atlas Obscura*, January 10, 2017, https://www.atlasobscura.com/articles/the-story-behind-gay-bob-the-worlds-first-outandproud-doll, accessed November 15, 2023; Donald Padgett, "Meet Gay Bob," *The Advocate*, July 22, 2023, https://www.advocate.com/news/gay-bob-out-ken-barbie, accessed November 15, 2023. The podcast episode mentions that Gay Bob could talk, but the one I met at the San Francisco Public Library was silent, and there appeared to be no button, string, place for battery storage, or other mechanism one could use to make him speak. "Queer as Frog," *Historically Really Good Friends*, Episode 22, July 6, 2022.
8. "A Plea to Ban 'Gay Bob' Doll," *San Francisco Chronicle*, August 17, 1978, 37.
9. According to Shaun Cole, gay men "sought to pass by dressing 'invisibly' and displaying their homosexuality only in more private settings or by using signals that were less easily recognized by outsiders." Cole, *Now We Don Our Gay Apparel: Gay Men's Dress in the Twentieth Century* (New York: Oxford University Press, 2000), 36.
10. Cole, *Now We Don Our Gay Apparel*, 32–33, 63. See also George Chauncey, *Gay New York: Gender, Urban Culture and the Making of the Gay Male World, 1890–1940* (New York: Basic Books, 1995), 52–54.
11. In his pathbreaking work *Gay New York*, George Chauncey explores how gay men gathered in Greenwich Village and Harlem to cruise, attend drag balls, and develop hidden codes of communication and dress. Since then, Colin Johnson and others have demonstrated the problems with "metronormative thinking" about gay history. Johnson makes the case for considering the homosocial agrarian origins of sexuality in rural America. Johnson, *Just Queer Folks* (Philadelphia: Temple University Press, 2013). It is also worth noting that the term "queer" has lived many lives in the past and present as an adjective, noun, and verb. Since the 1500s, the term has been used to describe something peculiar or eccentric. In the early twentieth century, the *Oxford English Dictionary* records its use as a derogatory term for gay people. In the 1990s, some LGBTQ+ people (and especially queer theorists) began to reclaim the term as a source of empowerment. I use the term here in that spirit as an umbrella category to describe any individual who does not identify as straight or cisgender. Queer, adj. *Oxford English Dictionary*, https://www.oed.com/dictionary/queer_adj1?tab=meaning_and_use#27444388, accessed February 10, 2025.
12. See David K. Johnson, *The Lavender Scare: The Cold War Persecution of Gays and Lesbians in the Federal Government* (Chicago: University of Chicago Press, 2006). See also Cole, *Now We Don Our Gay Apparel*, Chapter 4.
13. As Betty Luther Hillman has argued, in the mid-1960s, homophile activist organizations "transitioned into a larger, louder, and more militant gay liberation movement." However, many gay white men who desired assimilation and acceptance were often primarily concerned with "gender respectability." They attempted to silence transgender folks, drag queens, butch lesbians, and effeminate gay men who had few public spaces in which to congregate safely. Hillman, "'The most profoundly revolutionary act a homosexual can engage in': Drag and the Politics of Gender Presentation in the San Francisco Gay Liberation Movement, 1964–1972," *Journal of the History of Sexuality* 20, no. 1 (2011): 155.

14. According to Shaun Cole and Martin Duberman, Frank Kameny, of the Mattachine Society, enforced a strict gender dress code requiring women to wear dresses and men to don suits. Cole, *Now We Don Our Gay Apparel*, 60; Duberman, *Stonewall* (New York: Dutton, 1993), 111–112. Hillman argues that "disentangling homosexual and gender-transgressive identities became crucial to the political goals of gay activism." "The most profoundly revolutionary act," 156, 159.
15. I use the term "cross-dressing" somewhat reluctantly here and throughout this chapter with the awareness that it is an increasingly antiquated term. I do not seek to reinforce the idea that there are two "opposite" sexes and that all clothing is designed for either men or women. Though the term reinforces binary understandings of gender and sex, it is the word most often used in sources from the 1960s and 1970s and is still used by some individuals today. I agree with sociologist Clare Sears that the term erroneously assumes that the type of clothing that "belongs" to each sex is easily agreed on, when, in fact, such determinations are subject to fierce social debate. Sears also contends that "cross-dressing is a problematic concept because it assumes that people can also be easily and consensually classified as 'belonging' to one of two discrete, opposite sexes." Sears, *Arresting Dress: Cross-Dressing, Law, and Fascination in Nineteenth Century San Francisco* (Durham, NC: Duke University Press, 2015), 21.
16. The states of New York (1845) and California (1874) passed similar laws. William K. Eskridge, Jr., *Gaylaw: Challenging the Apartheid of the Closet* (Cambridge, MA: Harvard University Press, 1999), 27, Appendix A2, 338–341.
17. Sears notes that 34 U.S. cities outlawed "cross-dressing" between 1848 and 1900. Sears, *Arresting Dress*, 82. See also Susan Stryker, *Transgender History* (Berkeley, CA: Seal Press, 2017), 47.
18. According to Sears, this law was enacted by the San Francisco Board of Supervisors; it criminalized the act of appearing in public "in a dress not belonging to his or her sex." Sears, *Arresting Dress*, 2.
19. This change becomes evident when comparing the 1968 (2nd ed.) and 1980 (3rd ed.) of the *Diagnostic and Statistical Manual of Mental Disorders* published by the American Psychiatric Association. For further discussion, see Abram J. Lewis, "'We Are Certain of Our Own Insanity': Anti-Psychiatry and the Gay Liberation Movement, 1960–1980," *Journal of the History of Sexuality* 25, no. 1 (January 2016): 83–113.
20. See Fred Fejes, *Gay Rights and Moral Panic: The Origins of America's Debate on Homosexuality* (New York: Palgrave, 2008).
21. Worsened by the AIDS crisis of the 1980s and 1990s, the stakes were incredibly high for queer people who dared to live openly. Gay sex was still considered a criminal act until 2004, when the Supreme Court declared laws outlawing two people of the same sex from having anal or oral sex unconstitutional. John Lawrence and Tyron Carter had been arrested for violating Texas' "Homosexual Conduct Law" in 1998. *Lawrence v. Texas*, 2004, Lambda Legal, https://lambdalegal.org/case/lawrence-v-texas/, accessed November 20, 2023.
22. I use the word "trans" with the understanding that the term "transgender" was not commonly used in the United States before the 1990s. The language that people who did not fit into stereotypical gender categories were using was constantly changing, and there was little consensus as to what dynamic terms like "drag," "queen," and other terms that many now consider derogatory (i.e., transvestite, TV, transsexual) meant. When I am certain how a particular individual identified themself and what pronouns they used, I follow their example. At the risk of sounding ahistorical, I use the word "trans" in the hope of being as inclusive as possible. I do, however, also recognize that these terms were used by different people at

different times to signify different things. For example, Marsha P. Johnson has alternately been identified as a drag queen, trans woman, and "transvestite," though these terms are not necessarily interchangeable.
23. Liz Millward, *Making a Scene: Lesbians and Community across Canada, 1964–1984* (Vancouver: University of British Columbia Press, 2016). See also Nan Alamilla Boyd, *Wide-Open Town: A History of Queer San Francisco to 1965* (Berkeley: University of California Press, 2005).
24. Victor Silverman and Susan Stryker, dirs., *Screaming Queens: The Riot at Compton's Cafeteria* (San Francisco: KQED Production, 2005).
25. According to *Screaming Queens*, they often vied for window seats so they could both be seen by passersby and get the first look at who was coming in.
26. Silverman and Stryker, *Screaming Queens*. For case studies on how race impacted the homophile movement, see Kent Peacock, "Race, the Homosexual, and the Mattachine Society of Washington 1961–1970," *Journal of the History of Sexuality* 25, no. 2 (May 2016): 267–296, and Kevin J. Mumford, "The Trouble with Gay Rights: Race and the Politics of Sexual Orientation in Philadelphia, 1969–1982," *Journal of American History* 98, no. 1 (June 2011): 49–72.
27. According to Stryker, the management at Compton's resented the "uppity new political attitude some of its customers were starting to express. And that friction lit the fuse that led directly to the riot." Silverman and Stryker, *Screaming Queens*.
28. The exact date of the riot is unknown. Arrest records have allegedly been destroyed or gone missing. It is worth noting that approximately one month before the Compton riots, Dr. Harry Benjamin published *The Transsexual Phenomenon*, which served as a sort-of-how-to guide for drag queens in the Tenderloin District who began to learn about the concept of the "transsexual." Silverman and Stryker, *Screaming Queens*.
29. Silverman and Stryker, *Screaming Queens*.
30. See Nan Alamilla Boyd, *Wide Open Town: A History of Queer San Francisco to 1965* (Berkeley: University of California Press, 2003).
31. Susan Stryker, *Transgender History: The Roots of Today's Revolution* (Berkeley, CA: Seal Press, 2017), 86. On September 15, 1966 (roughly a month after the uprising at Compton's), Vanguard organized another protest, this time calling on the city to "clean up the streets" in the Tenderloin District. In October 2023, rare film footage documenting the two protests led by Vanguard was discovered in the archives of television station ABC7. In the protest staged in September, a large crowd of people can be seen literally sweeping the streets. A trans woman appears at the front of the crowd attempting to balance holding a large black purse while sweeping a broom in the streets. Vanguard disbanded after approximately two years. Ken Miguel and Reggie Acqui, "ABC7 archival film sheds light on earliest known 'gay liberation' uprising in US," https://abc7news.com/lgbtq-history-pre-stonewall-protests-comptons-cafeteria-vanguard/13868364/?mc_cid=21989037fa&mc_eid=7bab5be932&fbclid=IwAR2gZLDUxqNSq7OVOnFguLNvUUMWSS3mptjnq_XoqMLLLJodwQhroaAyyaA, accessed November 20, 2023. See also Joseph Plaster, *Kids on the Street: Queer Kinship and Religion in San Francisco's Tenderloin* (Durham, NC: Duke University Press, 2023).
32. Silverman and Stryker, *Screaming Queens*.
33. Whether or not this happened on the first or second night of the riots, multiple sources confirm Johnson's actions. Lillian Faderman argues that Johnson "stuffed a bag with the bricks, then shimmied up a lamppost despite her high heels and tight dress. Taking aim at the windshield of a squad car parked below, she let fly and heard the satisfying shatter of glass."

Faderman, *The Gay Revolution: The Story of Struggle* (New York: Simon and Schuster, 2015), 174. According to Matthew Riemer and Leighton Brown, "While everyone agrees Marsha was there near the beginning of the first night—and multiple sources confirm seeing her climb a lamppost to drop a bag on a cop car—she told Eric Marcus that she arrived *after* 'the riots had already started.'" Riemer and Brown, *We Are Everywhere: Protest, Power, and Pride in the History of Queer Liberation* (New York: Ten Speed Press, 2019), 338. In *Stonewall: The Riots That Sparked the Gay Revolution*, David Carter states that from just 6 feet away, Craig Rodwell saw Marsha P. Johnson "climb to the top of a lamppost and drop a bag containing a heavy object on the car's windshield, shattering it." Carter also claims that Johnson left New Jersey for New York City in 1966 (New York: St. Martin's Griffin, 2004), 65, 188.

34. "Life Story: Marsha P. Johnson," https://wams.nyhistory.org/growth-and-turmoil/growing-tensions/marsha-p-johnson/, accessed November 26, 2023. See also "Marsha P. Johnson's historic role in the LGBTQ+ rights movement," *PBS News,* June 11, 2023, https://www.pbs.org/newshour/show/marsha-p-johnsons-historic-role-in-the-lgbtq-rights-movement, accessed November 26, 2023.
35. See Elizabeth Clark-Lewis's discussion of "freedom bags" in *Living In, Living Out: African American Domestics in Washington, D.C. 1910–1940* (Washington, DC: Smithsonian Books, 1994), 94.
36. Dwight Garner, "He Was the Visual Voice of the Village Voice," *New York Times*, September 6, 2018.
37. "Thomas Lanigan-Schmidt Remembers Stonewall," *Artforum.com*, June 25, 2019, https://www.artforum.com/interviews/thomas-lanigan-schmidt-remembers-stonewall-80155, accessed October 30, 2019.
38. Silverman and Stryker, *Screaming Queens*.
39. Danny Lewis, "Men's Shirts Button on the Right. Why Do Women's Button on the Left?," *Smithsonian Magazine*, November 23, 2015, https://www.smithsonianmag.com/smart-news/mens-shirts-button-on-the-right-why-do-womens-button-on-the-left-180957361/, accessed December 12, 2024.
40. John F. Harris, "VA to Drop Its Ban on Gay Bars," *The Washington Post*, October 19, 1991, https://www.washingtonpost.com/archive/local/1991/10/19/va-to-drop-its-ban-on-gay-bars/827fa71c-37db-406f-9c12-29fcf9d5e6c5/, accessed November 9, 2023.
41. Carter, *Stonewall*, 18, 32.
42. Cole identifies Lanigan-Schmidt as one of the "'boys' . . . who looked like girls but who you knew were boys." *Now We Don Our Gay Apparel*, 52.
43. "Thomas Lanigan-Schmidt Remembers Stonewall."
44. Bradley Picklesimer, oral history interview by Kate Kunath, *Outwords*, March 28, 2018.
45. Manuela Soares, "The Purloined *Ladder*," in Sonya Jones, ed., *Gay and Lesbian Literature since World War II: History and Memory* (San Francisco: Haworth Press, 1998), 36.
46. Marcia M. Gallo, *Different Daughters: A History of the Daughters of Bilitis and the Rise of the Lesbian Rights Movement* (Emeryville, CA: Seal Press, 2007), xliii.
47. In the 1950s, the briefcase was a quintessential accessory for the straight white businessman. According to Shaun Cole, some drag balls featured competitions over "businessman drag, where the competitors walked and talked like surreal versions of white executives, complete with suit, wingtips, briefcase and *The Wall Street Journal*." Cole, *Now We Don Our Gay Apparel*, 53. For more information on briefcases, see Paul Atkinson, "Man in a Briefcase: The Social Construction of the Laptop Computer and the Emergence of a Type Form," *Journal of Design History* 18, no. 2 (Summer 2005): 191–205.
48. Sears, *Arresting Dress*.

49. Lyon and Martin Papers, 93–132, Daughters of Bilitis, Box 2 of 2, Minutes, 1955–1959, Administrative Files DOB SF Chapter, GLBT Historical Society.
50. Gallo, *Different Daughters*, 24. *The Ladder* was first published in October 1956 until August 1972. Soares, "The Purloined *Ladder*," 28.
51. Gallo, *Different Daughters*, 24. For an example of a brief discussion of "transvestism" among lesbians, see Barbara Stephens, "Tranvestism: A Cross-Cultural Survey," *The Ladder* 1, no. 9 (1957): 10–14.
52. Phyllis Lyon, "Lesbian Liberation Begins," *The Gay and Lesbian Review* (Winter 1995), https://glreview.org/article/lesbian-liberation-begins/, accessed September 12, 2022.
53. One of the first obstacles the group faced was how to safely maintain their social and political activities. In October 1956, they began publishing a monthly newsletter. To protect their identities, most DOB members used pseudonyms and 5 ½ by 8 ½ copies of *The Ladder* were distributed in dark bags. Gallo, *Different Daughters*, xix; Soares, "The Purloined *Ladder*," 32.
54. Jess Stearn, *The Grapevine: A Report on the Secret World of the Lesbian* (New York: Doubleday, 1964), 5.
55. Stearn, *The Grapevine*, 5.
56. Madeline Davis and Elizabeth Lapovsky Kennedy, *Boots of Leather, Slippers of Gold: The History of a Lesbian Community* (New York: Routledge, 1993), 159.
57. Davis and Lapovsky Kennedy, 160.
58. For a theoretical exploration of women's productions of masculinity, see J. Halberstam's seminal work, *Female Masculinity* (Durham, NC: Duke University Press, 1998).
59. Davis and Lapovsky Kennedy, 160.
60. Davis and Lapovsky Kennedy, 160.
61. In her pathbreaking anthropological study of drag, Esther Newton argues, "The principal opposition in which the gay world revolves is masculine-feminine." Furthermore, she states that there are a number of ways of "presenting this opposition through one's own person, where it becomes also an opposition of 'inside' = 'outside' or 'underneath' = 'outside.' Ultimately all drag symbolism opposes the 'inner' or 'real' self (subjective self) to the 'outer' self (social self)." It is possible, then, that wearing a purse was considered part of the performance of an outer self. Newton, *Mother Camp: Female Impersonators in America* (Chicago: University of Chicago Press, 1979), 100.
62. Davis and Lapovsky Kennedy, 160.
63. Halberstam, *Female Masculinity*, 88.
64. Here, Halberstam cites Hall's biography, Michael Baker, *Our Three Selves: The Life of Radclyffe Hall* (New York: William Morrow, 1985), 170.
65. Sasha Gregory-Lewis, "Dyke and Proud," *The Advocate*, no. 171, August 27, 1975, 32–33. Gregory-Lewis would later publish *Sunday's Women: A Report on Lesbian Life Today* (Boston: Beacon Press, 1979).
66. Gregory-Lewis, "Dyke and Proud," 32–33.
67. Hannah Carlson, *Pockets: An Intimate History of How We Keep Things Close* (Chapel Hill, NC: Algonquin Books, 2023), 82. See Chapter 3, 79–107.
68. Gregory-Lewis, "Dyke and Proud," 32–33.
69. SmpD, "Coming Out," *Amazon: A Feminist Journal* 8, no. 6 (October/November 1980): 52. Gale Archives of Sexuality and Gender.
70. Michael Wetherbee, "Cross-Dressing," *Sexual Law Reporter* 3, no. 1 (January/February 1977): 1.
71. Joan Nestle notes that, in the 1950s, older lesbians advised her to always wear three items of women's clothing, "so the vice squad can't bust you for transvestism." Nestle, *A Restricted Country* (Ithaca, NY: Firebrand Books, 1987), 162.

72. Wetherbee, "Cross-Dressing," 1.
73. *Cincinnati v. Adams*, November 1974, https://casetext.com/case/cincinnati-v-adams, accessed November 9, 2023.
74. *Cincinnati v. Adams*.
75. Betty Luther Hillman, *Dressing for the Culture Wars*, especially Chapter 5 titled "Everyone Should Be Accustomed to Seeing Long Hair on Men by Now" (Lincoln: University of Nebraska, 2015).
76. Larry Bush, "The Therapeutic State, Borderline Homophobia," *Inquiry*, June 9, 1980.
77. Exceptions could be made for those with special waivers, but the federal government did not change this policy until January 2010. Kimberly Gracia Jones, Esq., and Sande Gracia Jones, "U.S. Travel Policies and Immigration Laws for HIV-Infected Persons," *Journal of the Association of Nurses in AIDS Care,*" 19, no. 4 (July/August 2008): 325–329. See also the Center for HIV Law and Policy, https://www.hivlawandpolicy.org/issues/immigration, accessed November 19, 2023.
78. "Homosexuals Still Fight U.S. Immigration Limits," *New York Times*, August 12, 1979, 20.
79. Bush, "Borderline Homophobia," 8.
80. Bush, "Borderline Homophobia," 8.
81. Bush, "Borderline Homophobia," 8.
82. Liz Millward, *Making a Scene: Lesbians and Community across Canada* (Vancouver: University of British Columbia, 2015), 165. See note 50.
83. *The Alternative*, Syracuse, NY, June 1977. International Gay Information Center Archives, Manuscripts and Archives Division, Humanities and Social Science Library, NYPL.
84. Karla Jay and Allen Young, *The Gay Report: Lesbians and Gay Men Speak about Sexual Experiences and Lifestyles* (New York: Summit Books, 1979), 576.
85. Jay and Young, *The Gay Report*, 578.
86. Jay and Young, *The Gay Report*, 577.
87. Hillman, "The most profoundly revolutionary act," 156–159. See also Newton, who argues that there was "an enormous struggle within the gay community . . . , to come to terms with the stigma of effeminacy." She adds, "Even one feminine item [such as a purse] ruins the integrity of the masculine system; the male loses his caste honor." *Mother Camp*, xiii.
88. Cole, *Don We Now Our Gay Apparel*, 94.
89. E. Patrick Johnson, *Sweet Tea: Black Gay Men of the South, An Oral History* (Chapel Hill: University of North Carolina Press, 2008), 308.
90. Jessica, untitled, *Transvestia* 35 (Los Angeles, 1965), 20.
91. Johnson, *Sweet Tea*, 308.
92. Jennifer Brier, *Infectious Ideas: U.S. Political Responses to the AIDS Crisis* (Chapel Hill: University of North Carolina Press, 2009), especially Chapter 1.
93. Prior to 1994, the U.S. military effectively banned "homosexuals" from serving in the military.
94. According to the Department of Defense, DADT was not repealed until 2011, though over the previous seventeen years, 13,000 people had been kicked out of the military for being gay, https://www.defense.gov/Spotlights/Dont-Ask-Dont-Tell-Resources/, accessed August 13, 2024. See also Leisa Meyer, *Creating G.I. Jane: Sexuality and Power in the Women's Army Corps during World War II* (New York: Columbia University Press, 1998).
95. Johnson, *Sweet Tea*, 308.
96. Rhonda Evans, "The Alternative Press: A Look Back at *Transvestia*," June 22, 2017, https://www.nypl.org/blog/2017/06/21/look-back-transvestia, accessed January 17, 2022.
97. Beginning in January 1960, Prince also created what can best be described as monthly miniature scrapbooks (similar to zines) that included media clippings related to men dressing as

women. Prince distributed these for 1 dollar an issue or 5 dollars a year and titled the publication "T.V Clipsheet" (Los Angeles: Chevalier Publications).
98. Beatrice, "What Shall I Wear?," *Transvestia*, no. 31, Los Angeles, 1965, 62–63.
99. Kelly's bag was a highlight of an exhibition at the Victoria and Albert Museum in 2010. Jess Cartner-Morley, "Grace Kelly exhibition features famous battered handbag," *The Guardian*, April 16, 2010; Kelly, https://www.hermes.com/us/en/content/106196-kelly/, accessed November 12, 2023.
100. Beatrice, "What Shall I Wear?," *Transvestia* 31, Los Angeles, 1965, 64.
101. Genevieve, "Forethought Saved the Day," *Transvestia* 24, Los Angeles, 1963, 28.
102. Jessica, untitled, *Transvestia*.
103. Jessica, untitled, *Transvestia*. I do not know what pronouns Jessica used, but I have attempted to leave room for the fact Jessica may have used multiple pronouns. In this instance, I use the pronoun "her" because I am describing her actions while performing as a woman. Jessica described sustaining a unique professional female impersonation act for years. Unlike many gender impersonators in vaudeville who revealed their "real" sex on stage in the finale of the act, Jessica never revealed that she was a "man" during the performance. In fact, Jessica lived full-time as a woman throughout her stage career. It was only after Jessica decided to marry Connie that Jessica sporadically began dressing as a man again.
104. In another way, this story also provides an example of a model life from which others, whose families and partners were less supportive than Jessica's, might find hope and inspiration. The instruction and enduring support of Connie, who would later become Jessica's wife, play a key role in the story and align with the magazine's "Letters from Wives" column. Rhonda Evans, "The Alternative Press: A Look Back at *Transvestia*," June 22, 2017, https://www.nypl.org/blog/2017/06/21/look-back-transvestia, accessed January 17, 2022.
105. Folder "Gender Discrimination vs. Sex Workers," Victoria Schneider Papers 2000–57, Box 1, Dr. John P. DeCecco Archives and Special Collections, GLBT Historical Society, San Francisco.
106. Transcript, Interview of Victoria Schneider by LTC Investigator Mary White, 9, Schneider Papers.
107. Folder "Claims Against S.F.," Schneider Papers.
108. Folder "Claims Against S.F.," Schneider Papers. I wish to thank Isaac Fellman, reference archivist of the GLBT Historical Society, for this insight.
109. Hanna Rosin, "A Tubby Ache for Jerry Falwell," *The Washington Post*, February 11, 1999.
110. Michael Ellison, "Tinky Winky Falls Foul of the Moral Majority," *The Guardian*, February 11, 1999; Eric Zorn, "Tinky Winky Way Out in Front of Foolish Falwell" *Chicago Tribune*, February 11, 1999, https://www.chicagotribune.com/news/ct-xpm-1999-02-11-9902110405-story.html/, accessed November 12, 2023.
111. "Tinky Winky Debate Rages," *CBS News*, February 10, 1999, https://www.cbsnews.com/news/tinky-winky-debate-rages/, accessed November 12, 2023.
112. "Tinky Winky Debate Rages."
113. Bob Harris, "Parents Alert: Is Jerry Falwell Gay?," *Mother Jones*, February 19, 1999.
114. The show, which received mixed reviews, was performed at the Second City's Donny's Skybox Studio Theater from mid-June to the end of July. Gregg Shapiro, "Don't Ask, Don't Teletubby," *Outlines*, June 16, 1999, 21.
115. "Man Murdered for Carrying Fiancé's Purse," Feminist Majority Foundation blog, September 7, 2001. See also "News: Violence Continues," *Transgender Tapestry*, no. 96 (Winter 2001): 9.
116. *State of Tennessee v. Lewis M. Davidson III*, Court of Criminal Appeals of Tennessee at Nashville, December 6, 2004.

117. "Man mocked for holding a purse, then shot and killed," *Arizona Daily Sun*, July 29, 2001, https://azdailysun.com/man-mocked-for-holding-a-purse-then-shot-killed/article_2739de48-25a5-5836-a1dd-7f8c5a2d4000.html/, accessed September 17, 2022.

118. "Nashville man guilty of murder after shooting man with purse," Associated Press, May 28, 2003.

EPILOGUE

1. Fisher-Price Laugh & Learn My Pretty Learning Purse Playset, https://www.kohls.com/product/prd-992074/fisher-price-laugh-learn-my-pretty-learning-purse-playset.jsp, accessed December 12, 2024.

2. Emilia Petrarca, "Aretha Franklin's Chanel Handbags Carried More than Cash," *The Cut*, August 17, 2018, https://www.thecut.com/2018/08/aretha-franklin-purse-ode.html, accessed January 5, 2024; Matt Miller, "An Ailing Aretha Franklin Brought the House Down," *Esquire*, August 17, 2018. https://www.esquire.com/entertainment/music/a22757514/aretha-franklin-final-performance-video/, accessed August 13, 2024; "Aretha Franklin's handwritten will found in a couch," *CBS News*, July 12, 2023, https://www.cbsnews.com/news/aretha-franklin-will-couch-estate/, accessed August 13, 2024.

3. Jennifer Callahan, *Making the Case*, W & B Productions, 2020. See also Lilah Ramzi, "R.B.G.'s B.A.G.S," *Vogue*, November 19, 2020, https://www.vogue.com/article/in-a-new-short-film-the-late-ruth-bader-ginsburg-waxes-poetic-about-her-purses, accessed December 12, 2024.

4. Sally Beatty, "The Kitchen Sink Might Fit, Too, in Latest Tote Bags," *Wall Street Journal*, July 2, 2004.

5. For example, see "New line of purses for butches unveiled at handbag convention," *AfterEllen*, January 28, 2009, https://www.afterellen.com/new-line-of-purses-for-butches-unveiled-at-handbag-convention/, accessed November 12, 2023; Katie Boyden, "I Have Found the Best Wallet for the Purse-Averse Lesbian," *Pride.com*, July 21, 2014, https://www.Pride.com/women/2014/7/21/i-have-found-best-wallet-ever-purse-averse-lesbian, accessed November 12, 2023; "The Burse," https://www.pinterest.com/ondineleb/the-burse-butch-purse/, accessed November 12, 2023; Cindy Zelman, "What's in a butch's purse?," https://cindyzelman.com/2012/01/22/whats-in-a-butchs-purse/#:~:text=%E2%80%93%20An%20old%20vial%20that%20once,but%20now%20contains%20two%20Tylenol, accessed November 12, 2023.

6. Some readers will remember the *Seinfeld* episode about Jerry's "European carry all." Andy Ackerman, dir., "The Reverse Peephole," 1998, Season 9, Episode 12.

7. Yancy, oral history interview by author, Zoom, June 28, 2021.

8. Christina Buse and Julia Twigg, "Women with Dementia and Their Handbags: Negotiating Identity, Privacy and 'Home' through Material Culture," *Journal of Aging Studies* 30 (2014): 14–22. See also Buse and Twigg, "Dress, Dementia, and the Embodiment of Identity," *Dementia* 12, 3 (May 2013): 326–336.

9. "Closely connected to the individual," scholars Christina Buse and Julia Twigg argue, purses "contain an assortment of objects designed to provide support in the enactment of self: make up, scarves, identity cards, money, personal photographs, talismans, memory objects." Buse and Twigg, "Women with Dementia and Their Handbags," 14.

10. Statista, https://www.statista.com/outlook/cmo/accessories/luggage-bags/handbags/united-states, accessed February 12, 2025.

Bibliography

PRIMARY SOURCES

Born in Slavery Collection: Slave Narratives from the Federal Writers' Project, 1936–1938, Digital Collections, Library of Congress, United States of America
    Ashley, Sarah, "Texas Narratives," Vol. 16, Part 1
    Bacchus, Josephine, "South Carolina Narratives," Vol. 14, Part 1
    Bell, Laura, "North Carolina Narratives," Vol. 11, Part 1
    Butler, Isaiah, "South Carolina Narratives," Vol. 14, Part 1
    Bridges, Annie, "Missouri Narratives," Vol. 10
    Clinton, Joe by Watt McKinney, "Arkansas Narratives," Vol. 2, Part 2
    Hawkins, Tom, "Georgia Narratives," Vol. 4, Part 2
    Henry, Ida, "Oklahoma Narratives," Vol. 13
    Hunter, Lina, "Georgia Narratives," Vol. 4, Part 2
    Marshall, Adeline, "Texas Narratives," Part 3
    McIntosh, Waters, "Arkansas Narratives," Vol. 2, Part 5
    Orford, Richard, "Georgia Narratives," Vol. 4, Part 3
    Proctor, Jenny, "Texas Narratives," Vol. 16, Part 3
    Raines, Charlotte, "Georgia Narratives," Vol. 4, Part 3
    Simmons, Rosa, "Arkansas Narratives," Vol. 2, Part 6
    Tatum, Fannie, "Arkansas Narratives," Vol. 2, Part 6
    Todd, Albert, "Texas Narratives," Part 4
    Walker, Irella Battle, "Texas Narratives," Vol. 16, Part 4
    Wheeler, Fannie, "Arkansas Narratives," Vol. 2, Part 7
    Witt, Rube, "Texas Narratives," Vol. 16, Part 4
Dr. John P. DeCecco Archives and Special Collections, Gay, Lesbian, Bisexual and Transgender Historical Society, San Francisco
    Daughters of Bilitis Papers
    Schneider, Victoria Papers
    Transcript, Screaming Queens Collection
Eva Tanguay Papers, Benson Ford Research Center, The Henry Ford Museum, Dearborn, MI
Gale Archives of Gender and Sexuality
International Museum of Bags and Purses, Amsterdam (Tassen Museum, now closed)
James C. Hormel LGBTQIA Center, San Francisco Public Library
Katherine Keene Papers, 1941–1977, MC 817 8.3.1, Box 5, Arthur and Elizabeth Schlesinger Library on the History of Women in America, Harvard University, Cambridge, MA
Planned Parenthood Federation of America, 1918–1974, Sophia Smith Collection, Smith College Library
Library of Congress
National Museum of African American History and Culture, Digital Collections
National Woman's Party, Political Cartoon Collection
Newseum, Washington, DC (now closed)
New York Public Library Digital Collections, Photographs and Sheet Music

New York State Museum, Purse Collection
Outwords.com
Schomburg Center for Research in Black Culture, New York Public Library
Susan B. Anthony Museum and House, Rochester, NY
Trumpauer Mulholland, Joan. Arlington, Virginia, personal archives

Oral Histories

Arthur and Elizabeth Schlesinger Library on the History of Women in America, Harvard University, Cambridge, MA
    Black Women Oral History Project, 1976–1981
        Moore, Audley OH-31
        Parks, Rosa OH-31
The HistoryMakers, Oral History Digital Archive
    Steele, Honorable Bobbie. Interviewed by Larry Crowe, July 1, 2002
    Thomas, Reginald. Interviewed by Larry Crowe, July 27, 2004
International Ladies' Garment Workers' Union (ILGWU) Archives at the Kheel Center for Labor-Management Documentation and Archives, Cornell University, Ithaca, NY
    Oral History Interviews with survivors of the Triangle Shirtwaist Factory Fire, by Leon Stein
Picklesimer, Brad. Oral History Interview by Kate Kunath, *Outwords*, March 28, 2018
Trumpauer Mulholland, Joan. Interview by author, January 2020
Yancy, Roberta "Bobbi." Interview by author, Zoom, June 2021

Newspapers and Other Periodicals

Advocate
Afro-American
Alternative
American Jeweler
Arizona Daily Sun
Atlanta Constitution
Atlanta Daily World
Bismarck Tribune
Boston Daily Globe
Charleston Mercury
Chicago Daily Tribune
The Chicago Defender
Cosmopolitan
Daily Picayune (New Orleans)
Esquire
Evening Star
Frank Leslie's Ladies Magazine
Gay and Lesbian Review
Gaze
Good Housekeeping
The Guardian
Half-Century Magazine
Harper's Bazaar
Harper's Weekly

Inquiry
Jet
Ladies Home Journal
Los Angeles Times
Maryland Independent
McCall's
Mother Jones
Ms. Magazine
New York Amsterdam News
The New Yorker
New York Observer and Chronicle
The New York Times
New York Tribune
Outlines
Peterson's Magazine
The Pittsburgh Courier
Raleigh Register
Redbook Magazine
San Francisco Chronicle
Scientific American
Sears, Roebuck and Co. Catalogue
TIME Magazine
Transvestia
TV Clipsheet
US Weekly
Vogue
The Wall Street Journal
The Washington Post
The Washington Times
Wilmington Chronicle
Woman's Day
Woman's Home Companion
Women's Wear Daily
The Youth's Companion

Trial Transcripts

New York v. Harris and Blanck (1911)
Cincinnati v. Adams (1974)
New Jersey v. T.L.O. 469, U.S. 325 (1985)
State of Tennessee v. Lewis M. Davidson III, Court of Criminal Appeals of Tennessee at Nashville (2004)

Films

Arbuckle, Roscoe. *Coney Island*. Paramount Pictures, 1917.
Arbuckle, Roscoe. *Fatty's Chance Acquaintance*. Keystone Studios, 1915.
Arbuckle, Roscoe. *Mabel and Fatty's Wash Day*. Keystone Studies, 1915.
Griffith, D. W. *A New Trick*. Biograph, 1909.
Stevenson, Robert. *Mary Poppins*. Burbank, CA: Walt Disney Studios, 1964.

Published Primary Sources

Addams, Jane. *The Spirit of the Youth and the City Streets*. New York: Macmillan, 1909.
Addams, Jane. *Twenty Years at Hull House*. New York: Macmillan, 1911.
Angelino, Henry. "Shoplifting: A Critical Review." *The Midwest Sociologist* 15, no. 2 (Spring 1953): 17–22.
Angelou, Maya. *I Know Why the Caged Bird Sings*. New York: Random House, 2009. Originally published 1969.
Bates, Daisy. *The Long Shadow of Little Rock*. Fayetteville: University of Arkansas Press, 1986.
Bly, Nellie. *Around the World in Seventy-Two Days*. New York: Pictorial Weeklies, 1890. Electronic edition. https://digital.library.upenn.edu/women/bly/world/world.html.
Botume, Elizabeth Hyde. *First Days amongst the Contrabands*. Boston: Lee and Shepard, 1893.
Davidson, Lillias Campbell. *Hints to Lady Travelers: At Home and Abroad*. London: Elliott and Thompson Ltd., 2011. Originally published by Iliffe and Son, 1889.
Douglass, Frederick. *Narrative of the Life of Frederick Douglass, An American Slave*. London: H.G. Collins, 1851.
Dreiser, Theodore. *Sister Carrie*. New York: Doubleday, 1900. Reprinted Mineola: Dover, 2004.
Du Bois, W. E. B. "The Negro Criminal." In *The Philadelphia Negro*. Philadelphia: University of Pennsylvania, 1899.
Frederick, Christine. *Selling Mrs. Consumer*. New York: The Business Bourse, 1929.
Freud, Sigmund. *Dora: An Analysis of a Case of Hysteria*. New York: Collier Books/Macmillan, 1963. Reprinted New York: Touchstone, 1997.
Gilman, Charlotte Perkins. *Herland*. Originally published in serial in *The Forerunner*, 1915.
Gordon, Ann D., ed. *The Selected Papers of Elizabeth Cady Stanton and Susan B. Anthony*, Vol. 6, 1895–1906. New Brunswick, NJ: Rutgers University Press, 2013.
Holsaert, Faith S., and Martha Prescod Norman Noonan, et al. *Hands on the Freedom Plow: Personal Accounts by Women in SNCC*. Urbana: University of Illinois Press, 2010.
Jacobs, Harriet. *Incidents in the Life of a Slave Girl*. New York: Cosimo Books, 1861.
Jay, Karla, and Allen Young. *The Gay Report: Lesbians and Gay Men Speak about Sexual Experiences and Lifestyles*. New York: Summit Books, 1979.
Johnson, E. Patrick. *Sweet Tea: Black Gay Men of the South, An Oral History*. Chapel Hill: University of North Carolina Press, 2008.
Mitchell, Wesley C., and Charles E. Merriam, et al. *Recent Social Trends in the United States: Report of the President's Research Committee on Social Trends*. Vol. 1. New York: McGraw-Hill, 1933.
Moody, Anne. *Coming of Age in Mississippi*. New York: Dell, 1968.
Nestle, Joan. *A Restricted Country*. Ithaca, NY: Firebrand Books, 1987.
Northup, Solomon. *Twelve Years a Slave: Narrative of Solomon Northup, a Citizen of New-York, Kidnapped in Washington City in 1841, and Rescued in 1853*. Documenting the American South, Electronic edition. https://docsouth.unc.edu/fpn/northup/northup.html.
Odum, Howard. *Race and Rumors of Race: The American South in the Early Forties*. Chapel Hill: University of North Carolina, 1943. Reprinted Baltimore: Johns Hopkins University Press, 1997.
Parks, Rosa with Jim Haskins. *My Story*. New York: Puffin Books, 1992.
Robinson, JoAnn. *The Montgomery Bus Boycott and the Women Who Started It: The Memoir of Jo Ann Gibson Robinson*. Knoxville: University of Tennessee Press, 1987.
Rudolfsky, Bernard. "Are Clothes Modern? An Essay on Contemporary Apparel." Chicago: P. Theobold, 1947.

Silver, Carol Ruth. *Freedom Rider Diary: Smuggled Notes from Parchman Prison*. Jackson: University Press of Mississippi, 2017.
Statistical Abstract of the United States, Department of Commerce, Manufactures, by Specified Industries, 1910.
Statistical Abstract of the United States, Department of Commerce, Manufactures, by Specified Industries, 1925.
Stearn, Jess. *The Grapevine: A Report on the Secret World of the Lesbian*. New York: Doubleday, 1964.
Truth, Sojourner. *The Narrative of Sojourner Truth*. New York: Penguin Books, 1998. Originally published Boston, 1850.
U.S. Department of Labor, Bureau of Labor Statistics. *Regularity of Employment in the Women's Ready-to-Wear Garment Industries*. Bulletin 183. Washington, DC: Government Printing Office, 1915.
Wald, Lillian D. *The House on Henry Street*. New York: Henry, Holt, and Co., 1915.
Washington, Cynthia. "We started from different ends of the spectrum." *Southern Exposure*, "Generations: Women in the South" 4, no. 4 (Winter 1976): 14–15.

SECONDARY SOURCES

Abelson, Elaine. *When Ladies Go A-Thieving: Middle Class Shoplifters in the Victorian Department Store*. New York: Oxford University Press, 1989.
Ahmed, Sara. *Living a Feminist Life*. Durham, NC: Duke University Press, 2017.
Allen, Carmel. *The Handbag: To Have and to Hold*. London: Carltons Books, 1999.
Argetsinger, Amy. *There She Was: The Secret History of Miss America*. New York: Simon and Schuster, 2021.
Arsenault, Raymond. *Freedom Riders: 1961 and the Struggle for Racial Justice*. New York: Oxford University Press, 2006.
Atkinson, Paul. "Man in a Briefcase: The Social Construction of the Laptop Computer and the Emergence of a Type Form." *Journal of Design History* 18, no. 2 (Summer 2005): 191–205.
Baptist, Edward. *The Half Has Never Been Told: Slavery and the Making of American Capitalism*. New York: Basic Books, 2016.
Barkley-Brown, Elsa. "Negotiating and Transforming the Public Sphere: African American Political Life in Transition from Slavery to Freedom," in ed. Jane Dailey, Glenda Elizbeth Gilmore, and Bryant Simon, *Jumpin' Jim Crow: Southern Politics from Civil War to Civil Rights*. Princeton, NJ: Princeton University Press, 2000: 28–66.
Baumgarten, Linda. "'Clothes for the People:' Slave Clothing in Early Virginia," *Journal of Early Southern Decorative Arts* 14, no. 2 (1988): 26–70.
Bederman, Gail. *Manliness and Civilization: A Cultural History of Gender and Race in the United States, 1880–1917*. Chicago: University of Chicago Press, 1995.
Belk, Russell. "Possessions and the Extended Self." *Journal of Consumer Research* 15, no. 2 (September 1988): 139–168.
Black, Sandy, Amy De La Haye, Joanne Entwistle, Agnes Rocamora, Regina A. Root, and Helen Thomas, eds. *The Handbook of Fashion Studies*. London: Bloomsbury Academic, 2013.
Boyd, Nan Alamilla. *Wide-Open Town: A History of Queer San Francisco to 1965*. Berkeley: University of California Press, 2005.
Brier, Jennifer. *Infectious Ideas: U.S. Political Responses to the AIDS Crisis*. Chapel Hill: University of North Carolina Press, 2009.
Browne, Simone. *Dark Matters: On the Surveillance of Blackness*. Durham, NC: Duke University Press, 2015.

Buckley, Liam. "Self and Accessory in Gambian Studio Photography." *Visual Anthropology Review* 16, no. 2 (September 2000): 71–91.

Burman, Barbara. "'Pocketing the Difference': Gender and Pockets in Nineteenth Century Britain." *Gender & History* 14 (2002): 447–469.

Burman, Barbara, and Ariane Fennetaux. *The Pocket: A Hidden History of Women's Lives, 1660–1900*. New Haven, CT: Yale University Press, 2020.

Buse, Christina, and Julia Twigg. "Dress, Dementia, and the Embodiment of Identity." *Dementia* 12 (May 2013): 326–336.

Buse, Christina, and Julia Twigg. "Women with Dementia and Their Handbags: Negotiating Identity, Privacy and 'Home' through Material Culture." *Journal of Aging Studies* 30 (2014): 14–22.

Butler, Judith. *Gender Trouble: Feminism and the Subversion of Identity*. New York: Routledge, 2006.

Callahan, Jennifer, dir. *Making the Case*. New York: W&B Productions, 2020.

Camp, Stephanie M. H. *Closer to Freedom: Enslaved Women and Everyday Resistance in the Plantation South*. Chapel Hill: University of North Carolina Press, 2004.

Camp, Stephanie M. H. "The Pleasures of Resistance: Enslaved Women and Body Politics in the Plantation South, 1830–1861." *Journal of Southern History* 68, no. 3 (2002): 533–572.

Campbell, D'Ann. "Women in Combat: The World War II Experience in the United States, Great Britain, Germany and the Soviet Union." *Journal of Military History* 57, no. 2 (April 1993): 301–323.

Carlson, Hannah. *Pockets: An Intimate History of How We Keep Things Close*. Chapel Hill, NC: Algonquin Books, 2023.

Carmichael, Stokely with Ekwueme Michael Thelwell. *Ready for Revolution: The Life and Struggles of Stokely Carmichael (Kwame Ture)*. New York: Scribner, 2003.

Carter, David. *Stonewall: The Riots That Sparked the Gay Revolution*. New York: St. Martin's Press, 2004.

Casey, Kathleen B. "Pickets, Protests, and Purses in the American Civil Rights Movement." *Gender and History* 35, no. 3 (October 2023): 1070–1088.

Casey, Kathleen B. *The Prettiest Girl on Stage Is a Man: Race and Gender Benders in American Vaudeville*. Knoxville: University of Tennessee Press, 2015.

Casey, Kathleen B. "'This Sack So Full': Enslaved Women's Use of Sacks in Antebellum America," in ed. James Brown, Anna Jamieson, and Naomi Segal, *The Cultural Construction of Hidden Spaces: Essays on Pockets, Pouches and Secret Drawers*. Leiden: Brill, 2024, 37–51.

Chan, Sewell. "Marsha P. Johnson, a Transgender Pioneer and Activist." *The New York Times*, March 8, 2018.

Chauncey, George. *Gay New York: Gender, Urban Culture, and the Making of the Gay Male World, 1890–1940*. New York: Basic Books, 1995.

Chenoune, Farid, ed. *Carried Away: All About Bags*. New York: Vendome Press, 2005.

Chenoune, Farid. *A History of Men's Fashion*. Paris: Flammarion, 1993.

Clark-Lewis, Elizabeth. *Living In, Living Out: African American Domestics in Washington, D.C. 1910–1940*. Washington, DC: Smithsonian Books, 1994.

Clement, Elizabeth Alice. *Love for Sale: Courting, Treating, and Prostitution in New York City, 1900–1945*. Chapel Hill: University of North Carolina Press, 2006.

Clemente, Deirdre. *Dress Casual: How College Students Redefined American Style*. Chapel Hill: University of North Carolina Press, 2014.

Clinton, Catherine. *Harriet Tubman: The Road to Freedom*. New York: Little, Brown, 2004.

Cobb, Charles E., Jr. *This Non-Violent Stuff'll Get You Killed: How Guns Made the Civil Rights Movement Possible*. New York: Basic Books, 2014.

Cohen, Lizabeth. *A Consumer's Republic: The Politics of Mass Consumption in Postwar America*. New York: Vintage Books, 2003.

Cole, Shaun. *Now We Don Our Gay Apparel: Gay Men's Dress in the Twentieth Century*. New York: Berg, 2000.

Coleman, J. Winston, Jr. *Kentucky in Slavery Times*. Chapel Hill: University of North Carolina Press, 1940.

Collier-Thomas, Bettye, and V. P. Franklin. *Sisters in the Struggle: African American Women in the Civil Rights-Black Power Movement*. New York: New York University Press, 2001.

Conrad, Earl. *Harriet Tubman*. Washington, DC: Associated Publishers, 1943.

Cox, Caroline. *The Handbag: An Illustrated History*. New York: HarperCollins, 2007.

Crane, Diane. *Fashion and Its Social Agendas: Class, Gender, and Identity in Clothing*. Chicago: University of Chicago, 2000.

Crawford, Vicki L., Jacqueline Anne Rouse, and Barbara Woods, eds. *Women in the Civil Rights Movement: Trailblazers and Torchbearers, 1941–1965*. Bloomington: Indiana University Press, 1990.

Crenshaw, Kimberlé. "Demarginalizing the Intersection of Race and Sex: A Black Feminist Critique of Antidiscrimination Doctrine, Feminist Theory and Antiracist Politics." Paper presented at University of Chicago Legal Forum, 1989, 139–167.

Crenshaw, Kimberlé. "Mapping the Margins: Intersectionality, Identity Politics, and Violence against Women of Color." *Stanford Law Review* 43, no. 6 (1991): 1241–1299.

Deutsch, Sarah. *Women and the City: Gender, Space, and Power in Boston, 1879–1940*. New York: Oxford University Press, 2000.

Douglas, Ann. *Terrible Honesty: Mongrel Manhattan in the 1920s*. New York: Farrar, Straus, and Giroux, 1996.

Duberman, Martin. *Stonewall*. New York: Dutton, 1993.

Dudziak, Mary. *Cold War Civil Rights: Race and the Image of American Democracy*. Princeton, NJ: Princeton University Press, 2000.

DuRocher, Kristina. *Ida B. Wells: Social Activist and Reformer*. Abingdon, UK: Routledge, 2016.

Edwards, Laura F. "James and His Striped Velvet Pantaloons: Textiles, Commerce and Law in the New Republic." *Journal of American History* 107 (2020): 336–361.

Edwards, Laura F. *Only the Clothes on Her Back: Clothing and the Hidden History of Power in the Nineteenth-Century United States*. New York: Oxford University Press, 2022.

Enstad, Nan. *Ladies of Labor, Girls of Adventure: Working Women, Popular Culture, and Labor Politics at the Turn of the Twentieth Century*. New York: Columbia University Press, 1999.

Ephron, Nora. "I Hate My Purse." In *I Feel Bad about My Neck*. New York: Random House, 2007, 16–26.

Eskridge, William N., Jr. *Gaylaw: Challenging the Apartheid of the Closet*. Cambridge, MA: Harvard University Press, 1999.

Faderman, Lillian. *The Gay Revolution: The Story of Struggle*. New York: Simon and Schuster, 2015.

Farell-Beck, Jane, and Colleen Gau. *Uplift: The Bra in America*. Philadelphia: University of Pennsylvania Press, 2002.

Farell-Beck, Jane, and Laura Klosterman Kidd. "The Roles of Health Professional in the Development and Dissemination of Women's Sanitary Products, 1880–1940." *Journal of the History of Medicine and Allied Sciences* 3 (July 1996): 325–352.

Farmer, Ashley. *Remaking Black Power: How Black Women Transformed an Era*. Chapel Hill: University of North Carolina Press, 2019.

Fejes, Fred. *Gay Rights and Moral Panic: The Origins of America's Debate on Homosexuality* New York: Palgrave, 2008.
Fitch, Samantha. "The Gendered Pocket: Fashion and Patriarchal Anxieties about the Female Consumer in Select Victorian Literature." PhD diss., Indiana University of Pennsylvania, 2017.
Ford, Tanisha. *Liberated Threads: Black Women, Style and the Global Politics of Soul.* Chapel Hill: University of North Carolina, 2015.
Ford, Tanisha. "SNCC Women, Denim, and the Politics of Dress." *Journal of Southern History* no. 3 (August 2013): 625–658.
Foster, Helen Bradley. *New Raiments of Self: African American Clothing in the Antebellum South.* New York: Berg, 1997.
Foster, Vanda. *Bags and Purses.* London: B.T. Batsford Ltd., 1982.
Freidenfelds, Lara. *The Modern Period: Menstruation in Twentieth Century America.* Baltimore: Johns Hopkins University Press, 2009.
Friesen, Hannah S. "Skirted Soldiers: An Account of American Women's Military Service during World War II." Master's thesis, San Diego State University, 2021.
Gachet, Sophie. *The Handbag Book: 400 Designer Bags That Changed Fashion.* New York: Harry N. Abrams, 2024.
Gallagher, Winifred. *It's in the Bag: What Purses Reveal and Conceal.* New York: HarperCollins, 2006.
Gallo, Marcia M. *Different Daughters: A History of the Daughters of Bilitis and the Rise of the Lesbian Rights Movement.* Emeryville, CA: Seal Press, 2007.
Gilbert, Douglas. *American Vaudeville: Its Life and Times.* New York: McGraw Hill, 1940.
Glenn, Susan. *Female Spectacle: The Theatrical Roots of Modern Feminism.* Cambridge, MA: Harvard University Press, 2000.
Grigsby, Darcy Grimaldo. *Enduring Truths: Sojourner's Shadows and Substance.* Chicago: University of Chicago Press, 2015.
Grossman, Joanna. "Women's Jury Service: Right of Citizenship or Privilege of Difference." *Stanford Law Review* 46, no. 5 (May 1994): 1115–1160.
Guilfoyle, Timothy. "Street-Rats and Gutter-Snipes: Child Pickpockets and Street Culture in New York City, 1850–1900." *Journal of Social History* 37, no. 4 (Summer 2004): 853–882.
Hagerty, Barbara. *Handbags: A Peek Inside Woman's Most Trusted Accessory.* Philadelphia: Running Press, 2002.
Hagerty, Barbara. *Purse Universe: Portraits of Women and Their Purses from the Purse Project.* Birmingham, AL: Crane Hill, 2001.
Halberstam, J. *Female Masculinity.* Durham, NC: Duke University Press, 1998.
Hall, Martha, Belinda T. Orzada, and Dilia Lopez-Gydosh. "American Women's Wartime Dress: Sociocultural Ambiguity Regarding Women's Roles During World War II." *Journal of American Culture* 38, no. 3 (September 2015): 232–242.
Halttunen, Karen. *Confidence Men and Painted Women: A Study of Middle-Class Culture in America, 1830–1870.* New Haven, CT: Yale University Press, 1982.
Hampf, M. Michaela. "'Dykes' or 'Whores': Sexuality and the Women's Army Corps in the United States during World War II." *Women's Studies International Forum* 27, no 1 (January/February 2004): 13–30.
Harder, Kelsie B, and W. L. McAtee. "'Handbag' or 'Purse'?" *American Speech* 36, no. 2 (1961): 154–156.
Hartog, Hendrik. *Man and Wife in America: A History.* Cambridge, MA: Harvard University Press, 2000.

Hegarty, Marilyn. *Victory Girls, Khaki-Wackies, and Patriotutes: The Regulation of Female Sexuality during World War II*. New York: New York University Press, 2008.
Hickey, Georgina. *Breaking the Gender Code: Women and Urban Public Space in the Twentieth-Century United States*. Austin: University of Texas Press, 2023.
Higginbotham, Evelyn Brooks. "African American Women's History and the Metalanguage of Race." *Signs* 17, no. 2 (1992): 251–274.
Higginbotham, Evelyn Brooks. *Righteous Discontent: The Women's Movement in the Black Baptist Church, 1880–1920*. Cambridge, MA: Harvard University Press, 1993.
Hill, Lance. *Deacons for Defense: Armed Resistance and the Civil Rights Movement*. Chapel Hill: University of North Carolina Press, 2004.
Hillman, Betty Luther. *Dressing for the Culture Wars: Style and the Politics of Self-Presentation in the 1960s and 1970s*. Lincoln: University of Nebraska Press, 2015.
Hillman, Betty Luther. "'The Most Profoundly Revolutionary Act a Homosexual Can Engage in': Drag and the Politics of Gender Presentation in the San Francisco Gay Liberation Movement, 1964–1972." *Journal of the History of Sexuality* 20, no. 1 (2011): 153–181.
Hobson, Janell. "Between History and Fantasy: Harriet Tubman in the Artistic and Popular Imaginary." *Meridians* 12, no. 2 (2014): 50–77.
Hunter, Tera W. *To Joy My Freedom: Southern Black Women's Lives and Labor after the Civil War*. Cambridge, MA: Harvard University Press, 1997.
Ivo, Sigrid. *Bags: The Museum of Bags and Purses, Amsterdam*. Amsterdam: Pepin Press, 2011.
Johnson, Colin R. *Just Queer Folks: Gender and Sexuality in Rural America*. Philadelphia: Temple University Press, 2013.
Johnson, Nicholas J. *Negroes and the Gun: The Black Tradition of Arms*. New York: Prometheus, 2014.
Johnson, Walter. *Soul by Soul: Life Inside the Antebellum Slave Market*. Cambridge, MA: Harvard University Press, 1999.
Jones, Sonya, ed. *Gay and Lesbian Literature since World War II: History and Memory*. San Francisco: Haworth Press, 1998.
Jules-Rosette, Bennetta. *Josephine Baker in Art and Life: The Icon and the Image*. Urbana: University of Illinois Press, 2007.
Kennedy, Elizabeth Lapovsky, and Madeline Davis. *Boots of Leather, Slippers of Gold: The History of a Lesbian Community*. New York: Routledge, 1993.
Kessler-Harris, Alice. *Out to Work: A History of Wage-Earning Women in the United States*. New York: Oxford University Press, 1982.
Kroeger, Brooke. *Nellie Bly: Daredevil, Reporter, Feminist*. New York: Times Books, 1994.
Laite, Julia. "The Emmet's Inch: Small History in a Digital Age." *Journal of Social History* 53, no. 4 (Summer 2020): 963–989.
Lange, Allison K. *Picturing Political Power: Images in the Women's Suffrage Movement* Chicago: University of Chicago Press, 2020.
Leach, William. *Land of Desire: Merchants, Power, and the Rise of a New American Culture*. New York: Vintage Books, 1993.
Lee, Chana Kai. *For Freedom's Sake: The Life of Fannie Lou Hamer*. Urbana: University of Illinois, 2000.
Lesy, Michael. "Visual Literacy." *Journal of American History* 94, no. 1 (January 2007): 143–153.
Lewis, Abram J. "'We Are Certain of Our Own Insanity': Anti-Psychiatry and the Gay Liberation Movement, 1960–1980." *Journal of the History of Sexuality* 25, no. 1 (January 2016): 83–113.
Ling, Peter, and Sharon Montieth, eds. *Gender and the Civil Rights Movement*. New Brunswick, NJ: Rutgers, 2004.

Logan, Onnie Lee as told to Katherine Clark. *Motherwit: An Alabama Midwife's Story*. New York: E.P. Dutton, 1989.
Lurie, Alison. *The Language of Clothes*. New York: Random House, 1981.
Mandziuk, Roseanne. "'Ending Women's Greatest Hygienic Mistake': Modernity and the Mortification of Menstruation in Kotex Advertising, 1921–1926." *Women's Studies Quarterly* 38, no. 3 (Fall 2010): 42–62.
Massa, Steve. *Rediscovering Roscoe: The Films of "Fatty" Arbuckle*. Orlando, FL: Bear Manor Media, 2020.
Mayer, Heather. *Beyond the Rebel Girl: Women and the Industrial Workers of the World in the Pacific Northwest, 1905–1924*. Corvallis: Oregon State University Press, 2018.
McAdam, Doug. *Freedom Summer*. New York: Oxford University Press, 1988.
McGuire, Danielle. *The Dark End of the Street: Black Women, Rape, and Resistance, A New History of the Civil Rights Movement from Rosa Parks to the Rise of Black Power*. New York: Vintage Books, 2010.
Merkin, Daphne. *The Fame Lunches: On Wounded Icons, Money, Sex, The Brontës, and the Importance of Handbags*. New York: Farrar, Strauss and Giroux, 2015.
Merrit, Gregg. *Room 1219: The Life of Fatty Arbuckle, the Mysterious Death of Virginia Rappe, and the Scandal That Changed Hollywood*. Chicago: Chicago Review Press, 2013.
Meyer, Leisa. *Creating G.I. Jane: Sexuality and Power in the Women's Army Corps during World War II*. New York: Columbia University Press, 1998.
Meyerowitz, Joanne. *Women Adrift: Independent Wage Earners in Chicago, 1880–1930*. Chicago: University of Chicago, 1988.
Miles, Tiya. *All That She Carried: The Journey of Ashley's Sack, A Black Family Keepsake*. New York: Random House, 2021.
Mills, Kay. *This Little Light of Mine: The Life of Fannie Lou Hamer*. Lexington: University Press of Kentucky, 2007.
Millward, Liz. *Making a Scene: Lesbians and Community across Canada*. Vancouver: University of British Columbia, 2016.
Morgan, Jennifer. *Laboring Women: Reproduction and Gender in New World Slavery*. Philadelphia: University of Pennsylvania Press, 2004.
Motz, Marilyn F. "Visual Autobiography: Photograph Albums of Turn-of-the-Century Midwestern Women." *American Quarterly* 41, no. 1 (March 1989): 63–92.
Mulholland, Loki. *She Stood for Freedom: The Untold Story of a Civil Rights Hero, Joan Trumpauer Mulholland*. Shenzhen, China: Shadow Mountain, 2016.
Mumford, Kevin. "The Trouble with Gay Rights: Race and the Politics of Sexual Orientation in Philadelphia, 1969–1982." *Journal of American History* 98, no. 1 (June 2011): 49–72.
Nelson, Stanley, and Elizabeth Clark-Lewis, *Freedom Bags*. New York: Filmmakers Library, 1991.
Newton, Esther. *Mother Camp: Female Impersonators in America*. Chicago: University of Chicago Press, 1979.
Nunley, Tamika Y. *At the Threshold of Liberty: Women, Slavery, and Shifting Identities in Washington D.C.* Chapel Hill: University of North Carolina Press, 2021.
O'Brien, Michael J. *We Shall Not Be Moved: The Jackson Woolworth's Sit-in and the Movement It Inspired*. Jackson: University Press of Mississippi, 2014.
O'Brien, Tim. *The Things They Carried*. Boston: Mariner Books, 1990.
Orleck, Annelise. *Common Sense and a Little Fire: Women and Working-Class Politics in the United States, 1900–1965*. Chapel Hill: University of North Carolina Press, 1995.
Oxford English Dictionary. Oed.com
Ownby, Ted, and Becca Walton, *Clothing and Fashion in Southern History*. Jacksonville: University Press of Mississippi, 2020.

Pace, Courtney. *Freedom Faith: The Womanist Vision of Prathia Hall*. Athens: University of Georgia Press, 2019.

Pagan, Eduardo Obregon. *The Sleepy Lagoon: Zoot Suits, Race, and Riot in Wartime L.A.* Chapel Hill: University of North Carolina Press, 2003.

Painter, Nell Irvin. *Sojourner Truth: A Life, A Symbol*. New York: W.W. Norton, 1997.

Peacock, Kent. "Race, the Homosexual, and the Mattachine Society of Washington 1961–1970." *Journal of the History of Sexuality* 25, no. 2 (May 2016): 267–296.

Peiss, Kathy. *Cheap Amusements: Working-Women and Leisure in Turn-of-the-Century New York*. Philadelphia: Temple University Press, 1986.

Peiss, Kathy. *Hope in a Jar: The Making of America's Beauty Culture*. Philadelphia: University of Pennsylvania Press, 2011.

Penney, Darby, and Peter Stastny. *The Lives They Left Behind: Suitcases from a State Hospital Attic*. New York: Bellevue Literary Press, 2008.

Perdue, Charles L., Jr., Thomas E. Barden, and Robert K. Phillips, eds. *Weevils in the Wheat: Interviews with Virginia Ex-Slaves*. Charlottesville: University Press of Virginia, 1976.

Plaster, Joseph. *Kids on the Street: Queer Kinship and Religion in San Francisco's Tenderloin*. Durham, NC: Duke University Press, 2023.

Prude, Jonathan. "To Look upon the 'Lower Sort': Runaway Ads and the Appearance of Unfree Laborers in America, 1750-1800." *Journal of American History* 78, no. 1 (June 1991): 124–159.

Rabinovitch-Fox, Einav. *Dressed for Freedom: The Fashionable Politics of American Feminism*. Urbana: University of Illinois Press, 2021.

Ransby, Barbara. *Ella Baker and the Black Freedom Movement: A Radical Democratic Vision*. Chapel Hill: University of North Carolina Press, 2003.

Rawick, George P. *From Sundown to Sunup: The Making of a Black Community*. Westport, CT: Greenwood, 1972.

Remus, Emily. *A Shopper's Paradise: How the Ladies of Chicago Claimed Power and Pleasure in the New Downtown*. Cambridge, MA: Harvard University Press, 2019.

Ridge, Emily. "The Problem of the Woman's Bag from the New Woman to Modernity." *Modernism/Modernity* 21, no. 3 (September 2014): 757–780.

Riemer, Matthew, and Leighton Brown. *We Are Everywhere: Protest, Power, and Pride in the History of Queer Liberation*. New York: Ten Speed Press, 2019.

Robnett, Belina. *How Long, How Long? African American Women in the Struggle for Civil Rights*. New York: Oxford University Press, 1997.

Rooks, Noliwe M. *Ladies Pages: African American Women's Magazines and the Culture That Made Them*. New Brunswick, NJ: Rutgers University Press, 2004.

Rouse, Wendy L. *Her Own Hero: The Origins of the Women's Self-Defense Movement*. New York: New York University Press, 2017.

Sandweiss, Martha. "Image and Artifact: The Photograph as Evidence in the Digital Age." *Journal of American History* 94, no. 1 (2007): 193–202.

Santangelo, Lauren C. *Suffrage and the City: New York Women Battle for the Ballot*. New York: Oxford University Press, 2019.

Schorman, Rob. *Selling Style: Clothing and Social Change at the Turn of the Century*. Philadelphia: University of Pennsylvania Press, 2003.

Schuyf, Judith. "'Trousers with Flies!' The Clothing and Subculture of Lesbians." *Textile History* 24, no. 1 (1993): 61–73.

Scott, Joan Wallach. "Gender: A Useful Category of Historical Analysis." *American Historical Review* 1, no. 5 (1986): 1053–1075.

Sears, Clare. *Arresting Dress: Cross-Dressing, Law, and Fascination in Nineteenth-Century San Francisco*. Durham, NC: Duke University Press, 2015.

Severa, Joan. *Dressed for the Photographer: Ordinary Americans and Fashion, 1840–1900*. Kent, OH: Kent State University Press, 1995.
Sewell, Jessica Ellen. *Women and the Everyday City: Public Space in San Francisco, 1890–1915*. Minneapolis: University of Minnesota Press, 2011.
Silver, Carol Ruth. *Freedom Rider Diary: Smuggled Notes from Parchman Prison*. Jackson: University Press of Mississippi, 2014.
Silverman, Victor, and Susan Stryker, dirs. *Screaming Queens: The Riot at Compton's Cafeteria*. San Francisco: KQED Production, 2005.
Smith, Shawn Michelle. *American Archives: Gender, Race, and Class in Visual Culture*. Princeton, NJ: Princeton University Press, 1999.
Spain, Daphne. *How Women Saved the City*. Minneapolis: University of Minnesota Press, 2001.
Spencer, Robyn. "Engendering the Black Freedom Struggle: Revolutionary Black Womanhood and the Black Panther Party in the Bay Area, California." *Journal of Women's History* 20 (2008): 90–113.
Spencer, Robyn. *The Revolution Has Come: Black Power, Gender, and the Black Panther Party in Oakland*. Durham, NC: Duke University Press, 2016.
Stansell, Christine. *City of Women: Sex and Class in New York, 1789–1860*. Urbana: University of Illinois Press, 1987.
Stein, Leon. *The Triangle Fire*. Ithaca, NY: Cornell University Press, 2011.
Stryker, Susan. *Transgender History: The Roots of Today's Revolution*. Berkeley, CA: Seal Press, 2017.
Styring, Kelley. *In Your Purse: Archaeology of the American Handbag*. Bloomington, IN: Insightfarm, 2007.
Teukolsky, Rachel. "Cartomania: Sensation, Celebrity, and the Democratized Portrait." *Victorian Studies* 57, no. 3 (Spring 2015): 462–475.
Theoharris, Jeanne. *The Rebellious Life of Mrs. Rosa Parks*. Boston: Beacon Press, 2013.
Tobler, Douglas, and Nelson B. Wadsworth. *The History of Mormons in Photographs and Text: 1830 to the Present*. New York: St. Martin's Press, 1989.
Todd, Eileen Wiley. "Photojournalism, Visual Culture, and the Triangle Shirtwaist Fire." *Labor: Studies in Working Class History of the Americas* 2, no. 2 (Summer 2005): 9–27.
Tone, Andrea. *Devices and Desires: A History of Contraceptives in America*. New York: Hill and Wang, 2001.
Trethewey, Natasha. *Domestic Work*. St. Paul, MN: Graywolf Press, 2000.
Tyson, Timothy. *Radio-Free Dixie: Robert F. Williams and the Roots of Black Power*. Chapel Hill: University of North Carolina Press, 2001.
Ulrich, Laurel Thatcher. "Of Pens and Needles: Sources in Early American Women's History." *Journal of American History* 77, no. 1 (1990): 200–207.
Vapnek, Lara. *Breadwinners: Working Women and Economic Independence, 1865–1920*. Urbana: University of Illinois Press, 2009.
Vinikas, Vincent. *Soft Soap, Hard Sell: American Hygiene in an Age of Advertisement*. Ames: Iowa State University Press, 1992.
Volpe, Andrea. "Cartes de Visite Portrait Photographs and the Culture of Class Formation," in ed. Ardis Cameron, *Looking for America: The Visual Production of Nation and People*. Malden, MA: Blackwell, 2005: 42–57.
von Drehl. *Triangle: The Fire That Changed America*. New York: Grove Press, 2003.
von Schneidemesser, Luanne. "Purse and Its Synonyms." *American Speech* 55 (1980): 74–76.
Vostra, Sharra Louise. *Under Wraps: A History of Menstrual Hygiene Technology*. Lanham, MD: Lexington Books, 2008.

Welke, Barbara Y. "When All the Women Were White, and All the Blacks Were Men: Gender, Class, Race, and the Road to Plessy, 1855–1914." *Law and History Review* 13, no. 2 (Autumn 1995): 261–316.

Werner, Julia, and Dennis Braatz. *For the Love of Bags*. Augsburg, Germany: TeNeues: 2015.

White, Shane, and Graham White. "Slave Clothing and African-American Culture in the Eighteenth and Nineteenth Centuries." *Past & Present* 148 (1995): 149–186.

White, Shane, and Graham White. *Stylin': African American Expressive Culture, from Its Beginnings to the Zoot Suit*. Ithaca, NY: Cornell University Press, 1999.

Wilcox, Claire. *A Century of Handbags: Icons of Style in the 20th Century*. New York: Chartwell Books, 1998.

Wilcox, Claire, ed. *Handbags: The Making of a Museum*. New Haven, CT: Yale University Press, 2012.

Willey, Amanda Mae. "Fashioning Femininity for War: Material Culture and Gender Performance in the WAC and WAVES during World War II." PhD diss., Kansas State University, 2015.

Wolcott, Victoria. *Remaking Respectability: African American Women in Interwar Detroit* Chapel Hill: University of North Carolina Press, 2001.

Zakim, Michael. "A Ready-Made Business: The Birth of the Clothing Industry in America," *The Business History Review* 73, no. 1 (Spring 1999): 61–90.

Zakim, Michael. *Ready-Made Democracy: A History of Men's Dress in the American Republic, 1760-1860*. Chicago: University of Chicago Press, 2003.

Index

Note: Figures are indicated by an italic "*f*", following the page number.
For the benefit of digital users, indexed terms that span two pages (e.g., 52–53) may, on occasion, appear on only one of those pages.

Abbott, Simon 29
accessories. *See also* gloves; hats;
     purses; shoes
   of Black women 44*f*, 45, 110, 115
   of enslaved people 31
   ornamental 52, 64
   in portraits 40–5
   purse 64–6
   of working women 67–8
activism 14
   anti-rape 188 n.51
   Civil Rights Movement 108–31
   gay rights movement 14, 134–5, 137,
      139–42, 139*f*, 145–8
   women's rights 5
actresses 50, 77–8, 177 n.87
Addams, Jane 67–8
advertisements
   in Black-owned newspapers 96–7
   for contraceptives 101–2
   for Gay Bob 132
   for handbags, purses and pocketbooks
      64–7, 65*f*, 66*f*
   for personal and feminine hygiene
      products 86–91, 89*f*, 96–8, 105–6
   runaway 28–31, 30*f*
   for small purses 52
   for toiletries 81–2
   for Vachelle bags 95*f*
The Advocate 144
African Americans. *See also* Black men;
      Black women
   statues of 117*f*, 188 n.47
AIDS 146, 148–9, 155–6, 193 n.21
Alabama 18, 113
Allender, Nina 45–6
alligator bags 45, 64, 156–7
Alterman, Kate 69

Ambrosia Flask 91
American Birth Control League 83, 101,
     184 n.113
American Ladies Tailor Association 54
American Mercury 99–100
American Psychiatric Association 134–5
American South
   gay Black men from 148–9
   gun clubs 188 n.45
   language 99–100, 187 n.18
Andrews, Julie 5
Angelino, Henry 59–60
Angelou, Maya 99–100, 187 n.18
Anna B. H. (Willard Insane Asylum
      resident): suitcase and purses of 9–10,
      10*f*, 11*f*
antebellum America 12–13, 15–35
Anthony, Susan B. 12, 45, 156–7
apparel. *See* clothing
"Appeal" (Walker) 23–4
Arbuckle, Roscoe (Fatty) 48–50, 49*f*
Arden, Elizabeth 92–3
Arkansas
   desegregation crisis 112
   enslaved people in 25
armed self-defense 14, 112–16, 122–3
Armstrong, C. A. 102
Around the World in Seventy-Two Days
      (Bly) 36
Ashley (enslaved girl) 25–6
Ashley, Sarah 20–2, 21*f*
Atlanta Constitution 57
The Atlanta World 96–7
Ayvette White Plastic Syringe 183 n.110

backy sacks 26
bag (term) 6, 98
bag inspections. *See* inspections

bags. *See also* handbags; pocketbooks; purses
  enslaved women's use of sacks 12–13, 15–35
  recommendations for women 51–2
Baker, Ella 109, 120–1, 185 n.4
Baker, Josephine 187 n.25
Baptist, Edward 166 n.40
Barnard College 121–2
Barney (children's character) 152
Bates, Daisy 112, 120, 185 n.4, 187 n.24
Beals, Jessie Tarbox 43–5, 43*f*
Beard, Romare 33–4
Bell, Laura 26–7
Benjamin, Harry 194 n.28
Bennett, Billie 49–50
Bernstein, Samuel 74
Bible 125–6
bicycling 51–2, 64
Bir-Con-El (Lenori Laboratories) 101–2
Birkin, Jane 125–6
Birkin bags 125–6
birth control 100–2
Birth Control Federation of America
  (BCFA) 102
birth rates 100–1
Black Codes 115
Black men
  free 23–4
  runaways 28–30, 30*f*
  Southern gay 148–9
Black-owned newspapers 96–7
Black Panther Party (BPP) 115–16, 188 n.44
Blackwell, Fred 130–1
Black women
  accessories of 44*f*, 45, 110, 115
  advertisements aimed at 96–7
  in Civil Rights Movement 14, 108–25,
    111*f*, 127–31
  clothing of 16–19, 23, 27–31, 30*f*, 109–11,
    115–16, 121–2, 173 n.9
  college students 112, 114–15, 120–2,
    124, 128–31
  domestic workers 109
  enslaved, 12–13, 15–35, 30*f*
  Great Migration 34–5, 83, 138
  magazines aimed at 96
  menstruation rags 74, 182 n.87
  midwives 83
  migrants 34–5
  "Miss Black Middle Class," 121–2
  pathbreaking 56
  performers 155–6
  politics of respectability 109–10
  portraits of 41–5, 169 n.20
  purchasing power 177 n.7
  runaways 28–30, 30*f*
  soul style 186 n.5
  stereotypes of 44*f*, 45
  wealthy 56
  working 50–1, 108–11, 173 n.8, 181 n.69
Blake, James 108
Blanck, Max 71–2, 75–7
Bly, Nellie 12, 36–7, 38*f*, 156–7
body
  bags and 81–107
  cross-body bags 104, 105*f*, 158–9
  purses as proxies for 7, 83, 106
boho-chic 2
bookbags
  in 1930s 100
  author's 1–3, 1*f*
  of college students 125–6
booklets 84, 101–2
Booth, John 15
border control 146–7
Bornstein, Minnie 176 n.57
Boston bags 94
Boston Equal Suffrage and Good
  Government Association 51
Bostwick, Charles 75–6
Botume, Elizabeth 24–5
Bradford, Sarah H. 33–4
briefcases 120, 142
Bronx Slave Markets 109
Brown, Harvey 22–3
Brown, William Wells 32
Brunet, Ariane 147, 154
Bryant, Anita 134–5
Bucelli, Mary 71
Buckley, Liam 170 n.27
built environments 38–9
burglar-proof bags 13, 52
burlap bags
  author's army green burlap sack 1–3, 1*f*
  clothing made from 26–7
burses (butch purses) 158, 192 n.5
Bursky, Becky 74–6
Bush, Larry 146–7
businessman drag 195 n.47
butch femme dynamic 142
butch lesbians 14, 142–5, 192 n.5

butch purses (burses) 158, 192 n.5
Butler, Isaiah 18

Campana Corporation 105–6
Carmen Complexion Powder 91
Carmichael, Stokely 113–14, 124–8
carpetbags 5, 42f
"Carry Your Luggage, Lady!" (Allender) 46
Carter, Tyron 193 n.21
cartes de visite 32, 40–5
Casey, Kathleen B.: bookbag 1–3, 1f
Caty (enslaved woman) 31
Cellucotton Products Co. 87
Cerene 182 n.87
Chaffee, Lois 128–9
Chanel, Coco 83
Chanel bags 125–6, 155–6
Chaney, James 114
change purses 129–30, 130f
charity girls 77–8
Charleston Courier 29–30
The Charleston Mercury 29–30
chatelaine bags 68–9
Chauncey, George 192 n.11
Cherrydale Drug Fair (Arlington) 124–5, 125f
The Chicago Defender 54–8
Chicago Sunday Tribune 68–9
The Chicago Tribune 55–6
church lady look 109–11, 115
cigarette cases 93–4
City of Cincinnati v. Adams (a.k.a. Harris) 145
city spaces. *See* public space
Civil Rights Movement 14, 24, 34–5, 108–31
  Freedom Quilting Bee 26
  Freedom Rides 124, 126–8
  Freedom Summer 114
  Montgomery Bus Boycott 14, 116–18, 185 n.2
  sit-ins 124–6, 125f, 128–31, 130f, 158–9
Civil War 5, 33–4
Clark, Septima 185 n.4
Clinton, Bill 149
Clinton, Joe 22, 166 n.36
clothing
  accessories. *See* gloves; hats; purses; shoes
  businessman drag 195 n.47
  butch femme 142
  in Civil Rights Movement 120, 127–8, 186 n.5, 186 n.13

cross-dressing 14, 134, 136, 143, 145–8
dressing up 173 n.9
of enslaved people 16–19, 23, 27–31
feminine 144
of gay men 133–4, 148–9
gender-appropriate 120
of lesbians 134, 141–3, 145
made from sacks 16–18, 23, 27
men's 23, 66–7, 102–3, 142–4
ownership of 31
with pockets 4–5, 23, 43–5, 54–5, 144
in queer communities 133–4, 141
ready-to-wear 38–9, 50, 63–4, 100
Sunday clothes 115, 169 n.20
of transwomen 149–52
women's. *See* women's clothing
clutch purses (clutches) 95–6, 149–50, 157f, 172 n.69
Coach 158
Cobb, Charles, Jr. 122–3
Cochrane, Elizabeth. *See* Bly, Nellie
coded language 39, 98–100
coffles 25–6
coin purses 50–1, 64–7, 66f, 129
COINTELPRO 122–3
Cold War 134, 189 n.64
Colgate 81–2, 96–7
college students
  book bags 125–6
  sit-ins 124, 128–31
  women 112, 114–15, 120–2, 124–6, 128–31
colored plains 17
Colvin, Claudette 119
Gene Compton's Cafeteria (San Francisco) 135–8, 136f, 137f, 154
Comstock Act 84, 101
concentration camps 184 n.126
condoms 102
Coney Island (1917) 49–50
Congress of Racial Equality (CORE) 128–9
Connie 150
contraceptives 101–2
Cooke, Marvel 109
cosmetics 91–3, 103
Cosmopolitan magazine 90, 96
costs 64, 66f
courier bags 51–2
COVID-19 pandemic 159
Cox, Swepson H. 15
Craft, Ellen and William 29

crime 59–61, 59f
Crispin, Jon 9–10
Croker, Ed 69–70
cross-body bags 104, 105f, 158–9
cross-dressing 14, 134, 136, 143, 145–8
culture
    material 37, 162 n.27, 164 n.6
    popular 46–7, 59, 162 n.25
Cunningham, Mary M. 43–5, 43f

DADT ("Don't Ask, Don't Tell") 149
daily patterns 81–2
The Daily Picayune 29–30
Daub, Eugene 188 n.47
Daughters of Bilitis (DOB) 134, 141–2
Davidson, Lewis III 153–4
Davidson, Lillias Campbell 51–2
Delta State Teachers College 112
Democratic National Convention (1964) 122–3
denim 115
designer bags 125–6, 145
Diagnostic and Statistical Manual of Mental Disorders (DSM) 134–5, 146
Diamond, Dion 124–5, 125f
Dickey, James H., Jr. 166 n.49
Dietrich, Marlene 102–3
distribution systems 24
Dixon, Margaret 58
DOB (Daughters of Bilitis) 134, 141–2
Dobbs International 189 n.75
domestic servants 63
domestic workers 109–11
Domsky-Abrams, Mary 71, 173 n.6, 176 n.57
"Don't Ask, Don't Tell" (DADT) 149
Douglass, Frederick 19–20, 165 n.14
drag 196 n.61
drag balls 195 n.47
Drag Queen Chris 139–41, 140f, 154
drag queens 135–6, 137f, 138–9, 147–8
"Drapery Factory" (Trethewey) 176 n.60
Dreiser, Emma 78
Dreiser, Theodore 78–80
dress. *See also* clothing
    cross-dressing 14, 134, 136, 143, 145–8
dress codes
    for enslaved people 16–17
    gender 134
dresses
    pocket problem 161 n.11 (*See also* pockets)
    pop-over 102–3
    trailing 161 n.11

DuBois, W. E. B. 57–8
Durfee, Minta 49–50

electricity 81
elite women 4–5
Elizondo, Felicia 137–8
enslaved people
    accessories of 31
    clothing of 16–19, 23, 27–31
    runaways 28–31, 30f
    sacks and bags of 12–13, 15–35, 30f
    slave collars 18
envelope bags 66–7, 94–6, 172 n.69
Essence 182 n.83
etiquette books 171 n.63
etiquette guides 144
evening clutches 149–50
Evening Star 93, 98
Evers, Medgar 128–9

fabric bags 64, 158–9
Faderman, Lillian 194 n.33
Falwell, Jerry 152–3, 153f
fashion 94–6
    church lady look 109–11, 115
    designer bags 125–6, 145
    high 6–7
fashion accessories 67, 110
Fatty's Chance Acquaintance (1915) 49–50
FBI surveillance 120, 122–3, 142
Federal Writers' Project (FWP) 15–16
Female Society of Birmingham (England) 168 n.80
feminine clothing 144
feminine hygiene products 13–14, 52–3, 81–107, 89f
femininity
    emblems of 40, 138, 143–4
    gay men and 147–8
feminism 145
feminization 48–9, 82, 106–7, 135, 138, 144
Fibs (Kotex) 100
firearms
    Black Codes 115
    in Civil Rights Movement 118
    pocket pistols 113
    purses as portable arsenals 14, 112–15
    shotguns 122–3
Firmin, Rob 188 n.47
Fisher-Price
    My Pretty Learning Purse 14
    My Smart Purse 155, 156f

flappers 92*f*
flour sacks 15
Foley, Margaret 46, 47*f*
Franklin, Aretha 155–6, 157*f*
freedom bags 31, 34–5, 109, 116–17, 138, 186 n.5, 187 n.35
freedom papers 165 n.20
Freedom Quilting Bee 26
Freedom Rides 124, 126–8
Freedom Summer 114
French heels 64
Freud, Sigmund 98, 144

Garbo, Greta 102–3
Garcia, Javier Cruz 146
garment workers 67–8
Garvey, Marcus 118
gay Black men 148–9
Gay Bob (doll) 132–3, 133*f*
GayCo Productions 152
gaylaws 134
gay men 14, 133–6, 138–9, 143–4, 146–9, 154
Gay New York (Chauncey) 192 n.11
gay rights movement 14, 134–5, 137, 139–42, 139*f*, 145–8
Gees Bend, Alabama 26
gender-appropriate clothing 120
gender policing 147–8
gender respectability 134
General Jackson Showboat 152–3
Georgia: enslaved people in 25
Gilman, Charlotte Perkins 5, 54
Ginsburg, Ruth Bader 156–7
Gizmo Development 132
gloves 43–5, 109–12, 115, 119*f*
Good Housekeeping 81, 91, 94, 96–8, 179 n.32
Gorman, Margaret 83
Gottlieb, Camilla 184 n.126
Grant, Gordon 59*f*
Great Depression 16, 26–7, 84, 88, 94, 100–1, 109, 172 n.72
Great Migration 34–5, 83, 138
The Greensboro Four 121
Gregory, Lillian 189 n.75
Gregory-Lewis, Sasha 144
GRID (Gay-Related Immune Deficiency) 148–9
gripsacks 38*f*, 156–7
gun clubs 188 n.45
gun control 115
gunny sacks 18

guns
    in Civil Rights Movement 118
    pocket pistols 113
    purses as portable arsenals 14, 112–15
    shotguns 122–3

Half-Century Magazine for the Colored Woman and Homemaker 96
Hall, Prathia 189 n.75
Hall, Radclyffe "John," 144
Hamer, Fannie Lou 122–4, 124*f*, 185 n.4
handbag (term) 3–4, 6
handbag market 159
handbags 37
    advertisements for 64–7, 65*f*
    affordable 64, 65*f*
    designer 145
    leather 92*f*, 149–50
    of pathbreaking women 36–7
    recommendations for 51–2
handguns
    in Civil Rights Movement 118
    pocket pistols 113
    purses as portable arsenals 14, 112–15
"Hannah! (I Want My Hannah)" (Pendleton) 44*f*, 45
Harding, Warren G. 83
Harper's Weekly 52
Harris, Isaac 71–2, 75–7
Harris, Leslie 166 n.40
Harvard University 8
hats 67, 109–11, 115, 179 n.19
    pillbox 116, 117*f*, 121
    tall theater hats 169 n.11
haversacks 33–4, 33*f*
Hawkins, Tom 27
Height, Dorothy 185 n.4
Hemings, Sally 17
Henry (enslaved boy) 22–3
Henry, Ida 27
Hepburn, Audrey 125–6
Hepburn, Katherine 102–3
Herland (Gilman) 54
Hermès 149–50
Hickey, Georgina 51
Higginbotham, Mr. 17
high fashion 6–7
Hinds County Jail, Mississippi 126–8
HIV/AIDS 146, 148–9, 155–6, 193 n.21
Hodges, Mary Laney 112–13
Holocaust 184 n.126
Holt, Valerie and Melvin 152–4

homophile movement 136, 147–8
Homosexual Conduct Law (Texas) 193 n.21
homosexuality 146–7
hoop-skirts 169 n.11
Hoover, Herbert 82
Hopkins, L. A. 177 n.76
Houston, Willie 152–4, 158
Howard University 124–5
Hull House 67–8
Hunter, Lina 28
Hunter, Tera 110–11
Hurston, Zora Neale 99–100, 187 n.18

"If I Were a Man" (Gilman) 54
immigrant working women 13, 61, 63–4, 73–4, 77
Immigration and Naturalization Service (INS) 146–7
indigenous people 162 n.26
In Friendship 120
inspections
    to confirm gender identity 151–2
    to deter theft 61–2, 71, 74–5, 106, 178 n.14
    to identify gay interlopers 146–7
    under skirts 110–11
    strip searches 151–2
    vaginal cavity searches 128
International Ladies' Garment Workers' Union 67, 73–4
internment camps 184 n.126
Italy: working women from 63

Jackson, Mississippi 128–9
Jackson Daily News 130
Jacobs, Harriet 19–20, 31, 34–5
Jaime (Southern gay Black man) 148–9
Japanese American women 184 n.126
Jay, Karla 147–8
Jefferson, Thomas 17
Jessica (author) 150
Jet magazine 122, 189 n.75
jeweled purses 171 n.48
Jim Crow segregation. *See* segregation
J.M. High Company 96–7
John, Elton 155–6
Johnson, Colin 192 n.11
Johnson, E. Patrick 148
Johnson, Lyndon B. (LBJ) 123–4
Johnson, Marsha P. ("Pay it no mind") 138–9, 139*f*, 154, 193 n.22
Johnson, William 29, 33–4

Johnson-Reed Immigration Act 174 n.15
Jones, Nedra 152–3
journalism
    press coverage of purse-snatching 39, 57–9
    yellow 58
journalistic approach 162 n.25
Judson, Whitcomb 93

Kameny, Frank 193 n.14
Keene, Katherine Mildred 104, 104*f*
Keith (purse-carrying gay military man) 148–9
Kelly, Grace 125–6, 149–50
Kennedy, Davis and Lapovsky 142–3
Kennedy, John F. 186 n.16
Keystone Pictures 48–9
Kimberly Clark Corporation 100
King, Coretta Scott 185 n.4
King, Martin Luther, Jr. 120, 123–4
Kleenex 96–7
kleptomania 59–60
Koppelman, Becky and Gussie 61–2, 64, 69
Korean War veterans 188 n.45
Kotex booklets 84
Kotex cabinets 179 n.34
Kotex products 13–14, 84–5, 87
    advertisements for 86–91, 96–8, 105
    Fibs 100
Ku Klux Klan 18, 115–16, 187 n.24
Kurb 90

labor activists 173 n.8
The Ladder 196 n.51
Ladies Home Journal 87, 89–91, 93, 96, 177 n.2
Lady Cyclists' Association 171 n.62
Landers, Ann 132
Langford, Charles 119*f*
language
    coded 39, 98–100
    terminology 3–6
Lanigan-Schmidt, Thomas (Tommy) 140*f*, 141
Lauder, Estée 92–3
Lavender Scare 134
Lawrence, John 193 n.21
leather, patent 115
leather bag industry 82
leather bags
    affordable 64, 65*f*

in Civil Rights Movement 112–13, 115, 121–2
envelope purses 94
freedom bags 186 n.8
handbags 92f
  in queer community 139–41, 140f, 149–50
  toy purses 132, 133f
  WAC-issue 103–4, 104f, 105f
  of working women 13, 66–7
Lemlich, Clara 72–3
Lenori Laboratories 101–2
lesbians 134–5, 141–3, 145, 147, 158
  butch 14, 142–5, 192 n.5
  butch femme dynamic 142
  clothing of 134, 141–3, 145
Levi's jeans 144
Lewis, Pearlena 129
Lewis, Tareka 115–16
LGBTQ+ people 14, 135–6, 192 n.11
Listerine 81–2
Little Rock Nine 112
locks 52
Logan, Onnie Lee 84–5
long purses 5
long straps 53–4
Los Angeles Sentinel 182 n.87
Los Angeles Times 50–1
The Los Angeles Times 93, 95–6
Louisiana: enslaved people in 16–17
Lydia Pinkham's Vegetable Compound 88–9, 89f, 96–7
Lyon, Phyllis 142

Mabel and Fatty's Wash Day (1915) 48–9, 49f
Mafia 139–41
magic bags 152
make-shift bags 128
makeup 92–3
Malone, Annie Turnbo 92–3
man purse (murse) 14, 158
March on Washington (1963) 112
marginalized communities 137
marital hygiene products 182 n.87
married women 37, 181 n.69
Martin, Carol 187 n.31
Martin, Del 142
Martinez, Edwardo Roman 146
Maryland Independent 88
Mary Poppins 5

masculinity
  threats to 154
  women's productions of 142–3
Mason, Perry 66–7
material culture
  historical textiles 164 n.6
  role in women's lives 37, 162 n.27
Mattachine Society 134
Matty (lesbian bartender) 143–4
Mayers, Rose 75
McCall's 105
McCardell, Claire 102–3
McCoy, Harry 49f
McDarrah, Fred 138–9
McIntosh, Waters 27–8
men
  in Civil Rights Movement 113–14, 120, 123–9
  drag queens 135–6, 137f, 138–9, 147–8
  gay 14, 133–6, 138–9, 143–4, 154
  Spirit Cave Man 7
men's briefcases 120
men's clothing
  pants with pockets 23, 142–4
  in queer community 142–4
  suit pockets 66–7
  waistcoats 102–3
men's pocketbooks and purses 3–5, 82. *See also* briefcases
  in queer community 132, 133f, 148–50
  at the turn of the century 48, 49f
  of working men 66–7, 66f, 78–9
menstrual or menstruation rags 74, 85–6, 182 n.87
menstrual products 13–14, 74, 84–90, 89f, 96–8, 100–1, 103–7
mesh bags 162 n.26
MFDP (Mississippi Freedom Democratic Party) 122–3
Michigan Womyn's Music Festival 147
middle-class women 67–8, 77, 169 n.20
Middleton, Ruth 25
Midol 13–14, 83, 87–8, 90, 96–7
midwives, Black 83
migrants. *See also* immigrant working women
  Black women 34–5
Miles, Tiya 25
military service 148–9
Milk, Harvey 146
Milledgeville Federal Union 29–30

miniature purses. *See* reticules
miser's bags 5
Miss America Pageant 83
"Miss Black Middle Class," 121–2
Mississippi: enslaved people in 25
Mississippi Freedom Democratic Party (MFDP) 122–3
Missouri: enslaved people in 25
Modess 182 n.87
moll-buzzers 57
monogramming 174 n.20
Montgomery Bus Boycott 14, 116–18, 185 n.2
Moody, Anne 129–31, 130*f*
Moore, Howard 122
Moses, Bob 121
Mother Jones 152
MUM 89–91
murse (man purse) 14, 158
My Pretty Learning Purse 14
My Smart Purse (Fisher-Price) 155, 156*f*

NAACP (National Association for the Advancement of Colored People) 128–9
Nash, Diane 185 n.4
National Association for the Advancement of Colored People (NAACP) 14, 118, 120, 128–9
National Liberty Journal 152
National Urban League 43–5
National Woman's Party 45–6
necklace bags 37
Negro cloth 17
New Journal and Guide 96–7
Newman, Pauline M. 73–4
New Testament 125–6
New Woman 36, 181 n.67
New York
  gaylaws 193 n.16
  People of the State of New York v. Isaac Harris and Max Blanck 71–2, 75–7
New York City, New York
  Gay New York (Chauncey) 192 n.11
  treating 64
  Uprising of the 20,000 (1909) 67–8, 72, 72*f*
  urban women 173 n.8
New York Evening Journal 72–3
The New York Observer 53–4
New York State Museum (Albany) 8, 10–11

New York Times 189 n.75
The New York Times 71
Nixon, E. D. 117–18, 185 n.2
Non-Violent Action Group (NAG) 124–5
Norman, Memphis 129
Normand, Mabel 48–9, 49*f*
Northen, Janet 158
Northup, Solomon 19–22, 24

Odum, Howard 115–16
Oklahoma
  enslaved people in 25
  Tulsa Race Massacre 83
old bag (term) 6, 98, 144
Olsen, Mary 106
Orford, Richard 20–2
ornamental accessories 52, 64
overalls 115
overnight bags 126–7
ownership 31
Oxford heels 117*f*
Ozols, Mara 182 n.92

Pace, Courtney 189 n.75
painted women 91
pamphlets, purse-size 84, 101
paper bags 109
Parchman prison 128
Parks, Raymond 118–19
Parks, Rosa 12, 108–9, 116–21, 117*f*, 119*f*
Parrish, Amos 95–6
patent leather 115
pathbreaking women 12, 36–60
Patsey (enslaved woman) 20
Payn, Martha 31
Pendleton, E. H. 44*f*
penny purses 46–7
People of the State of New York v. Isaac Harris and Max Blanck 71–2, 75–7
Pepe, Pauline 68–70
Perfu-mist (Ronson) 96
personal hygiene products 13–14, 52–3, 81–107, 89*f*
personalization 174 n.20
Per-stik 90–1
The Philadelphia Tribune 96–7
photographic portraits 39–45
Picciotto, Salvatore 52–3, 53*f*
pickets 108–31
Picklesimer, Bradley 141

INDEX

Picklesimer, Elizabeth 141
pickpocketing 37, 39, 57
pillbox hats 116, 117f, 121
Lydia Pinkham's Vegetable Compound 88–9, 89f, 96–7
Planned Parenthood Federation of America 101
pocketbook (term) 3–4, 6, 16, 66–7, 99–100, 110
pocketbook inspections. *See* inspections
pocketbooks. *See also* handbags; purses
  in antebellum America 24, 34–5
  in Civil Rights Movement 120–1
  of pathbreaking women at the turn of the century 48, 54–5
  per capita output 82
  in queer communities 137
  of working women 13, 61–80, 70f, 72f
pocket pistols 113
pockets
  detachable 16, 27–8, 31–2
  as distribution systems 24
  extra 144
  hidden 28
  history of 4–5
  home-made 15, 18–20
  interior or integrated 4–5, 23, 43–5, 54–5, 100, 102–3, 142–4
  pickpocketing 37, 39, 57
  power of 23–4, 54, 66–7, 144
  private 23–4
  tie-on 4
  value of 156–7
  visible 4
Poland: working women from 63
politics
  political cartoons 45–6
  of respectability 108–11, 114, 123–4, 124f, 130f, 131
Poore, Johnny 27
pop-over dresses 102–3
popular culture 46–7, 59, 162 n.25
portable douches 101–2
Porter, Robert 150–2
portmanteaus 31
Pretlow, T. J. 31
Pretty Learning Purse (now marketed as My Smart Purse) 14, 155, 156f
prices 64, 66f
Prince 197 n.97

Prince, Virginia 149
privacy
  in 1920s 83
  in antebellum America 12–13, 16, 26
  in Civil Rights Movement 121
  in queer community 135
  at the turn of the century 55–6
  of working women 61–80
Progressive Era 51
prostitution 50, 77–8
protests 108–31
proto-purses 12–13, 18–19
public health boards 178 n.14
public space 38–9, 77
public transportation
  Jim Crow segregation on 186 n.13
  Montgomery Bus Boycott 116–18, 185 n.2
  streetcars 50–1, 64
public women 50, 77–8
Puck 59, 59f
purse (term) 3–6, 16, 66–7
purse industry 82, 159
purse inspections. *See* inspections
purse organizers 149–50
purses 1–14, 155–60. *See also* handbags; pocketbooks
  1920s–1940s 81–107
  accessories 64–6
  advertisements for 65f, 66–7, 66f
  burglary-proof 13
  in Civil Rights Movement 34–5, 108–31
  compartments of 64–7
  contents of 55–6, 156–9, 192 n.9
  cultural significance of 37
  durability of 13, 52, 94, 143
  evolution of 105–6
  handling 46, 143, 148–50
  miniature. *See* reticules
  origin of 3–7
  of pathbreaking women 12, 36–60
  and personal hygiene 81–107
  personalization of 174 n.20
  political value of 108–11, 114, 123–4, 124f, 130f, 131
  as portable arsenals 14, 112–16
  as private spaces 61–80
  proto-purses 12–13, 18–19
  as proxies for the female body 7, 83, 106
  in queer communities 132–54, 139f, 140f
  safety features of 52

purses (*Continued*)
  security of 52–3
  size of 13, 48–9, 52, 143
  turn of the century 36–60
  value of 74, 159–60
  of working women 13, 61–80
purse-sized personal products 13–14
purse-sized pamphlets 84, 101
purse-snatching 3, 13, 59–60
  allegations against Black people of 57–8, 129–30
  average profits from 57
  coding of 39
  moll-buzzers 57
  press coverage of 39, 57–9
  protection against 52–3, 58
  public concern about 56
  victims of 34
Pursette tampons 105–6

queer (term) 192 n.11
queerness
  and purses 132–54
  symbols of 146–8, 152
Quest 90–1
quilts 26

racial differences. *See* Black women; white women
Raines, Charlotte 15, 17
Raleigh Register 29–30
Randolph, Mrs. 17
rats (hairpieces) 74
Rauh, Ida 72*f*
razor straps 175 n.36
Red Book Illustrated 179 n.44
Red Book Magazine 81, 91, 96–8
Regency era 31–2
respectability
  gender 134
  politics of 108–11, 114, 123–4, 124*f*, 130*f*, 131
reticules 16, 31–2, 42*f*, 52
  history of 4–5
  make-shift 128
Richardson, Judy 122
Richmond, Virginia 171 n.60
rights
  to carry a purse 121
  civil rights movement 14, 24, 34–5, 108–31

  gay rights movement 14, 134–5, 139–41, 139*f*, 194 n.31
  of married women 37
  women's rights activists 5
  women's right to vote (suffrage) 83, 91–2
Ringwood's Afro-American Journal of Fashion 96
rituals 141
Rivera, Sylvia 138
Robinson, Bill "Bojangles," 191 n.118
Robinson, Jo Ann 185 n.4, 189 n.61
Ronson's Perfu-mist 96
Roosevelt, Franklin D. 103
Rose (enslaved Black mother) 25
Rosenberg, Harvey 132
Ross, Araminta. *See* Tubman, Harriet
Rothstein, Beckie 61–2, 74
Rubin, Robert 76
rucksacks 163 n.37
runaway advertisements 28–31, 30*f*
Russia: working women from 63
Rustin, Bayard 120

sacks
  clothing made from 16–18, 23, 27
  detachable pockets made from 27–8
  enslaved women's use of 12–13, 15–35
  illicit use of 27–8
safety 50–1
safety features 52
Sagl, Helen 105*f*
Salter, John 129–30, 130*f*
San Francisco Board of Supervisors 193 n.18
San Francisco Chronicle 45, 132
San Francisco Police Department 142
San Francisco Public Library 132
Sanger, Margaret 83–4, 184 n.113
sanitary napkins 13–14, 74, 83–7, 100
Sarah (runaway) 29
Save Our Children campaign 134–5
Schlesinger Library, Harvard University 8
Schneider, Victoria 150–2, 151*f*, 154
Scott, Elizabeth 31
Sears, Roebuck and Co. 64, 66–7, 81, 94, 115–16
security 52–3
segregation
  Arkansas desegregation crisis 112
  Jim Crow 119, 124, 131, 186 n.13
  urban gender 169 n.10

Seinfeld 192 n.6
self-defense 3, 50–1, 124, 131, 143, 149–50, 188 n.45
    armed 14, 112–16, 122–3
Sellers, Cleveland 114
sexuality
    associations between pockets and purses and 4
    Homosexual Conduct Law (Texas) 193 n.21
    homosexuality 146–7
    symbols of 106, 135, 144
sex workers 50, 77–8, 136, 150–1, 151*f*
Shaw University 121
Shelby, Levi, Jr. 164 n.4
Sheldon, Isabel 93
Sheppard Towner Act 83
shoes
    heels 64, 67, 117*f*
    leather 115
    wooden 165 n.14
shoplifting 58–60
shopping 173 n.95
shotguns 122–3
shoulder bags 103
silent films 38–9, 48–50, 49*f*
Silver, Carol Ruth 126–8
Simmons, Rosa 26
Singer, Ida 74
Sister Carrie (Dreiser) 78–80
sit-ins 124–6, 125*f*, 128–31, 130*f*, 158–9
slave coffles 25–6
slave collars 165 nn20–21, 18
Smithson, Ida 85, 87
smoking 93–4, 128
SmpD 145
SNCC (Student Nonviolent Coordinating Committee) 14, 113–15, 121, 128–9, 186 n.13
soldiers 170 n.37
soul style 186 n.5
South Carolina: enslaved people in 16–18, 25, 27
Southern Christian Leadership Conference (SCLC) 120
Southern gay Black men 148–9
Southern terms 99–100, 187 n.18
souvenir bags 162 n.26
space
    women in public space 38–9, 77
    of working women 61–80

SPARS (Coast Guard) 103
specialty bags 64–6
Spirit Cave Man 7
spotters 128–9
state public health boards 178 n.14
Statistical Abstract of the United States 178 n.8
Stearn, Jess 142
Steele, Bobbie 112
stereotypes
    of Black women 44*f*, 45
    of lesbians and gay men 133–4
    in runaway advertisements 28–30, 30*f*
    of women in public spaces 38–9
Steuer, Max 75–6
Stonewall Riot (1969) 135, 137–9, 154
straps
    long 53–4
    razor 175 n.36
Student Nonviolent Coordinating Committee (SNCC) 14, 113–15, 121, 128–9, 186 n.13
students
    college students 112, 114–15, 120–2, 124–6, 128–31
    formerly enslaved 24–5
    Little Rock Nine 112
studio portraits 38–45
Suckle, Mark 122
suffrage 83, 91–2
suffrage bags 8, 9*f*, 45–6, 47*f*
The Suffrage News 47*f*
suffragette suit 54
The Suffragist 46
suitcases 34–5, 109, 126–7
Sunday clothes 115, 169 n.20
    church lady look 109–11, 115
Suttles, Sherry 189 n.77
sweet bags 4–5
symbolism
    of agency 46
    of femininity 40, 138, 143, 152–3
    of gay-pride 152
    in political cartoons 45–6
    of power 50, 60
    purses as proxies for the female body 7, 83, 106
    of queerness 141, 146–8, 152
    of sexuality 106, 135, 144
    in studio portraits of women 39–45

226 INDEX

Tampax 84, 97–8, 100, 105–6
tampons 13–14, 84–6, 100, 126–7
  Pursette 105–6
  Tampax 84, 97–8, 100, 105–6
Tanguay, Eva 46–8
Tassen Museum of Bags (Amsterdam) 8
Tatum, Fannie 26
Taylor, Lou 12
Taylor, Recy 188 n.51
Teletubbies (1998–2001) 152, 153*f*
Tenderloin District 194 n.28, 194 n.31
terminology 3–6
  in advertisements 66–7
  coded language 39, 98–100
Texas
  enslaved people in 25
  Homosexual Conduct Law 193 n.21
Thatcher, Margaret 8
theater hats, tall 169 n.11
theft. *See also* purse-snatching
  inspections to deter 61–2, 71, 74–5, 106, 178 n.14
  pickpocketing 37, 39, 57
  shoplifting 58–60
  women thieves 59*f*, 60
Thomas, Reginald 109–10
Tinky Winky 152, 153*f*
Tolstoy, Leo 67–8
tote bags 46, 47*f*, 158
Tougaloo College 128–9
Towns, William Henry 164 n.4
tow sacks 25–6
toy purses
  Gay Bob's 132, 133*f*
  My Smart Purse (Fisher-Price) 14, 155, 156*f*
trailing dresses 161 n.11
trans (term) 193 n.22
transgender (term) 193 n.22
trans people 135
Transvestia 149–50
transvestism 145–8, 196 n.71, 196 n.51
transvestites (TVs) 149–50
trans women 136–9, 149–52
travel bags 31, 109
travel papers 18
treating 64
Trethewey, Natasha 176 n.60
Triangle Shirtwaist Factory 13, 61–4, 73–4, 80
  People of the State of New York v. Isaac Harris and Max Blanck 71–2, 75–7

Triangle Shirtwaist Factory Fire (1911) 61–2, 68–74, 70*f*
  Uprising of the 20,000 (1909) 72–3
trick purses 93–4
Trumpauer, Joan 124–31, 125*f*, 130*f*, 185 n.4
Trumpower, Joan 190 n.91
Truth, Sojourner 41–3, 42*f*
Tubman, Harriet 31–4, 33*f*, 41
Tulsa Race Massacre 83
"T.V Clipsheet" (Prince) 197 n.97
twentieth century
  early 173 n.95
  late 132–54

underarm bags 94
Underground Railroad 33–4
uniforms 103, 105*f*
Uprising of the 20,000 (1909) 67–8, 72–3, 72*f*
urban women 77, 82–3, 91–2, 169 n.10, 173 n.8
U.S. Air Force 103
U.S. Coast Guard 103
U.S. Constitution 156–7
  First Amendment 145–6
  Nineteenth Amendment 83, 181 n.69
U.S. Department of Defense 149
U.S. military service 148–9
U.S. Navy 103
U.S. Supreme Court 181 n.69
Utah 181 n.69
utility bags 103

Vachelle bags 94, 95*f*
Vandeurs, Kady 139*f*
Vanguard 136, 194 n.31
vanity cases 13, 52–3, 53*f*
Van Wagenen, Isabella. *See* Truth, Sojourner
vaudeville 38–9, 46–7, 64, 150
Victoria and Albert Museum 198 n.99
Victorian Americans 37, 67–8, 77, 144, 162 n.26
Vietnam War 163 n.37
The Village Voice 138–9
violence against women 57–8
Virginia
  enslaved people in 25
  gay rights 139–41
  gun control 115

INDEX

Vogue magazine 7, 86–7, 90–1
voting rights (suffrage) 83, 91–2

WAAC (Women's Auxiliary Army Corps) 103–4, 105*f*
WAC (Women's Army Corps) 103–5
   leather bags 103–4, 104*f*, 105*f*
   uniforms 103, 105*f*
waist bags 52
Wald, Lillian 67–8
Walker, David 23–4
Walker, Irella Battle 20–2
Walker, Madame C. J. 92–3
The Wall Street Journal 158
Washington, Cynthia 114–15
Washington, D.C. 116
Washington, George 17–18
The Washington Times 88–9
WASPS (Air Force) 103
WAVES (Women Accepted for Volunteer Emergency Service) 103
wealth
   jeweled purses 171 n.48
   public displays of 58–9
   wealthy Black women 56, 186 n.13
Weems, Anna Maria 29
Wells, Ida B. 51
Wheeler, Fannie 26
white men
   businessmen 195 n.47
   gay men 192 n.13
White Slave Traffic Act (Mann Act) 50
white supremacy 16–17
white women
   in Civil Rights Movement 14, 124–31, 125*f*
   clothing of 31–2
   college students 124–6, 128–9
   lesbians 142–3
   middle-class 77
   purchasing power 81–2
   suffrage 83, 91–2
   urban 91–2
   working 51, 91–2
wicker purses 124–6, 125*f*
Wilkerson, Doris 187 n.31
Willard Asylum for the Insane 8–10
Williams, Mabel 110–11
Williams, Robert F. 188 n.45
window shopping 38–9

Witt, Jess 23
Witt, Rube 23
The Woman's Era 33–4
The Woman's Journal 46, 47*f*
women
   activists 14
   African American. *See* Black women
   aging 6
   birth rates 100–1
   butch femmes 142
   in Civil Rights Movement 14, 108–31
   college students 112, 114–15, 120–2, 124–6, 128–31
   cosmetic use 181 n.67
   cultural property of 82
   elite 4–5
   enslaved 12–13, 15–35, 30*f*
   immigrants 13, 61, 63–4, 73–4, 77
   Japanese American 184 n.126
   lesbians 14, 134–5, 141–5, 147, 158, 192 n.5
   married 37, 181 n.69
   middle-class 77, 169 n.20
   midwives 83
   migrants 34–5
   New Woman 36
   painted 91
   pathbreaking 12, 36–60
   portraits of 39–45
   productions of masculinity 196 n.58
   public 50, 77–8
   public roles 37
   purchasing power 177 n.7
   runaways 28–30, 30*f*
   sex workers 50, 77–8, 136, 150–1, 151*f*
   and shopping 173 n.95
   as taking up space 38–9
   thieves 59*f*, 60
   trans women 136–9, 149–52
   urban 77, 82–3, 91–2, 169 n.10, 173 n.8
   violence against 57–8
   wealthy 56, 186 n.13
   white American. *See* white women
   working-class. *See* working women
Women Accepted for Volunteer Emergency Service (WAVES) 103
Women's Army Corps (WAC) 103–5
   leather bags 103–4, 104*f*, 105*f*
   uniforms 103, 105*f*
Women's Auxiliary Army Corps (WAAC) 103–4, 105*f*

women's clothing 162 n.27, 189 n.77, 196 n.71
  accessories. *See* gloves; hats; purses; shoes
  in antebellum America 16–19, 23, 27–31
  Black women 109–11, 122, 173 n.9, 189 n.77
  church lady look 109–11, 115
  in Civil Rights Movement 109–11, 115–16, 120–2
  denim pants and overalls 115
  with extra pockets 144
  hoop-skirts 169 n.11
  with pockets 5, 100, 102–3
  ready-to-wear 63–4, 100, 102–3
  slacks 105–6
  suffragette suit 54
  trailing dresses 161 n.11
  at the turn of the century 38–9, 50, 54, 169 n.20
  underwear 143
  uniforms 103, 105*f*
  white women 31–2
  working women 38–9, 64, 67–8, 173 n.9, 174 n.29
  during World War II 5, 102–3
women's etiquette books 171 n.63
women's magazines 81–2
women's rights activists 5
women's right to vote (suffrage) 83, 91–2
Women's Wear Daily 60, 93–4
wooden shoes 165 n.14
Wood's Cut Rate store 96–7
Woolworth's 121, 128–31

working women 13, 61–80, 72*f*
  accessories of 67–8
  actresses 50, 77–8, 177 n.87
  Black 50–1, 108–9, 173 n.9, 181 n.69
  clothing of 38–9, 64, 67–8, 173 n.9, 174 n.29
  domestic servants 63
  domestic workers 109–11
  enslaved 17–18
  immigrants 13, 61, 63–4, 73–4, 77
  labor activists 173 n.8
  lesbians 143
  married 181 n.69
  pathbreaking 37–9, 47–8, 50–1, 58
  portraits of 40
  racial differences 181 n.69
  tie-on pockets 4
  urban 91–2
Works Progress Administration (WPA) 26
World War I 82–3
World War II 5, 102–3
World War II veterans 188 n.45
Wyoming 181 n.69

Yancy, Roberta "Bobbi" 110–11, 121–2, 158–9
yellow journalism 58
Young, Allen 147–8
Yuill, Robert "Bob," 132–3

zipper bags 93
zippers 52, 93